GREAT BRITAIN & IRELAND
Railway Letter Stamps 1957 - 1998

A Handbook and Catalogue

compiled by
Neill Oakley

RAILWAY PHILATELIC GROUP

INDEX

Alderney Packet	102
Bagley Wood Railway	102
Bala Lake Railway	102
Bardsey	102
Bluebell Railway	6, 11, 103
Bodmin & Wenford Railway	103
British Rail	11, 103
Calf of Man	104
Channel Tunnel	16, 106
Coras Iompair Eireann	14
Cumann Caomhnaithe Iarnróid na h-Éirann	70
Downpatrick & Ardglass Railway	14, 74
Dublin & Kingstown Railway	104
Dublin - Belfast Emergency Postal Service	104
East Somerset Railway	15
Eurotunnel	16
Festiniog Railway	18, 102
Gloucestershire Warwickshire Railway	24
Great Central Railway	25
Great Eastern Railway	104
Great Little Trains of Wales	26
Great Western Railway Airmail Service	105
Great Western Society T.P.O. 814 Group	27
Gwili Railway	105
Isle of Man Railway	29, 30
Isle of Man Victorian Steam Railway	30
Isle of Wight Railway	105
Keighley & Worth Valley Railway	11, 32
Kent & East Sussex Railway	36
Llanberis Lake Railway	37
Llechwedd Slate Caverns Railway	39
Localpost	106
London, Brighton & South Coast Railway	106
London Underground	106
Lundy	107
Manchester Express	107
Manx Electric Railway	42, 104
Mid-Hants Railway	42
Mid-Suffolk Light Railway	107
Middleton Railway	110
Midland Railway/Midland Railway Centre	47
Nene Valley Railway	47
Network SouthEast	112
North Yorkshire Moors Railway	53
Northern Ireland Railways	111
Railway Philatelic Group	111
Railway Preservation Society of Ireland	70, 74
Ravenglass & Eskdale Railway	75
Rheilffordd Ceudyllau Llechwedd	39, 102
Rheilffordd Ffestiniog	102
Rheilffordd Llyn Llanberis	37
Rheilffordd Llyn Padarn	37
Rheilffordd Llyn Tegid	102
Rheilffordd Talyllyn	84
Rheilffordd Trallwng a Llanfair	97
Rheilffordd Yr Wydda	102
Romney, Hythe & Dymchurch Railway	79
Snaefell Mountain Railway	42, 104
Snowdon Mountain Railway	83
Somerset & Dorset Railway Trust	112
Talyllyn Railway	84
Trenau Bychain Enwog Cymru	26
Vale of Rheidol Railway	95
Welsh Highland Railway	112
Welshpool & Llanfair Light Railway	97, 103
West Anglia	112
West Somerset Railway	100
Worth Valley Railway	11, 32
Ynys Enlli	102

*Dedicated to Miriam,
and Thomas and Sarah who think
railway letter stamps are "cool".*

© Neill Oakley 1999

Designed and typeset by Neill Oakley

Printed by Dorking Litho Limited,
Graphic House, Vincent Lane,
Dorking, Surrey RH4 3SA

Distribution by the Railway Philatelic Group
(Publications Officer: H. S. Wilson,
17 Heath Avenue, Littleover, Derby DE23 6DJ)

ISBN 0 901667 24 2

INTRODUCTION

It has been six long years since the last edition of this catalogue. Such an extended interval was not my intention but compiling, funding and producing it is a big undertaking. Although never published to make money, sufficient copies have to be sold to cover costs. If greater use of computer technology proves successful it should guarantee that future editions appear at more frequent intervals.

Since the last volume a new Railway Letter Service Agreement came into effect between Royal Mail and the operating railways. New services started at the Midland Railway Centre, on the Isle of Man Railways, a commemorative only service through the Channel Tunnel, and, almost, one on the Gloucestershire Warwickshire Railway. The Talyllyn Railway Letter Service, the first modern operation, celebrated its 40th anniversary in 1997. Some railways continue from strength to strength and it is encouraging to see more co-operation and support between those running day-to-day operations.

With the growing thematic interest in railways I have tried to include more information about the labels produced by railways and others which have neither been issued, nor used, to provide an authorised railway letter service. To avoid confusion with the genuine railway letter service material their status is indicated both in the introductory paragraphs below each railways heading and by the use of "L" to indicate a label. With the size of this catalogue increasing with every edition a decision will have to be made whether they can continue to be included.

It is becoming increasingly obvious that much early material is in short supply and is rarely offered for sale through dealers or at auction. Collectors will also note many other prices have been increased, some quite dramatically, and this is my best opinion of current trends. Prices are in sterling and for mint copies. Where two or more designs form a pair, strip, or block, a price is given only for the se-tenant format and not individual stamps, since the latter are generally neither sold by dealers nor bought by collectors and have a lower market value. Exceptions to these rules, particularly where the majority of an issue were used on covers, are noted. I have compared prices realised at auction with the trends and availability indicated in both railways' and dealers' price lists. Where I consider there to be insufficient information to value a rare and/or expensive item a "-" appears in the price column.

Stamps prepared by non-specialist printers can have minor flaws on a proportion of the printing. A few varieties which have special significance, some because they identify different printings, are listed as a full catalogue entry. "Specimen" stamps are listed although many were produced primarily for collectors rather than genuine publicity purposes. Essays, proofs and colour trials are noted when known to be held in private hands. Collectors should be wary of items not mentioned in this volume since they are unlikely to be official issues from the railways concerned. I would welcome more information on such items appearing for sale.

Illustrations are shown at 75% of actual linear size and are inserted as close to the relevant catalogue entries as page layouts permit. Exceptions are noted beside the illustration's number. An innovation in this edition is that, by using computers more, almost all the illustrations are now numbered for further clarity. Sheets of stamps which have been made more attractive by the addition of illustrative decorations in the margins are identified for the first time.

Post Office one-day postmarks and special railway letter cancels, produced by individual railways, that appear on their official covers are listed at the end of each relevant section. Other rubber handstamps, except letter fee cachets, are not covered by this catalogue. The listing and pricing of first day covers also lies outside the scope of this present volume.

I am grateful to all my correspondents at the various railways, the Railway Philatelic Group, Fred Taylor, Roger Dymond, Les Winn, Chris Whitehead and other R.P.G. members who have generously given information and made comments which have improved the contents. I apologise some information is missing. Despite my best efforts some details were not made available before the printing deadline.

Collectors wishing to keep up-to-date with new issues and discoveries are reminded that the R.P.G. publishes the latest information in their quarterly journal *Railway Philately* - for membership see the advert on the back cover. To contact a railway's letter service please use the address at the end of the appropriate introductory section. For other dormant services please contact a dealer. I do not deal in railway letter stamps and have none for sale.

If you have any information about new or past issues, wish to make corrections or comments about the catalogue, or have a query you think I might be able to answer, please write to the address below. I reply to correspondence, but when answering questions I would appreciate return postage.

I hope the format of this new edition is easy to use and a useful tool which increases your enjoyment of this fascinating and colourful hobby. See you again?

NEILL OAKLEY   28 February 1999
7 Toll Bar Court, Basinghall Gardens, Sutton, Surrey
SM2 6AT

RAILWAY LETTERS & RATES

On 1 February 1891, an agreement between the Post Office and a number of railway companies came into force under which letters could be carried more quickly than by the normal postal service. For this benefit the railways could charge an additional fee, payment being shown by a special adhesive stamp affixed to the bottom left-hand corner of the envelope. As their successor British Railways continued to operate the service until 1984. Of the independent railways, the Talyllyn Railway was the first to introduce a modern letter service in 1957, followed by the Festiniog, and the Ravenglass and Eskdale in 1969, and the Vale of Rheidol (then B.R. owned) in 1970. The Northern Ireland Railways Company Limited also operated a service.

A new agreement with the Post Office, superseding that of 1891, became operational on 3 June 1974. It contained two important provisions: i) Railways who were members of the Association of Minor Railway Companies (later renamed the Association of Independent Railways Ltd., and then the Association of Independent Railways and Preservation Societies, on merger with the A.R.P.S.) were enabled to apply to operate a railway letter service; ii) Authority was given to the Association to fix rates on behalf of member companies, thus ending British Rail's monopoly, whilst requiring an additional fee to be paid for the transfer of letters from minor railways to B.R.

Under the agreements letters are to be carried by the first available passenger train, and two forms of the service operate: i) Rail & post: Letters endorsed "to be posted on arrival at ..." are transferred to the normal postal system at the destination station; ii) Rail only: Letters endorsed "to be called for at ..." are collected by the addressee from the specified station. The railway acts as the agent of the Post Office for the latter service and cancels the R.M. stamp(s) as well as its own.

Until June 1976, the fee was related to three weight bands: up to 2oz, 4oz, and 1lb (the maximum permitted weight), and their metric equivalents. Subsequently there was one fee for any weight up to 450 grams. Enhanced rates applied to many destinations outside Great Britain, but within the British Isles. (The Northern Ireland Railways had their own tariff.)

From 1 April 1973, services were required to charge Value Added Tax (V.A.T.) at the following rates:
1 April 1973 - 10%; 29 July 1974 - 8%; 18 June 1979 - 15%; 1 April 1991 - 17½ %.

The basic rates (up to 2oz) for all railways until 2 June 1974, and for British Rail thereafter, during the period covered by this catalogue were as follows (the rates from 16 June 1974 include V.A.T.):

23 April 1956	11d	13 July 1975	24p
1 August 1957	1s0d	4 January 1976	29p
30 January 1966	1s1d	20 June 1976	65p
1 July 1968	1s2d	27 March 1977	81p
26 May 1969	1s3d	1 January 1978	97p
27 September 1970	2s0d	31 December 1978	£1.07
15 February 1971	10p	9 September 1979	£1.31
6 June 1971	15p	20 April 1980	£1.44
21 May 1972	16p	4 January 1981	£1.65
1 April 1973	18p	3 January 1982	£1.84
16 June 1974	21p	3 January 1983	£1.97
29 December 1974	23p	1 January 1984	£2.08

The last day of the B.R. service was 8 June 1984.

The A.I.R. levied the following basic rates (inclusive of V.A.T.):
3 June 1974 - 10p; 1 January 1978 - 15p; 19 November 1980 - 20p. The Vale of Rheidol continued with the B.R. rate until 24 March 1975, when it introduced a 15p rate, falling into line with the other minor railways on 1 January 1978.

At the end of 1988 the Association announced a rate increase commencing 1 January 1990, with the application of three weight bands:
up to 100g - 25p; 250g - 50p; and 450g (the maximum weight permitted) - 75p.

In the mid-1990s Royal Mail began to modernise its postal services, ready for the 21st Century, in an attempt to achieve charter mark status. Negotiations were held with representatives from railway letter services and the Association (now Heritage Railways Ltd.) with the intention of announcing the termination of the 1974 Agreement and introducing the new document early in 1998. Further discussions delayed its implementation until 18 December 1998.

The agreement is a contract directly between Royal Mail and the individual railway companies. It removes anacronisms in the previous document, such as references to BR's national service, lays down similar procedures as before but in more legalistic terms, and recognises only one weight band of up to 100g. The rate will remain unchanged at 25p until at least September 2000.

PHILATELIC ABBREVIATIONS

Decor.	Illustrations decorate the sheet margins
Des	Designer
Dsgn	Design
E	English
FDC	Number of official first day covers
fdc	First day cover/s
horiz.	horizontally
Illus	Illustration by
illus.	illustrated with
imperf	imperforate
No.	Catalogue number of stamp / Loco number in design description
Nos	Number of stamps printed / issued
num.	Sheets numbered (individual stamps numbered where indicated)
ovptd	overprinted
P	Number of perforations within 20mm
perf	perforated
perfs	perforations
pg	page
PHQ	Postcards illustrated with R.M. stamp designs. Also Postal Headquarters
P.O.	Post Office
Prf	Proof sheet, normally imperf / untrimmed
Ptr	Printer
R	Number of roulettes within 20mm
R.M.	Royal Mail
Sp	Stamp, or multiples, overprinted with the word "SPECIMEN". Colour of overprint as indicated
T.P.O.	Travelling Post Office
vert.	vertically
W	Welsh

RAILWAY ABBREVIATIONS

A.I.R.	Association of Independent Railways
A.P.T.	Advanced Passenger Train
A.R.P.S.	Association of Railway Preservation Societies
B.&E.R.	Bristol & Exeter Railway
B.&W.R.	Bodmin & Wenford Railway
BEV	Battery Electric Vehicle
B.R.	British Railways / British Rail
Bl.R	Bluebell Railway
C.I.E.	Coras Iompair Eireann
C.V.R.	Colne Valley Railway
D.&A.R.	Downpatrick & Ardglass Railway
D.&K.R.	Dublin & Kingstown Railway
D.&S.E.R.	Dublin & South Eastern Railway
D.B.	Deutsche Bundesbahn
E.S.R.	East Somerset Railway
F.R.	Festiniog / Ffestiniog Railway
G.C.R.	Great Central Railway
G.E.R.	Great Eastern Railway
G.N.R.	Great Northern Railway
G.N.R.(I.)	Great Northern Railway (Ireland)
G.S.&W.R.	Great Southern & Western Railway
G./W.R.	Gloucestershire Warwickshire Railway
G.W.R.	Great Western Railway
I.o.M.R.	Isle of Man Railway
I.o.M.V.S.R.	Isle of Man Victorian Steam Railway
I.W.R.	Isle of Wight Railway
K.E.S.R.	Kent & East Sussex Railway
K.W.V.R.	Keighley & Worth Valley Railway
L.&F.	Lynn & Fakenham Railway
L.&M.	Liverpool & Manchester Railway
L.&Y.R.	Lancashire & Yorkshire Railway
L.B.S.C.R.	London, Brighton & South Coast Railway
L.H.&J.C.	Lambton, Hetton & Joicey Collieries
L.L.R.	Llanberis Lake Railway
L.M.S.	London Midland & Scottish Railway
L.N.E.R.	London North Eastern Railway
L.N.W.R.	London & North Western Railway
L.S.C.R.	Llechwedd Slate Cavern Railway
L.S.W.R.	London & South Western Railway
L.T.	London Transport
M.E.R.	Manx Electric Railway
M.H.R.	Mid-Hants Railway
M.R.	Midland Railway
M.S.L.R.	Mid-Suffolk Light Railway
N.C.C.	Northern Counties Committee
N.E.L.P.G.	North Eastern Locomotive Preservation Group
N.E.R.	North Eastern Railway
N.I.R.	Northern Ireland Railways
N.V.R.	Nene Valley Railway
N.Y.M.H.T.	North York Moors Historical Trust
N.Y.M.R.	North Yorkshire Moors Railway
R.&E.R.	Ravenglass & Eskdale Railway
R.H.D.R.	Romney, Hythe & Dymchurch Railway
R.P.S.I.	Railway Preservation Society of Ireland
S.&D.	Somerset & Dorset Railway
S.E.C.R.	South Eastern & Chatham Railway
S.M.R.	Snowdon Mountain Railway
S.R.	Southern Railway
T.R.	Talyllyn Railway
U.S.A.T.C.	United States Army Transportation Corps
U.T.A.	Ulster Transport Authority
V.o.R.	Vale of Rheidol Railway
W.&P.R.	Whitby & Pickering Railway
W.D.	War Department
W.L.L.R.	Welshpool & Llanfair Light Railway
W.S.R.	West Somerset Railway
Y.&N.M.R.	York & North Midland Railway
Y.N.&B.R.	York, Newcastle & Berwick Railway
Y.N.R.	Yarmouth & Norfolk Railway

BLUEBELL RAILWAY

This standard gauge line was opened in 1882, as part of the Lewes & East Grinstead Railway, and was later owned by the London, Brighton & South Coast Railway. The five miles between Sheffield Park and Horsted Keynes opened to passengers under private ownership in 1960 as a museum to steam in a branch line setting. Sheffield Park has the pre-1923 atmosphere of the L.B.S.C.R., while Horsted Keynes recalls the post-1923 era of the Southern Railway. The railway is currently extending the line northwards along the old trackbed to reconnect with Connex services at East Grinstead. The current, temporary terminus is Kingscote Station (8½), about 2½ miles short of this goal. In 1997 the Railway purchased the trackbed of the branch linking Horsted Keynes to Ardingly, intending to restore it in the future.

In 1972 when the railway issued its original 10p label, during celebrations for the centenary of the locomotive *Fenchurch*, it was not party to the railway letter agreement. The label was still available, and became respectable, when the Company signed the document on 28 July 1974. The railway has signed the 1998 Agreement.

Enquiries to: Bluebell Railway Letter Service, 64 Gordon Road, Carshalton, Surrey SM5 3RE.

7/9/72. Railway Label. Des & Ptr: Dunn's, Eastbourne; Illus: Brian Haresnape (oil painting). Lithography in sheets of 4 (2 rows of 2) with selvedge at left, made up into booklets of 12 panes. R7 with imperf sheet edges.

Dsgn: S.E.C.R. 0-6-0T No.323 *Bluebell*

1	10p Deep blue on pale blue (imperf on upper edge)	£22.50
1a	10p Deep blue on pale blue (imperf on upper and right edge)	£22.50
1b	10p Deep blue on pale blue (imperf on lower edge)	£22.50
1c	10p Deep blue on pale blue (imperf on lower and right edge)	£22.50

	Pane of 4 with selvedge	£100.00
	Booklet of 48	-

Nos: 2000.

3/8/75. Definitive. Des & Ptr: Faulwood & Herbert Ltd., Brighton; Illus: Bluebell Railway (photo). Lithography in sheets of 10 (5 rows of 2). R5.

Dsgn: L.S.W.R. 4-4-2T No.488

2	10p Green	.75
	Sheet of 10	£8.50

Nos: Accurate figures are not known - figures quoted in early editions of this catalogue (1st printing 2500; 2nd printing 2000; later 1600 were surcharged for No.3-3c) were shown to be impossible when the railway announced the numbers for No.10 (2000). The printings cannot be separated because of the wide range of shades. A further 500 were surcharged for the provisional overprint, No.12. See also footnote for No.3-3c. FDC: 1000

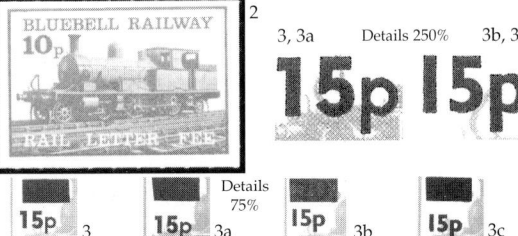

1/4/78. Provisionals. Surcharged in black by Faulwood & Herbert Ltd.

3	15p on 10p (2) (Serif 1, narrow spacing)	£7.50
3a	15p on 10p (2) (Serif 1, wide spacing)	£7.50
3b	15p on 10p (2) (Sans serif 1, narrow spacing)	£6.00
3c	15p on 10p (2) (Sans serif 1, wide spacing)	£6.00
(3)	Sheet of 10	£90.00
(3a)	Sheet of 10	£90.00
(3b)	Sheet of 10	£70.00
(3c)	Sheet of 10	£70.00

Nos: The railway announced 1600 were surcharged. The two distinct versions have a serif 1 with a narrow p, or a sans serif 1 with a bold p. Narrow spacing: 1mm between the masking block and the top of the "15p"; wide spacing: 2 - 2.5mm. No.3 was the type used on fdc and sold out first; it is not clear if the other types were separate printings, or if No.2 was reprinted as multiple panes and the overprint applied at the same time. FDC: 60

31/5/78. Definitive. Des: Roy Adams Studio, Brighton. Ptr: Faulwood & Herbert Ltd. Lithography in panes of 2 (2 rows of 1) with selvedge at top, bound in booklets of 100 panes. R5 with imperf sheet edges.

Dsgn: L.B.S.C.R. 0-6-0T No.72 *Fenchurch*

4	15p Black, and red (imperf on 2 sides)	.70
4a	15p Black, and red (imperf on 3 sides)	.70
	Pane of 2 with selvedge	£1.75
	Booklet of 200	£250.00

Nos: 5000. Copies are known with the red printing offset on the reverse. FDC: 1500

21/3/79. Definitive. Des & Ptr: Faulwood & Herbert Ltd.; Illus: Brian Haresnape (oil painting). Lithography in sheets of 10 (5 rows of 2). R5.

Dsgn: As No.1 but different format

5	15p Multicoloured	£2.00
	Sheet of 10	£22.50

Nos: 10000. FDC: 5500

2/8/80. 20th Anniversary of the Bluebell Railway. Des & Ptr: Faulwood & Herbert Ltd., to the Company's specification. Lithography in sheets of 4 (2 rows of 2). R5.

Dsgn: L.B.S.C.R. 0-6-0T No.55 *Stepney*

6	15p Red, black, brown and tan	£3.00
	Sheet of 4	£15.00

Nos: 6000. The railway stated that 4000 were subsequently surcharged; but see also footnote for No.7. FDC: 1000

19/11/80. Provisional. Surcharged in black by Faulwood and Herbert Ltd.

7	20p on 15p (6)	£3.00
	Sheet of 4	£15.00

Nos: 4000. Differences in colour shade and sheet margin markings between No.6 and 7 suggest that a new printing was made. FDC: 275

1/8/82. Centenary of the Lewes & East Grinstead Railway. Des: Roy Adams Studio. Ptr: Faulwood & Herbert Ltd. Lithography in sheets of 4 (2 rows of 2). R5.

Dsgn: Contractor's Manning Wardle 0-6-0ST loco *Sharpthorne*

8	20p Black, green and red	£1.00
	Sheet of 4	£5.00

Nos: 8000. FDC: 200

19/9/82. Bluebell Railway and Keighley & Worth Valley Railway Joint Issue. For full details see pg 11.

9	20p Red, green and black

30/7/85. Provisional. Surcharged in black by Faulwood & Herbert Ltd.

10	20p on 10p (2)	£1.50
	Sheet of 10	£16.00

Nos: 2000. The position of the overprint varies, with the obliteration block clear or touching the chimney. Two registrations can be detected on complete sheets: the different distances between the left edge of the block and the frame of the design being due to the position of the green printing on the original stamp. FDC: 500

2/8/90. Definitive. Des: Bluebell Railway. Ptr: Faulwood & Herbert Ltd. Offset lithography in sheets of 4 (2 rows of 2). R4.75.

Dsgn: B.R. Standard Class 9F 2-10-0 No.92240, inscribed "B.R. 9F Restored Bluebell Railway 1990"

11	25p Black and red	£1.00
	Sheet of 4	£5.00

Nos: 2000. FDC: 500

23/4/94. Provisional. Surcharged in black by P. Forrestier Smith.

12	25p on 10p (2)	£25.00

Nos: 500. Issuing these to cover the resumption of passenger services to Kingscote Station, the newly appointed organiser of the service did not appreciate the significance to collectors of this stopgap provisional, and produced too small a quantity for actual demand. No complete sheets exist since the top margins were removed to improve the registration of the surcharge and the stamps were broken up into singles, and a few pairs, before issue. Most of the first day covers were sold to passengers on trains operating that day who addressed the envelopes to themselves.   FDC: 150

21/5/94. Official Reopening of Kingscote Station. Des: Peter Forrestier Smith and the printers; Illus: Frank Field (drawing, from a photo by Peter Fellingham). Ptr: Faulwood & Herbert Ltd. Lithography in sheets of 4 (2 rows of 2). R9.5.

Dsgn: Kingscote Station with S.R. Class S15 4-6-0 No.847 at the down platform

13	25(p) Black and red	.40
	Sheet of 4	£1.60

Nos: 8000.   FDC: 300

27/8/94. "Golden Arrow Pullman". Des: Peter Forrestier Smith and the printers. Ptr: Faulwood & Herbert Ltd. Lithography in sheets of 4 (2 rows of 2). R9.5.

Dsgn: S.R. "Merchant Navy" Class 4-6-2 in "Golden Arrow" livery, inscribed "Golden Arrow Pullman"

14	25(p) Black	.40
	Sheet of 4	£1.60

Nos: 2000.
FDC: 300 covers and 150 postcards rail and post.

5/8/95. Thirty Five Years of Bluebell Railway Operation. Des: Peter Forrestier Smith; Illus: Mike Esau (photo). Ptr: Faulwood & Herbert Ltd. Lithography in sheets of 4 (2 rows of 2). R14.

Dsgn: S.E.C.R. 0-6-0T No.323 *Bluebell*

15	25(p) Black and red	.40
	Sheet of 4	£1.60

Nos: 4000.
FDC: 300 covers and 150 postcards rail and post.

28/10/95. Return to Steam of *Camelot*. Des: Peter Forrestier Smith; Illus: David A. Idle (photo). Ptr: Faulwood & Herbert Ltd. Lithography in sheets of 4 (2 rows of 2). R14.

Dsgn: B.R. Standard Class 5MT 4-6-0 No.73082 *Camelot*, inscribed "Camelot Return to Steam 1995"

16	25(p) Black and red	.40
	Sheet of 4	£1.60

Nos: 4000. When the photograph was reproduced on each of the four stamps the cropping of the images was not identical. The number of windows visible on the second carriage at the extreme right of the frame, for example, varies in the left and right-hand columns.
FDC: 300 covers and 150 postcards rail and post.

6/4/96. Diamond Jubilee of S.R. Class S15 No.847. Des: Neill Oakley; Illus: Mike Esau (photo). Ptr: Walsall Security Printers. Offset lithography in sheets of 4 (2 rows of 2). P14.

Dsgn: S.R. Class S15 No.847 and Pullman carriages

17	25(p) Multicoloured	.40
(17)	Sheet of 4	£1.60
(17a)	Sheet of 4 - imperf	£10.00

Nos: 17) 8000; 17a) 240. 60 imperf sheets were supplied by the printers to the railway. One sheet was presented to the designer and the remaining 59 numbered and signed by the designer and photographer.
FDC: 17) 250 covers and 200 postcards rail & post.

24/8/96. Golden Jubilee of *Blackmore Vale*. Des: Neill Oakley; Illus: Mike Esau (photo). Ptr: Walsall Security Printers. Offset lithography in sheets of 4 (2 rows of 2). P14.

Dsgn: S.R. "West Country" Class 4-6-2 No.34023 *Blackmore Vale*

18	25(p) Multicoloured	.40
(18)	Sheet of 4	£1.60
(18a)	Sheet of 4 - imperf	£10.00

Nos: 18) 8000; 18a) 240. 60 imperf sheets were supplied by the printers to the railway. One sheet was presented to the designer and the remaining 59 numbered and signed by the designer and photographer.
FDC: 18) 250 covers and 200 postcards rail & post.

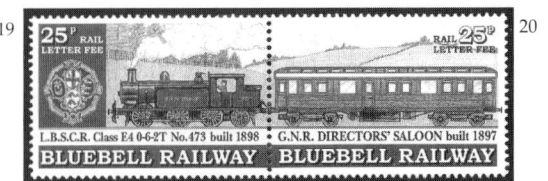

29/3/97. *Birch Grove* & Centenary of the G.N.R. Director's Saloon. Des: Neill Oakley. Ptr: Walsall Security Printers. Offset lithography in sheets of 4 (2 rows of 2, se-tenant horiz.). P14.

Dsgn: 19) L.B.S.C.R. Class E4 0-6-2T No.473 *Birch Grove* and detail from company's crest; 20) G.N.R. Director's Saloon

19	25p Multicoloured	
20	25p Multicoloured	
(19+20)	Se-tenant pair	.80
(19-20)	Sheet of 4	£1.60
(19a-20a)	Sheet of 4 - imperf	£10.00

Nos: 19-20) 4000 of each; 19a-20a) 120 of each. 60 imperf sheets were signed by the designer.
FDC: 192 covers and 150 postcards rail & post.

23/8/97. Locomotive *Baxter* 120 Years of Service. Des: Neill Oakley; Illus: Mike Esau (photo). Ptr: Walsall Security Printers. Offset lithography in sheets of 4 (2 rows of 2), num. 0001 - 2000. P14.

Dsgn: Contractor's locomotive 0-4-0T *Baxter* and goods wagons

21	25p Multicoloured	.40
(21)	Sheet of 4	£1.60
(21a)	Sheet of 4 - imperf	£10.00

Nos: 21) 8000; 21a) 240. 60 imperf sheets were signed by the designer and photographer.
FDC: 200 covers and 150 postcards rail & post.

21   22

11/4/98. Centenary of *Birch Grove*. Des: Neill Oakley; Illus: Klaus Marx (photo). Ptr: Walsall Security Printers. Offset lithography in sheets of 4 (2 rows of 2). P14.

Dsgn: L.B.S.C.R. No.473 *Birch Grove* awaiting the next duty during the summer of 1970

22	25p Multicoloured	.40
(22)	Sheet of 4	£1.60
(22a)	Sheet of 4 - imperf	£10.00

Nos: 22) 8000; 22a) 100. The printer supplied a number of imperf sheets, of which the railway issued 25 signed by the designer and photographer.
FDC: 200 covers and 150 postcards rail & post.

 23

15/8/98. B.R. Class 4 No.75027 Re-enters Service. Des: Neill Oakley; Illus: Peter Forrestier Smith (photo). Ptr: Walsall Security Printers. Offset lithography in sheets of 4 (2 rows of 2). P14.

Dsgn: B.R. Standard Class 4MT No.75027 passing Horsted Keynes signalbox on a test run on 23/10/97

23	25p Multicoloured	.40
(23)	Sheet of 4	£1.60
(23a)	Sheet of 4 - imperf	£10.00

Nos: 23) 8000; 23a) 100. The printer supplied a number of imperf sheets, of which 25 were issued, signed by the designer and photographer.
FDC: 250 covers and 200 postcards rail & post.

Bl.R. SPECIAL CANCELLATIONS

1	1/4/78	First Day of Issue
2	21/3/79	Bluebell Railway, Sheffield Park Station [illus. *Bluebell* 0-6-0T loco - blue]
3	2/8/80	First Day of Issue
4	29/7/81	Carried on Royal Wedding Day Special [illus. Prince of Wales' feathers]
5	15/9/90	Carried by Inaugural Train Hauled by Bluebell 9F
6	30/9/90	Carried by Train Hauled by Battle of Britain Engine "257" *Squadron*
7	24/12/90	Carried by Santa's Special Train on 24th Dec 1990
8	5/8/95	Horsted Keynes - Celebrating 35 Years of Bluebell Railway Operation 1960-1995 [blue]
9	28/10/95	Sheffield Park - *Camelot* Returns to Steam [blue]
10	25/1/96	Horsted Keynes - New Post Office Cancellation
11	6/4/96	Horsted Keynes - Southern Railway Class S.15 No.847 Diamond Jubilee 1936-1996
12	14/5/96	Horsted Keynes - Footballing Legends
13	9/7/96	Horsted Keynes - Olympics '96
14	27/7/96	Horsted Keynes - L.B.S.C.R. 150th Anniversary [illus. Company crest]
15	6/8/96	Horsted Keynes - Women of Achievement
16	24/8/96	Horsted Keynes - 1946 1996 *Blackmore Vale* Golden Jubilee [illus. front view of loco]
17	3/9/96	Horsted Keynes - Childrens TV
18	28/10/96	Horsted Keynes - Christmas
19	29/3/97	Horsted Keynes - G.N.R. Director's Saloon 1897-1997 [illus. end view of carriage]
20	13/5/97	Horsted Keynes - Classic Horror [illus. vampire bat]
21	10/6/97	Horsted Keynes - Aircraft Designers

22	8/7/97	Horsted Keynes - Horses [illus. horse's head]
23	12/8/97	Horsted Keynes - Sub-Post Offices [illus. pillarbox with "Post Office" direction sign on top]
24	23/8/97	Horsted Keynes - 120 Years of Service Fletcher Jennings & Co. *Baxter* [illus. the loco and wagons]
25	9/9/97	Horsted Keynes - Enid Blyton [illus. open book and signature]
26	27/10/97	Horsted Keynes - Christmas [illus. Nativity scene]
27	14/3/98	Sheffield Park - 40th Anniversary of Closure The End of the Line 1882-1958 [illus. headstone - blue]
28	11/4/98	Horsted Keynes - *Birch Grove* 100 [illus. front view of loco]
29	20/6/98	Horsted Keynes - Renaming and Return to Service of *Birch Grove* [arch of lettering]
30	23/6/98	Horsted Keynes - Health [illus. "London Jack" charity dog]
31	21/7/98	Horsted Keynes - Magical Worlds [illus. child asleep in bed dreaming of a loco and train]
32	15/8/98	Horsted Keynes - [illus. front view of B.R. Standard Class 4MT]
33	25/8/98	Horsted Keynes - Carnival [illus. face mask]
34	29/9/98	Horsted Keynes - Speed [illus. side view of front of L.N.E.R. Class A4 loco]

P.O. ONE-DAY POSTMARKS

7/8/70	Uckfield - 10th Anniversary [illus. side view of 0-6-0T loco. Used on a commemorative cover before the railway letter service started]
7/9/72	Sheffield Park, Uckfield - *Fenchurch* Centenary [illus. side view of 0-6-0T loco. Used for No.1 as above]
30/9/76	Horsted Keynes, Haywards Heath - Centenary Formation Lewes & East Grinstead Railway [illus. side view of 0-6-2T loco]
21/3/79	Sheffield Park, Uckfield - 20th Anniversary Founders' Day Bluebell Railway [illus. sprig of bluebells]
2/8/82	Horsted Keynes, Haywards Heath - Centenary of Lewes & East Grinstead Railway [illus. Stephenson's *Rocket*]

R.M. moveable date cancellations were sponsored to advertise the railway:

| 25/1/96 | East Grinstead - Bluebell Railway 'Where Steam Lives' |
| 29/3/97 | East Grinstead - Bluebell Railway making tracks [illus. side view of 0-6-2T *Birch Grove*] |

A P.O. slogan postmark was used to advertise the railway:

| 1/6/81 | Sheffield Park - Steam Trains in Sussex Bluebell Railway [illus. front view of loco] |

OLD & NEW

Rev R A de Lacy-Spencer

St John's Lodge ~ Quidenham
NORWICH ~ NR16 2PG

Railway Letter, Parcel & Newspaper Stamps
T.P.O. & other Railway Postal History
FOR SALE & WANTED

New price list available on request.

SPECIAL OFFERS FROM LIST:

5 different 1891-type Railway Letter Fee Stamps
£4 post free

NYMR 1989 20p (20th anniversary of the first NYMR engine movement) No.26 - IMPERF sheet of 6   £25

British Rail APT 55p - No.2a 'prepared but not issued' Sheet of 10   £8

BLUEBELL RAILWAY AND KEIGHLEY & WORTH VALLEY RAILWAY JOINT ISSUE

19/9/82. Centenary of the Birth of O. V. S. Bulleid. Des & Ptr: Larkfield Printing Co. Ltd., Brighouse; Illus: Worth Valley Railway (artwork). Lithography in sheets of 20 (5 rows of 4). Rough P11.

Dsgn: S.R. "West Country" Class 4-6-2 No.21C123 *Blackmore Vale* and shield

1	20p Red, green and black	.75
	Sheet of 20	£15.00

Nos: 4000. Sheets are known with perfs omitted to the left of the first column of stamps, misaligned perfs, and colour shifts. Two types of paper, white and a creamier shade, have been identified since the last edition of the catalogue.

FDC: 2000 (1000 by each company)

Note: This stamp will also be found catalogued in chronological sequence under the respective railways: Bluebell No.9; K.W.V.R. No.11.

BRITISH RAIL

British Rail did not normally issue special stamps for the general transportation of railway letters. Collectors who are interested in the stamp designs issued for this purpose by the pre-nationalisation companies should refer to H. T. Jackson's catalogue *The Railway and Airway Letter Stamps of the British Isles 1891 - 1971*, published by Harry Hayes.

The British Rail letter service ceased in June 1984, and the agreement with the Post Office lapsed. Until the introduction of the 1998 Agreement Royal Mail allowed British Rail to issue railway letter stamps and operate a letter service on certain special occasions. Listed below are stamps and cachets issued by, or with the authority of, British Rail to commemorate a particular journey or event.

STAMPS

12/3/80. 150th Anniversary of the Liverpool & Manchester Railway. Des: B.R. and the printers. Ptr: T. Stephenson & Sons Ltd, Prescot. Lithography in sheets of 10 (5 rows of 2), num. 1 - 10000. P11.

Dsgn: *Rocket* and "Rocket 150" badge

1	55p Black, red, brown and pale yellow	£2.50
1a	55p - imperf	-
(1)	Sheet of 10	£25.00
(1a)	Sheet of 40 - imperf	-
(1ab)	Sheet of 10 - imperf	-

Nos: 100000. The sheet was originally sold at the discounted rate of £5.00. Imperf proofs exist in sheet formats of 10 (5 rows of 2), and 40 (10 rows of 4). Large quantities of No.1 were used on covers and postcards carried on the replica locomotives in the L.&M. Cavalcade held near Rainhill on 12/3/80.

7/12/81. Introduction of the Advanced Passenger Train. Des: B.R. and the printers. Ptr of No.2: T. Stephenson & Sons Ltd. Lithography in sheets of 10 (5 rows of 2). P14.

Dsgn: The Advanced Passenger Train

2	55p Red, black and yellow	£2.00
2a	55p Black, red and yellow	£1.25
(2)	Sheet of 10	£22.50
(2a)	Sheet of 10	£12.00

Nos: 2) 10000; 2a) not known. No.2a (with a white background) was designed and printed ready for the inauguration of the A.P.T., possibly by the charity that had produced the series of labels (L1 - L9). At a late stage B.R. decided their quality was not appropriate and organised a reprint (with a red background), this time from T. Stephenson to ensure a high standard. The status of No.2a can be regarded as 'prepared but not issued'. FDC: 2) 3440

22/1/85. 150th Anniversary of the Incorporation of the Great Western Railway. Des: Douglas Cameron. Ptr: T. Stephenson & Sons Ltd. Lithography in miniature sheets of 4 (2 rows of 2), containing one example of each. P14.

Dsgn: 3) G.W.R. 4-2-2 *Iron Duke*; 4) G.W.R. 4-4-0 No.3440 *City of Truro*; 5) B.R. Class 47 Co-Co diesel No.47500 *Great Western*; 6) B.R. InterCity 125 power car

3	55p Multicoloured	
4	55p Multicoloured	
5	55p Multicoloured	
6	55p Multicoloured	
(3-6)	Miniature sheet of 4	£6.00
(3a-6a)	Miniature sheet of 4 - imperf	£10.00

Nos: 3-6) 49000 of each; 3a-6a) 1000 of each. Later 10000 perf and 200 imperf sheets were surcharged "Vale of Rheidol" (see pg 96); a further 2500 perf and 100 imperf sheets were overprinted for L10-L13 as cinderella labels with No.3 and 4 having the inscription "Paddington Station 1838-1988", and No.5 and 6 "London / Birmingham 1838-1988" (see pg 13). This left an issue of 3-6) 36500 of each; 3a-6a) 700 of each. Some letter stamp sheets were sold in presentation packs. Some individual stamps on foreign covers have been seen by the compiler that have been unofficially overprinted in black with "*Flying Scotsman* 1988 / Australian Bicentenial Tour". FDC: 3-6) 1000 with sheets; 3000 of each

Other adhesive designs bear the B.R. motif; those issued by the Vale of Rheidol Railway are dealt with on pg 95 onwards.

CACHETS

7/6/68. Buxton - Manchester.

C1	1/1d in black	£8.00
C1a	1/1d in plum	£12.00
C1b	1/1d in red	£10.00

A total of 1840 carried

3/5/70. Whitstable - Canterbury.

C2	1/3d in red. Approx 400 carried	£12.00

31/7/71. London - Brighton.

C3	15p in green. 300 carried	£12.00

31/1/72. Holyhead - Bangor.

C4	15p in red. 400 carried	£12.00

Note the the above cachets were numbered H1 - H4 in the last edition of the catalogue.

LABELS

A number of labels have been issued by bodies claiming that their productions are official B.R. letter stamps. In fact they were privately printed and sold, albeit for charitable purposes in many cases. The labels had no franking validity at other British Rail stations. The organisers simply paid B.R. for each cover carried at the time of posting, so at best they were an accountancy check. The organisers kept all receipts from the sale of mint labels. These issues are listed below for convenience.

3/10/71. Front Views of G.W.R./B.R. "Castle" Class 4-6-0 No.7029 *Clun Castle* and B.R. Class 86 Bo-Bo Electric Locomotives

L1	15p Multicoloured	£3.00
	Sheet of 12	£37.50

The legend "Standard Gauge Steam Trust" is printed in the upper margin of the sheet. Most examples on covers were carried between the Birmingham Railway Museum, Tyseley, and New Street Station, Birmingham, by car. Some envelopes appear to have been accepted as genuine railway letters, or as grace and favour items, by B.R. staff at more isolated locations.

29/4/72. B.R. Class 52 Bo-Bo "Western" Diesel

L2	15p Purple and black	£3.00
	Sheet of 10	£35.00

30/4/72. "Brighton Belle"

L3	15p Blue, yellow and black	£3.00
	Sheet of 10	£35.00

30/9/72. "Golden Arrow"

L4	15p Green and black	£3.50
	Sheet of 10	£40.00

1/1/73. L.M.S. "Coronation" Class 4-6-2

L5	16p Maroon and black	£3.50
	Sheet of 10	£40.00

1/1/73. L.N.E.R. Class A4 4-6-2

L6	16p Blue and black	£3.50
	Sheet of 10	£40.00

1/1/73. S.R. "West Country" 4-6-2

L7	16p Green and black	£3.50
	Sheet of 10	£40.00

1/1/73. B.R. Class 52 "Western" Diesel Surcharge

L8	16p on 15p (L2) in black	£3.50
	Sheet of 10	£40.00

1/1/73. "Brighton Belle" Surcharge

L9	16p on 15p (L3) in black	£3.50
	Sheet of 10	£40.00

Labels L2 - L9 were produced by the charity Southern Railwayman's Homes, Brighton.

31/5/88 onwards. 150th Anniversary of Paddington Station, and London & Birmingham Railway. As B.R. stamps No.3-6, except L10 and L11 overprinted "Paddington Station 1838-1988", and L12 and L13 "London / Birmingham 1838-1988" in black by Milbrooke Printers, Folkestone.

L10	55p (BR 3)	
L11	55p (BR 4)	
L12	55p (BR 5)	
L13	55p (BR 6)	
(L10-13)	Miniature sheet of 4	£6.00
(L10a-L13a)	Miniature sheet of 4 - imperf	£15.00

Nos: L10-13) 2500 of each; L10a-L13a) 100 of each. Although overprinted on the GWR150 sheet these stamps have no franking value, being produced as a cinderella issue. L10 was first used on covers postmarked 31/5/88, commemorating the 150th anniversary of Paddington Station. L11-L13 first appeared, as part of the complete sheet, on covers postmarked 4/6/88, celebrating the first public rail service to Maidenhead.

Note the labels of the above miniature sheet were numbered C1 - C4 in the last edition of the catalogue.

CORAS IOMPAIR EIREANN

Coras Iompair Eireann (C.I.E.) is the Republic's national transport company. Set up by the Irish Government in 1945, initially as a private company with some public funding, it was responsible for road, rail and canal services south of the border. In 1950 it was fully nationalised.

It produces various denominations of ticket-style labels, which are affixed to letters carried on its trains, to indicate the appropriate railway letter fee has been paid. In 1984, to celebrate the 150th Anniversary of the first Irish railway, it issued a commemorative railway letter stamp.

25/6/84. 150th Anniversary of the Dublin & Kingstown Railway. Des: Peter Sluis. Ptr: Irish Security Stamp Printing Ltd., Dublin. Lithography in sheets of 20 (5 rows of 4). P14.25 x 14.75.

Dsgn: D.&K.R. locomotive of 1834, beside Dublin Area Rapid Transit (DART) System railcar of 1984, and inscribed "Traen 150"

1	IR£1 Multicoloured	£4.50
	Sheet of 20: Plate 1A or 1B	£80.00

Nos: 40000; but approx 35000 were withdrawn leaving an issue of approx 5000. Each stamp was sold at IR£1.23 to include 23% V.A.T. The issue was withdrawn from sale on 25/6/84, after only one day, because the Post Office objected to the design's 'postage stamp' appearance. They required an overprint should be applied to indicate its exclusive use for railway letters. Envelopes with the stamps cancelled on the fdi by a special "Traen 150" cancel are known.

?/11/84. "Transport Fee" Overprint. Details as for No.1 but overprinted "Táille Iompair CIE" in black by Irish Security Stamp Printing Ltd.

2	IR£1 (1)	£4.00
	Sheet of 20: Plate 1A or 1B	£65.00

Nos: Approx 35000. See also footnote to No.1. Issue was withdrawn from sale on 31/12/84.

C.I.E. SPECIAL CANCELLATION

1   25/6/84 Heuston - Traen 150   Lá a Chéad Eisiúna [illus. 2-2-0 loco]

DOWNPATRICK & ARDGLASS RAILWAY

This railway is rebuilding part of the Belfast & County Down branch which ran southeast to Ardglass, which lies on the coast, from the Belfast to Newcastle line. It opened between Downpatrick and Ardglass for goods traffic on 27 May 1892, and for passengers on 8 July 1892. The harbour section closed by 1932, and the rest of the line was closed by the U.T.A. on 16 January 1950.

The southwestern curve of the Downpatrick triangle was re-opened by the D.&A.R. on 7 May 1990. $1^{3}/_{4}$ miles of 5'3" gauge track has now been built between Downpatrick and Magnus' Grave and the railway is being extended towards Ballydugan Mill to the south, and northwards to Inch Abbey, crossing the River Quoile early in 1999.

Although the railway arranged for an agent to organise the introduction and operation of a railway letter service this was never completed. The sheet of No.1-2 was officially released, and items carried on the first day of issue with the permission of Royal Mail, but no service was subsequently offered. The railway has not seen or had knowledge of the other stamps listed below.

When steam returns to the line in the summer of 1999 the railway hopes to introduce a full service and also utilise a restored T.P.O. carriage complete with public letterbox

Enquiries to: Downpatrick & Ardglass Railway Co. Ltd., Market Street, Downpatrick, Co. Down BT30 6LZ.

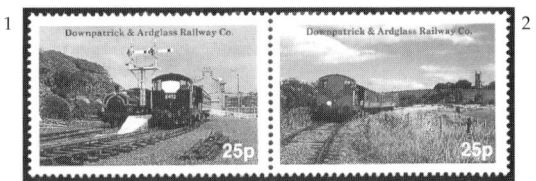

17/8/91. Definitives. Des: Peter McBride; Illus. Colin Holliday (photos). Ptr: The House of Questa, London. Offset lithography in miniature sheets of 6 (2 rows of 3), se-tenant horiz. & vert., row 1: 1+2+1; row 2: 2+1+2). P14.1.

Dsgn: 1) Hudswell Clarke 0-4-0ST No.3BG *Guinness* and C.I.E. Class 421 diesel E432 beneath signals at Downpatrick Station; 2) C.I.E. Class 421 diesel E421 and train, with Down Cathedral in background

1	25p Multicoloured	
2	25p Multicoloured	
(1+2)	Se-tenant pair	.85
(1-2)	Se-tenant block of 4	£1.75
(1-2)	Sheet of 6	£3.50

(1a-2a)   Sheet of 6 - imperf   £100.00

Nos: 15000 of each. Five imperf proof sheets exist. The photographs which appear on this D.&A.R. sheet originally bore the legend "R.P.S.I. and D.&A.R.C." on the proof sheets, with the upper margin inscribed "Railway Preservation Society of Ireland", the lower margin inscribed "First Class Postage will be paid by the Railway Company if one of these stamps is affixed to a railway letter and posted on a preserved train in Northern Ireland", and each stamp with a 50p value (see pg 74). Royal Mail allowed the use of a special railway cancellation to publicise the railway, for about 50 covers signed by the driver of the train etc., which were sent to local dignitaries and other officials and not available to the public.   FDC: 250 of each

17/8/91. R.P.S.I. and D.&A.R. Joint Railway Operation Definitives. For full details see pg 74.

3   50p Multicoloured
4   50p Multicoloured

6/8/93. "Downpatrick" Overprint. Overprinted "Downpatrick" or "Ardglass" in black (2 rows of 3, se-tenant horiz. and vert., row 1: 5+6+5; row 2: 7+8+7).

5   25p ovptd "Downpatrick" (1)
6   25p ovptd "Ardglass" (2)
7   25p ovptd "Downpatrick" (2)
8   25p ovptd "Ardglass" (1)
    Se-tenant block of 4   £2.00
    Sheet of 6   £2.50

Nos: 5 and 7) 1000 of each; 6 and 8) 500 of each. The Downpatrick & Ardglass Railway was not aware, until contacted during the compiling of this volume, that issues No.3-4 and No.5-8 had been released by their agent. These stamps have not been available for sale from the railway. Their status will be reviewed before the publication of the next edition of the catalogue.

D.&A.R. SPECIAL CANCELLATION

1   6/8/93   First Day of Issue
             Downpatrick Ardglass Railway
             Company   Posted on Board Train

EAST SOMERSET RAILWAY

The original East Somerset Railway was broad gauge and opened on 9 November 1858, from Witham Friary to Shepton Mallet, extending to Wells on 1 March 1862. It was taken over by the G.W.R. (who owned the Wells - Cheddar Valley - Yatton line) and, after a quiet history, British Railways withdrew passenger services on 9 September 1963.

It was reopened to the public in 1975, and originally ran from Cranmore to Merryfield Lane, a journey of 2 miles. It has since been extended to a halt at Mendip Vale, a further 3/4 mile. The strength of the railway is in its collection of locomotives and carriages and the replica Victorian engine shed and workshops.

In order to operate a letter service the railway made a formal application to the Post Office on 7 December 1983, which received acceptance on 3 February 1984. After several years the railway announced it had no plans to issue more stamps and the service was effectively suspended. It did not sign the 1998 Agreement.

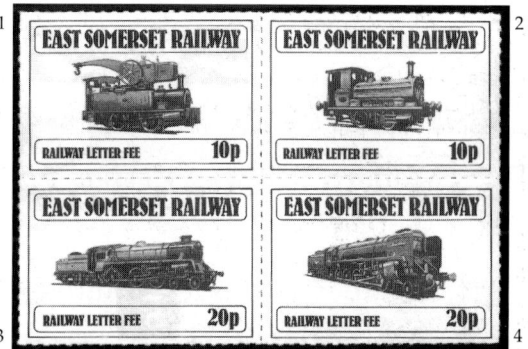

22/4/84. Definitives. Des: Gerald Patterson; Illus: East Somerset Railway (postcards). Ptr: Blackett Press, Bath. Lithography in miniature sheets of 4 (2 rows of 2), containing one example of each. R10.

Dsgn: 1) Dubs 0-4-0T crane loco No.4101; 2) Barclay 0-4-0ST No.1398 *Lord Fisher*; 3) B.R. Class 4 4-6-0 No.75029 *Green Knight*; 4) B.R. Class 9F 2-10-0 No.92203 *Black Prince*.

1   10p Multicoloured
2   10p Multicoloured
3   20p Multicoloured
4   20p Multicoloured
    Sheet of 4   £4.50

Nos: 2000 of each. A sheet is known with misplaced perforations. FDC: 550 with block of four, 100 with single stamps.

E.S.R. SPECIAL CANCELLATION

1   22/4/84   Merryfield Lane

P.O. SPECIAL HANDSTAMPS

5/7/92   Cranmore - Post Office K4 Official Opening
          [illus. telephone box which stands on
          Cranmore Station platform]

EUROTUNNEL

The first plans to build a link between England and France beneath the Channel date from 1802. Construction has begun three times: in 1881, at the beginning of the 1970s, and 1 December 1987 - the last occasion seeing the construction of the bores which now form the completed project. The service tunnel 'holed through' first, on 1 December 1990, and tunnelling was completed in June 1991. It was officially opened by H.M. The Queen and President Mitterand on 6 May 1994.

The link is made by three tunnels: two rail tubes, each with a track to carry trains in one direction, with a narrower service tunnel, linked to the others by shafts for maintenance and safety purposes, in between. The tunnel is 31 miles long, of which 24 are under the seabed at an average depth of 40 metres.

The Anglo-French private sector company CTG-FM, owned by Eurotunnel, won the concession to construct and operate the tunnel and its services in 1986. Delays and rising costs resulted in financial difficulties for the company which has had to renegotiate its loans with creditors more than once.

Passenger services by Eurostar run from Waterloo, London, to Paris and Brussels. The first fare paying Le Shuttle car services between Folkestone and Calais began on 22 December 1994. The high speed rail link between the Folkestone tunnel mouth and St. Pancras, London, has yet to be built.

The railway letter service was set up by Benhams (A. Buckingham) Ltd, acting as agents for Eurotunnel. Despite gaining approval from Royal Mail to operate the service prior to its launch the practical and legal complications of an international postal service has resulted in only official commemorative covers being carried. Despite the intention to operate a regular souvenir postal service the public has yet to be able to send their own mail on demand.

Enquiries to: Benhams Ltd, Benham House, Tontine Street, Folkestone, Kent CT20 1SD.

RAILWAYS OF GREAT BRITAIN

Modern Railway Letter
Stamps & Covers
Earlier R.L.S.,
Newspaper & Parcel Stamps
T.P.O.s, Pre-1940
General Postal History

Any of the above purchased. Please send details of what you have to offer - whether it be a single item or a collection.

CHRIS WHITEHEAD
77 Long Gore, Farncombe,
Godalming,
Surrey GU7 3TW
Tel: 01483 417563 - POSTAL ONLY

6/5/94. Channel Tunnel 1994 Sheet. Illus: Eurotunnel (artwork). Ptr: The House of Questa. Offset lithography in miniature sheets of 4 (2 rows of 2), containing one example of each. P14.

Dsgn: 1) Artist's impression of cross-section of Tunnel with, left to right, Le Shuttle train, engineering battery loco in service tunnel, and Eurostar; 2) Le Shuttle train facing right; 3) Le Shuttle train facing left; 4) Eurostar train leaving twin portal tunnel

1	55p Multicoloured		
2	55p Multicoloured		
3	55p Multicoloured		
4	55p Multicoloured		
(1-4)	Decor. sheet of 4		£5.00
(1a-4a)	Decor. sheet of 4 - imperf		£20.00

Nos: (1-4) 50000; later stamps were overprinted for No.5-8. Although the sheet margins indicated the stamps were issued by Eurotunnel, by the use of the Company's logo, there was no indication of their origin or the fact they were for the carriage of railway letters on the stamps themselves. Royal Mail objected that the absence of such text could result in them being mistaken for postage stamps and the overprint was ordered.

27/6/94. Eurotunnel Overprint. Overprinted 'Railway Letter' in black.

5	55p Multicoloured		
6	55p Multicoloured		
7	55p Multicoloured		
8	55p Multicoloured		
(5-8)	Decor. sheet of 4		£5.00
(5a-8a)	Decor. sheet of 4 - imperf		£12.00

See footnote to No.1-4.

26/6/95. Channel Tunnel 1995 Sheet. Illus: QA Photography (photos). Ptr: The House of Questa.. Offset lithography in miniature sheets of 4 (2 rows of 2), containing one example of each. P14.

Dsgn: 9) Eurostar locomotive emerging from tunnel portal; 10) Le Shuttle locomotive; 11) Le Shuttle locomotive viewed head-on in tunnel; 12) Eurostar train

9	55p Multicoloured		
10	55p Multicoloured		
11	55p Multicoloured		
12	55p Multicoloured		
(9-12)	Decor. sheet of 4		£4.00
(9a-12a)	Decor. sheet of 4 - imperf		£10.00

Nos: 50000.

EUROTUNNEL ONE-DAY CANCELLATIONS

A special cachet was prepared by Eurotunnel and used on 1 December 1990: "1st/ier Mail Through the Tunnel   Courier a Travers Le Tunnel" when the service tunnel breakthrough occurred. Cancels used for the railway letter service include:

1	27/4/94	Folkestone - Through the Channel Tunnel Trial Freight Train
2	6/5/94	Waterloo - Coquelles - Waterloo Carried Aboard the Royal Train
3	6/5/94	Folkestone - Grand Inauguration Day Carried on Celebration Eurostar Through the Channel Tunnel [illus. Eurostar train and British and French flags]
4	19/5/94	Folkestone - Through the Channel Tunnel 1st Lorry Shuttle [illus. Le Shuttle logo]
5	27/6/94	Folkestone - Through the Channel Tunnel 1st Rail Freight Trains de Marchandises Mise en Service
6	3/10/94	Folkestone - Through the Channel Tunnel 1st Car Shuttle [illus. Le Shuttle logo]
7	14/11/94	Brussels - Through the Channel Tunnel First Eurostar [illus. Eurostar train]
8	14/11/94	Paris - Through the Channel Tunnel First Eurostar [illus. Eurostar train]
9	22/12/94	Folkestone - Through the Channel Tunnel 1st Public Car Shuttle [illus. Le Shuttle logo]
10	26/6/95	Folkestone - Through the Channel Tunnel 1st Coach Run [illus. Le Shuttle logo]
11	8/1/96	Eurostar Services · Ashford International Terminal Carried on 1st Train from Ashford to Paris [illus. stylised tunnel - undated]
12	8/1/96	Ashford International Terminal Eurostar Services Ashford to Paris Through the Channel Tunnel Carried on First Train [undated]
13	28/2/96	Carried on Royal Eurostar Special Ashford-Paris
14	10/12/96	Car Shuttle Services Resumed
15	15/6/97	Carried Through the Tunnel Transportee sous la Manche [illus. stylised tunnel bore and British and French flags]

P.O. CANCELLATIONS

Eurotunnel sponsored postal cancellations before the introduction of the railway letter service:

1/12/90	Folkestone - Service Tunnel Breakthrough [illus. Eurotunnel logo]
22/5/91	Folkestone - Running Tunnel North Breakthrough [illus. Eurotunnel logo]

Cancellations used for the railway letter service include:

3/5/94	Folkestone - The Opening of the Channel Tunnel [illus. artist's impression of cross-section through Tunnel with British and French flags in portals]
3/5/94	Folkestone - Célébration '94 [illus. Eurotunnel logo and stylised figures with flags and bunting]
3/5/94	62 Calais - Tunnel Sous La Manche [illus. stylised track and tunnel]
3/5/94	62 Coquelles - Tunnel Sous la Manche Premier Jour [illus. Big Ben clocktower and Eiffel Tower]
3/5/94	Folkestone - The Channel Tunnel Le Tunnel Sous La Manche [illus. Le Shuttle logo]
3/5/94	Folkestone - Channel Tunnel [illus. British lion and French cockerel]
6/5/94	Folkestone - The Channel Tunnel The Inauguration by Her Majesty the Queen and President Mitterand [illus. crossed British and French flags]
19/5/94	Folkestone - First Lorry Shuttle Through the Channel Tunnel [illus. Le Shuttle loco in tunnel and British and French flags]
27/6/94	Folkestone - First Rail Freight Train Through the Tunnel [illus. Railfreight Distribution logo]
3/10/94	Folkestone - First Car Shuttle Through the Channel Tunnel [illus. cross-section through tunnel bore and doubledeck car transporter with British and French flags]
14/11/94	Folkestone - Eurostar Through the Channel Tunnel [illus. Eurostar train and British and French flags]
26/6/95	Folkestone - Through the Channel Tunnel 1st Coach Run [illus. coach and Le Shuttle wagon]
8/1/96	Ashford - Ashford International Terminal Launch of Eurostar services [illus. Eurostar train]
28/2/96	Ashford - Ashford International Terminal Royal Opening [illus. Eurostar train]
10/12/96	Folkestone - The Historic Channel Tunnel

FESTINIOG RAILWAY

This famous narrow gauge (1'11½") line is the oldest independent railway company in the world. It was incorporated by Act of Parliament in 1832, and opened in 1836, for the conveyance of slates from the quarries at Blaenau Ffestiniog to the harbour at Port Madoc, Caernarvonshire (now Porthmadog, Gwynedd). Passenger trains first ran in 1865. The decline of the slate industry and the Second World War led to closure in 1946, but revival, under a new administration, began in 1955 with the operation of passenger services between Porthmadog and Boston Lodge. In the years that followed the line was restored and reopened to Dduallt.

Beyond this point part of the original route was purchased compulsorily in connection with the building of the Tanygrisiau pumped-storage hydro-electric power station. A new deviation line was therefore constructed including the only spiral on a passenger carrying railway in Great Britain. In 1982 services were restored through to Blaenau Ffestiniog where a new station was shared with British Rail and currently with North Western Trains. From Porthmadog trains now serve Boston Lodge (1), Minffordd (2), Penrhyn (3½), Tan-y-Bwlch (7½), Dduallt (9½), Tanygrisiau (12¼), and Blaenau Ffestiniog (13½ miles).

In 1891 the railway was party to the agreement with the Postmaster General for the carrying of railway letters. The Company still has its copy of the original agreement, although no record appears in the Post Office Guide of the period. The continuing validity of the agreement was confirmed by Postal HQ, London, on 2 December 1968, and the service was reintroduced on 28 May 1969. The railway has achieved continuity of operation by signing both the 1974 and 1998 Agreements when they were introduced.

Every F.R. issue has been designed by Michael Seymour, the Company's archivist. All stamps were printed by T. Stephenson & Sons Ltd, Prescot, Merseyside, until 1983; subsequent issues have been printed by Faulwood & Herbert Ltd., Brighton. The railway does not announce the number of fdc serviced for each issue.

Enquiries to: The Festiniog Railway Company (RLS Dept), Porthmadog, Gwynedd LL49 9NF.

28/5/69 - 15/11/69. Definitives. Lithography in sheets of 12 (4 rows of 3), num. as below. P11, except where noted.

Dsgn: 1) Horse-drawn slate train c1849; 2) Portmadoc c1870, with *Mountaineer* and train; 3) 'The Twenties', No.2 *Prince* with 'Bullnose' Morris car; 4) F.R. 0-4-4-0T No.10 *Merddin Emrys* and train

1	1d Black and turquoise blue	.60
1a	1d - Rough perf.	.75
1b	1d - P11.2	.75
2	6d Black and salmon	£2.50
2b	6d - P11.2	.50
3	1s Black and yellow brown	£2.50
3b	1s - P11.2	£2.50
4	1s2d Black and sage green	.65
	Sheets of 12:	
(1)	Num: 00001 - 01000 (28/5/69)	£10.00
(1a)	Num: 01001 - 02100 (1/7/69)	£12.50
(1)	Num: 02101 - 03500 (13/8/69)	£10.00
(1b)	Num: 03501 - 04000 (15/11/69)	£12.50
(2)	Num: 00001 - 01000 (28/5/69)	£30.00
(2)	Num: 01001 - 02000 (13/8/69)	£30.00
(2b)	Num: 02001 - 03000 (15/11/69)	£7.50
(3)	Num: 00001 - 01000 (28/5/69)	£30.00
(3)	Num: 01001 - 02000 (13/8/69)	£30.00
(3b)	Num: 02001 - 02550 (15/11/69)	£30.00
(4)	Num: 00001 - 03275 (28/5/69)	£10.50

Nos: 1) 12000; 1a) 30000; 1b) 6000; 2) 24000; 2b) 12000; 3) 24000; 3b) 6600; 4) 39300. These figures are net after deducting sheets later surcharged for No.7-10 and 16, or spoilt. See also No.6.

Complete sheets may be identified by the number which appears to the right of the lower margin. In addition perforation methods vary: 28/5/69 left and right margins are perf; 1/7/69 perfs are very rough, both sides and the lower margin are perf; 13/8/69 quality of perfs is better, only the left margin is perf, but many of the vertical rows are incomplete leaving a 2mm gap above the lower row. 15/11/69 sheets are perf 11.2.

There is considerable variation in colour due to uneven inking. Examples of No.2 are known with double black printing.

Four stamps were prepared for the new service but British Rail unexpectedly increased the basic letter fee from 1s2d to 1s3d a few days before it started, so all covers had to bear at least two stamps.

15/9/69. Fairlie Centenary. Lithography in sheets of 12 (4 rows of 3), num. 00001 - 01000. P11.

Dsgn: 0-4-4-0T No.7 *Little Wonder* and portrait of Robert Francis Fairlie.

5	1s3d Black and carmine red	£2.50
	Sheet of 12	£32.50

Nos: 12000. A few examples exist with double red printing.

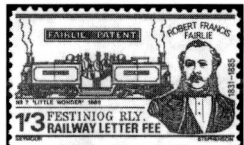 

3/6/70. Definitive. Lithography in sheets of 12 (4 rows of 3), num. 0001 - 1500. P11.2.

Dsgn: As No.4

6	1s3d Black, emerald and rosine	.50
	Sheet of 12	£7.50

Nos: 18000.

15/2/71 - 7/7/71. Decimal Provisionals. Surcharged by T. Stephenson & Sons Ltd., num. as below.

7	5p on 1d (1b) in claret	£3.00
8	10p on 1s3d (6) in cornflower blue	£3.00
9	10p on 1s2d (4) in dark red-lilac	£3.00
10	15p on 1s2d (4) in black and red	£3.00
	Sheets of 12:	
(7)	Num: 04001 - 04500 (15/2/71)	£45.00
(8)	Num: 1501 - 2000 (15/2/71)	£45.00
(9)	Num: 03651 - 04000 (28/5/71)	£45.00
(10)	Num: 03276 - 03650 (7/7/71)	£45.00

Nos: 7) 6000; 8) 5952; 9) 4188; 10) 4464. These figures take into account spoilt sheets. See also No.16.

28/7/71. Decimal Definitives. Letterpress in sheets of 12 (4 rows of 3, 5p values se-tenant horiz. 11+12+13), num. as below. P11.2.

Dsgn: 11) Portmadoc in the 1870s; 12) 0-4-4-0T No.8 *James Spooner*; 13) Hunslet 2-4-0ST *Linda*; 14) Tan-y-Bwlch station in the 1870s.

11	5p Black and bistre (used on cover)	£2.00
12	5p Black and reddish lilac (used on cover)	£2.00
13	5p Black and orange (used on cover)	£2.00
	Se-tenant strip of 3	£25.00
14	15p Black, slate blue and vermilion	.40
	Sheets of 12:	
(11-13)	Num: 0001 - 2500	£100.00
(14)	Num: 0001 - 1900, 1902	£5.50

Nos: 11-13) 10000 of each; 14) 30000; later 7176 of No.14 were surcharged for No.30, leaving an issue of 22812. Despite the large printing of No.11-13 the majority were used on covers to meet the 10p rate.

Hence the high value of mint se-tenant strips and sheets.

25/10/72. Centenary of the First Bogie Coaches Built for Regular Service in Great Britain. Letterpress in sheets of 12 (4 rows of 3), num. 0001 - 1250. P11.2.

Dsgn: First Festiniog Railway bogie coaches

15	15p Black, chocolate and sage green	.40
	Sheet of 12	£5.00

Nos: 15000.

28/2/73. Decimal Provisionals. Surcharged by T. Stephenson & Sons Ltd., num. as below.

16	1p on 1s (3) in dark red	£10.00
16a	1p on 1s (3) in vermilion	£60.00
16a	1p on 1s (3) in vermilion (used on cover)	£14.00
	Sheets of 12:	
(16)	Num: 02651 - 03000	£135.00
(16a)	Num: 02551 - 02650 (7/7/73)	-

Nos: 16) 4200; 16a) 1200. The rate increase of 21/5/72 was deferred, by arrangement with B.R., until 28/2/73, when No.16 was issued. No.16a was brought into use as a hastily ordered reprint in mid-season and was assumed to be the same as No.16. The description of the colours is my view - No.16, a maroon shade, appeared on the F.R. fdc (28/2/73), while No.16a, an orange-red shade, was primarily used on F.R. covers for the first day of at least two P.O. issues.

31/10/73. Low Value Definitives. Lithography in sheets of 20 (4 rows of 5), num. 0001 - 0800. P14.

Dsgn: 17) W. A. Madocks, M.P. and local landowner; 18) C. E. Spooner, engineer and F.R. Manager; 19) Sir H. W. Tyler, Board of Trade Inspector

17	1p Black on yellow	.35
18	2p Black on pink	.30
19	3p Black on green	.30
(17)	Sheet of 20	£9.00
(18)	Sheet of 20	£7.00
(19)	Sheet of 20	£7.00

Nos: 16000 of each. Examples of No.17 and 18 are known with an offset print on the reverse, and partial dry prints.

30/10/74. 150th Anniversary of Port Madoc Harbour. Lithography in sheets of 12 (4 rows of 3), num. 0001 - 1000. P14.

Dsgn: Slate ship in harbour, inscribed 'Port Madoc 1824-1974'

20	10p Orange and dark blue on pale blue	£1.75
	Sheet of 12	£22.50

Nos: 12000.

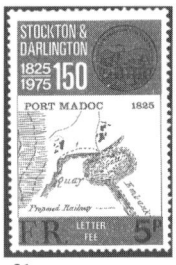 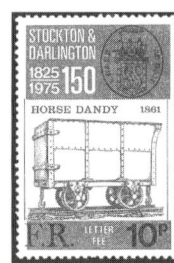 

13/8/75. 150th Anniversary of the Stockton & Darlington Railway. Lithography in sheets of 12 (3 rows of 4), num. 001 - 750. P14.

Dsgn: 21) Seal of the Stockton & Darlington Railway and plan of Port Madoc, 1825; 22) Seal of George Stephenson and F.R. horse dandy wagon, 1861; 23) Silhouette of Robert Stephenson and George England 0-4-0T *The Princess*, 1863

21	5p Black and rose red	£1.25
22	10p Black and yellow brown	£1.25
23	15p Black and violet blue	£1.25

(21)	Sheet of 12	£17.50
(22)	Sheet of 12	£17.50
(23)	Sheet of 12	£17.50

Nos: 9000 of each.

31/5/78. Definitives. Lithography in sheets of 12 (4 rows of 3), num. as below. P14.

Dsgn: 24) George England 0-4-0ST No.2 *Prince*, built 1863-4; 25) 0-4-4T *Taliesin*, built 1876; 26) Alco 2-6-2T *Mountaineer*, built 1917

24	5(p) Salmon and light blue	£2.00
25	10(p) Black and rose red	£2.00
26	15(p) Bronze green and yellow brown	£3.00
26a	15(p) Olive green and brown	£3.00
	Sheets of 12:	
(24)	Num: 0001 - 0650, plus others	£27.50
(25)	Num: 0001 - 0700	£27.50
(26)	Num: 0001 - 0700	£40.00
(26a)	Num: 0701 - 1150 (16/7/79)	£40.00

Nos: 24) 8592; 25) 8400; 26) 8400; 26a) 5400. No.26a was issued after stocks of No.26 became exhausted.

31/10/79. *Merddin Emrys* **Centenary.** Lithography in sheets of 12 (4 rows of 3), num. 001 - 750. P14.

Dsgn: No.10 *Merddin Emrys* at Boston Lodge

| 27 | 15(p) Indigo and purple brown | £2.60 |
| | Sheet of 12 | £35.00 |

Nos: 9000.

4/8/80. Great Little Trains of Wales Joint Issue. For full details see pg 26.

| 28 | 15p Black and red (E) |
| 29 | 15c Black and red (W) |

24/6/81. Provisional. Surcharged in black by Jones & Son, Penrhyndeudraeth, num. 1903 - 2500.

| 30 | 20(p) on 15p (14) | £1.15 |
| | Sheet of 12 | £14.00 |

Nos: 7176.

22/7/81. Definitive. Lithography in sheets of 12 (4 rows of 3), num. 0001 - 1250. P14.

Dsgn: Hunslet 2-4-0ST *Blanche*, built 1893

| 31 | 20(p) Green and black | .50 |
| | Sheet of 12 | £6.00 |

Nos: 15000.

25/5/82. 150th Anniversary of Incorporation and the Return to Blaenau Ffestiniog. Lithography in miniature sheets of 4 (2 rows of 2), containing one example of each, num. 1 - 10000. R6.

Dsgn: 32) Seal of Company, extract from Act of Incorporation and portrait of James Spooner; 33) *Taliesin* at Blaenau Ffestiniog (L.M.S. Station) in 1936; 34) No.6 *Little Giant*, built 1867, and Duffws 100 years ago; 35) F.R. 0-4-4-0T *Earl of Merioneth*, built 1979

32	10(p) Red, yellow and blue
33	10(p) Red, yellow, blue and green
34	20(p) Green, yellow, blue and red
35	20(p) Green, yellow, blue and red
	Sheet of 4	£1.25

Nos: 10000 of each.

18/4/86. 150th Anniversary of the Festiniog Railway. Lithography in miniature sheets of 3 (1 row of 3, se-tenant horiz. 36+37+38), num. 0001 - 12000. R5.

36-38

Dsgn: 36) Slate trains crossing 1836; 37) F.R. 0-4-4-0T No.3 *Livingston Thompson*, built at Boston Lodge 1886; 38) Hunslet 2-4-0ST *Linda*, built 1893

36	20(p) Green, brown and grey	
37	20(p) Green, brown and grey	
38	20(p) Green, brown and grey	
	Sheet of 3	£1.25

Nos: 10000 of each. Sheets from the original printing were num. 0001 - 10000. The P.O. spoilt the entire consignment of fdc and agreed to pay the Railway for replacement stamps and covers (the originals were destroyed at a later date). A second printing of 2000 sheets, num. 10001 - 12000 was ordered. Slight shade differences occur in the printings. Later 4000 of each were surcharged for No.43-45, from both printings, leaving a total issue of 6000 of each.

8/9/87. Henry Archer Commemorative. Offset lithography in sheets of 10 (5 rows of 2, se-tenant horiz. 39+40), num. 0001 - 1500. R4.75.

Dsgn: 39) Gravity slate train pre-1863, and Prince Albert stamp essay; 40) *Mountaineer*, built 1863, and perf Penny Red stamp

39	20(p) Grey, black and brown	
40	20(p) Grey, black and brown	
	Se-tenant pair	£1.10
	Sheet of 10	£6.00

Nos: 7500 of each; later 2100 of each were surcharged for No. 46+47, and 1400 of each were surcharged for No.48+49, leaving an issue of 4000 of each.

10/5/88. 125 Years of Steam on the Festiniog Railway. Offset lithography in sheets of 10 (5 rows of 2, se-tenant horiz. 41+42), num. 0001 - 1000. R4.75.

Dsgn: 41) No.2 *Prince*, built 1863-4, in its present form; 42) No.10 *Merddin Emrys* on shed

41	20(p) Red, black and yellow	
42	20(p) Black, red and yellow	
	Se-tenant pair	£1.25
	Sheet of 10	£7.00

Nos: 5000 of each.

10/4/90. Provisional. Surcharged in black by Faulwood & Herbert Ltd.

43	25(p) on 20(p) (36)	
44	25(p) on 20(p) (37)	
45	25(p) on 20(p) (38)	
	Sheet of 3	£1.75

Nos: 4000 of each. Sheets from both printings of No.36-38 were surcharged.

15/7/91. Provisional. Overprinted in grey and surcharged in red by Faulwood & Herbert (se-tenant horiz. and vert., rows 1, 3, & 5: 46+47; rows 2 & 4: 48+49), num. 0601 - 1300.

46	25(p) on 20(p) (39)	
47	5(p) on 20(p) (40)	
48	5(p) on 20(p) (39)	
49	25(p) on 20(p) (40)	
46+47	Se-tenant pair	£1.00
48+49	Se-tenant pair	£1.50
46-49	Se-tenant block of 4	£2.50
	Sheet of 10	£7.50

Nos: 46+47) 2100 of each; 48+49) 1400 of each. The poor quality of much of the overprinting means the clearest surcharges may be priced at a premium.

1/5/93. Definitives. Offset lithography in miniature sheets of 4 (2 rows of 2), containing one example of each. R9.5.

Dsgn: 50) Penrhyn Quarry loco *Charles*, built 1882; 51) *Linda* in 1962; 52) *Blanche*, in 1981; 53) *Linda* in 1992

50	5(p) Black, blue and red		
51	10(p) Black, blue and red		
52	25(p) Black, blue and red		
53	25(p) Black, blue and red		
	Decor. sheet of 4		£1.25

Nos: 3000 of each.

6/5/95. "All Our Yesterdays" Gala. Offset lithography in sheets of 10 (5 rows of 2, se-tenant horiz.). R14.

Dsgn: 54) George England 0-4-0ST No.4 *Palmerston* in 1920s condition (inset), and as built in 1864; 55) Simplex internal combustion shunting loco in the 1930s (inset), and in France during WWI guarded by a soldier

54	25(p) Multicoloured		
55	25(p) Multicoloured		
	Se-tenant pair		.80
	Sheet of 10		£4.00

Nos: 3750 of each.

9/7/96. Low Value Definitive. Offset lithography in sheets of 20 (4 rows of 5). P14.

Dsgn: F.R. 0-4-4-0T No.12 *David Lloyd George*, inscribed 1992

56	5(p) Black on coral red		.25
	Sheet of 20		£1.60

Nos: 10000.

F.R. SPECIAL CANCELLATIONS

1	28/5/71	Portmadoc - Railway Letter Post 1891-1971 Festiniog Railway Agreement with G.P.O. Signed 28 May 1891 [illus. letter stamp design with 80 in centre]
2	1/8/72	Minffordd Junction for Passengers Goods and Coal Slates Centenary 1872-1972 [illus. end views of narrow and standard gauge wagons at transfer wharf]
3	8/8/73	Tan-y-Bwlch Station Centenary 1873-1973 [illus. station staff and passengers]
4	26/5/75	Dduallt, Gelliwiog - Onward to Blaenau 1975 [illus. diagram of Dduallt spiral]
5	23/7/76	F.R. Revival 1955-1976 First train 23 vii 1955 21 Years of Passenger Services [illus. Simplex loco and train]
6	11/5/77	Loyal Greetings from Festiniog Railway Company [double ring cancel illus. Welsh dragon. Used to commemorate the Silver Jubilee of H.M. the Queen]
7	25/6/77	Llyn Ystradau - Another Step Towards Blaenau 1977 [illus. view towards hills]
8	31/5/78	1953-1978 Long Live the Queen [illus. crown, sceptre, and F.R. crest]
9	24/6/78	Tanygrisiau - Blaenau : Here we come! 1978 [illus. view of station]
10	15/9/78	1828-1978 W. A. Madocks Obiit 15 Sept. 1828 [illus. classical urn and floral swags]
11	25/6/79	A. F. Pegler 1954-1979 25 [years] The New Era [illus. portrait]
12	22/8/79	Minffordd Junction - Sir Rowland Hill 1879-1979 Wall letter-box 1913 [illus. platform scene with lady posting letter - black and red]
13	31/10/79	Boston Lodge - 1879-1979 *Merddin Emrys* [illus. loco nameplate and brass plate lettering]
14	12/3/80	Liverpool & Manchester Railway 1830-1980 Geo. Stephenson Esq. Engineer [illus. portrait]
15	21/4/80	*Prince* Back to Work 1980 [illus. loco]
16	22/7/81	The Royal Wedding 1981 [illus. celtic motif]
17	25/5/82	1832-1982 Porthmadog Bl Ffestiniog [illus. Prince of Wales' feathers]
18	30/4/83	Official Opening Blaenau Ffestiniog Station [illus. Prince of Wales' feathers and heraldic portcullis]
19	22/1/85	G.W.R. London to Bristol 150 First Parliamentary Act 1835 [ticket design]
20	23/7/85	30th Anniversary 23 vii 1955 / 1985 [illus. Simplex loco and train within ticket design]
21	18/4/86	Festiniog Railway Co. 1836-1986 [illus. horse hauling slate wagon - undated]
22	1/5/86	B.R. Class 47 named *Robert F. Fairlie* [illus. diesel and portrait]
23	8/9/87	Henry Archer First Director Eminent Victorian [illus. signature and frame of perforations]
24	10/5/88	The Festiniog Railway Co. 1863-1988 125 Years of Steam G. England & Co. Engineers, Hatcham Iron Works S.E. [illus. contemporary 2-2-2 loco]
25	10/5/88	Railway Post Office 1838-1988 London

26	4/5/90	Steam Gala 5th-7th May 1990 Railway Letter Service 21 Years 1969-1990
27	24/4/91	Visit of the Secretary of State for Wales [illus. Welsh dragons and stars]
28	28/5/91	Railway Letter Service 1891-1991 Agreement 28.v.1891 [illus. portrait of Henry Cecil Raikes, P.M.G., letterbox and F.R. train]
29	16/4/93	Naming of F.R. No.12 *David Lloyd George* [illus. portrait and nameplate]
30	1/5/93	The Festiniog Railway Co. Hunslet Hundred 1893-1993 [illus. Hunslet loco - undated]
31	20/7/93	From Scrap 1974 into Steam 1993 *Palmerston* [illus. front view of loco and nameplate - undated]
32	18/1/94	The World's Oldest The Festiniog Railway Company 1832 The Age of Steam Lives On [oval builder's plate design - undated]
33	28/5/94	1969-1994 Silver Jubilee of the Modern Service [illus. Railway Letter Service posting box decorated by company crest]
34	6/5/95	All Our Yesterdays [illus. Simplex internal combustion shunting loco - undated]
35	23/7/95	1955 - 1995 Forty Years of F.R. Progress [illus. 0-4-0ST *Prince* hauling two bogie carriages - undated]
36	9/7/96	New Stamp First Day of Issue [illus. draughtsman's pen and stamp artwork]
37	3/5/97	Festival of Steam 1997 [undated]
38	8/7/97	Penrhyn Re-opening 1957-1997 [illus. view of station building and ticket - undated]
39	13/11/97	E P 1947-1997 [Used to commemorate the Golden Wedding anniversary of H.M. The Queen and Prince Philip]

P.O. ONE-DAY POSTMARKS

17/6/85 Blaenau Ffestiniog - G.W.R. Celebrations [illus. *Taliesin*]

18/4/86 Porthmadog - 150th Anniversary Festiniog Railway Co. [illus. front view of loco within medallion]

8/9/87 Porthmadog - Henry Archer Victorian Stamp & Railway Pioneer [illus. *Mountaineer* in C19th condition]

GLOUCESTERSHIRE WARWICKSHIRE RAILWAY

This standard gauge line, at present 6 miles long, is part of an ambitious project which will eventually link Cheltenham Racecourse with Stratford Racecourse, the majority of the old G.W.R. route. There are at present two public stations, at Toddington and Winchcombe (2²/₃), with a further extension of track to the west towards Gotherington, where there is no passenger access or egress.

Volunteers planned the introduction of a railway letter service well in advance of its proposed introduction and passed the necessary papers to the railway company. The service was launched in the belief that these had been acted on and was run according to the agreement's regulations, but the railway had not completed the procedure. In July 1996, the service was terminated, with no notice, by the railway company which issued a statement that it would be re-introduced as soon as possible. No items are on sale at the railway and, at the time of writing, the company has not indicated a date when they plan to relaunch the service.

15/10/94. Definitive. Des: Stuart Hudson. Ptr: Walsall Security Printers. Offset lithography in sheets of 8 (4 rows of 2), num. 1 - 750. P13.5.

Dsgn: Crest of the G./W.R. (based on an early G.W.R. crest) on a background in the style of an 1891 railway letter stamp

L1	25p Brown and yellow	.40
L1Sp	25p Brown and yellow	-
(L1)	Sheet of 8	£3.50
(L1Sp)	Sheet of 8 - ovpt black	-

Nos: L1) 6000; L1Sp) Not known. Only very few 'specimen' sheets were prepared and most were used for publicity purposes. A couple of sheets had the stamps cancelled "19 SEP 1994", using the Toddington station handstamp, which were released as publicity. FDC: 426 rail & post; 95 rail only

L1

L2

21/6/95. Definitive. Des: Neill Oakley. Ptr: Walsall Security Printers. Offset lithography in sheets of 8 (4 rows of 2), num. 1 - 750. P13.5.

Dsgn: G.W.R. express train at speed, adapted from a "Cheltenham Flyer" luggage label design, and the G./W.R.'s crest

L2	25p Multicoloured	.40
L2Sp	25p Multicoloured - ovptd in black	-
(L2)	Sheet of 8	£3.50
(L2Sp)	Sheet of 8 - ovptd black	-

Nos: L2) 6000; L2Sp) Not known. Only very few 'specimen' sheets were prepared and most were used for publicity purposes.   FDC: Not known

G./W.R. SPECIAL CANCELLATIONS

Two cachets, dated 2/4/94 (10th Anniversary G./W.R.) and 3/5/94 (90 Years of Greet Tunnel), were applied to commemorative covers before the service began. The following cancels were used during the unofficial service:

1	25/12/94	G.[/]W.R. - Merry Christmas from Santa [illus. Santa aboard cartoon-style train]
2	1/2/95	Winchcombe - Booking Office [illus. belt and buckle border from G.[/]W.R. crest]
3	10/6/95	Winchcombe - Land's End to John O'Groats via the G.[/]W.R. [illus. cyclist beside G.W.R. Pannier tank loco]
4	21/6/95	Great Western Railway 1st Day of Issue [illus. "Cheltenham Flyer" train and G./W.R. crest]
5	21/6/95	G.[/]W.R. T.P.O. NT. UP
6	21/6/95	G.[/]W.R. T.P.O. NT. DOWN

An additional cancel, prepared before the service was terminated was applied to 20 covers which were carried by train after the official cessation of the service on the first day of issue of the RM 'Shakespeare Theatre' stamps:

7	8/8/95	Toddington - Gloucestershire Warwickshire Railway [illus. signature and portrait of Mr William Shakespeare with parchment frame]

P.O. ONE-DAY CANCELLATION

16/10/94	Toddington - First Day of Service [illus. Gloucester Station cancellation dated MR 25 1840]
12/5/95	Stonehouse - GWR150 Great Western Railway [illus. G.W.R. 4-6-0 loco in steam]

GREAT CENTRAL RAILWAY

The Manchester, Sheffield and Lincolnshire Railway changed its name to the Great Central Railway on the completion of its London Extension in 1899. It later became part of the London and North Eastern Railway in 1923, and British Railways in 1948. Many parts of the former G.C.R. were closed in the 1960s, including the 5 mile section between Loughborough Central, Quorn (2 miles), and Rothley, where the last B.R. train ran in May 1969. This length served the preserved railway for many years until the 3 mile southerly extension to Leicester North opened in 1990. There are plans to extend northwards to the outskirts of Nottingham in the future where the Nottingham Heritage Centre, with almost 1 mile of track, is already open to the public. The G.C.R. is the only standard gauge line which operates a mainline-style service over a 3 mile stretch of double track.

Letters and postcards were carried from 1982, but the railway never signed the Post Office Agreement, although for a while it appeared to be operating correct r.l.s. procedures. It cannot be regarded as a true railway letter service and items are no longer available from the railway.

8/5/82. Definitives. Des & Ptr: Walsall Security Printers; Illus: Great Central Railway (photos). Lithography in sheets of 10 (5 rows of 2, se-tenant horiz. L1+L2). P14.

Dsgn: L1) G.N.R. 4-2-2 No.1; L2) L.N.E.R. 0-6-2T No.4744 (G.N.R. No.1744)

L1	20p Multicoloured	
L2	20p Multicoloured	
	Se-tenant pair	£1.25
	Sheet of 10	£7.00

Nos: 25000 of each.

25/5/83. Definitives. Details as for No.1+2.

Dsgn: L3) G.C.R. 4-4-0 No.506 *Butler Henderson*; L4) L.N.E.R. 4-6-0 No.1306 *Mayflower*

L3   25p Multicoloured
L4   25p Multicoloured
          Se-tenant pair   £1.00
          Sheet of 10   £5.00

Nos: 25000 of each. Since it was not a signatory to the Post Office Agreement the Railway should not have been operating a service. Nevertheless it issued the incorrectly denominated 25p labels at a time when the appropriate rate was 20p.

G.C.R. SPECIAL CANCELLATION

1   18/1/94   Great Central T.P.O.   R.V.P.

P.O. ONE-DAY POSTMARKS

8/5/82   Loughborough - Inaugural Run of T.P.O. Service [illus. detail from G.C.R. crest]

27/7/86   Quorn - Leicester Mercury Fun Weekend [two postmarks were illus. Mercury newspaper van and G.C.R. No.506 facing either left or right]

18/1/94   Loughborough - Great Central Railway [illus. the company's crest]

THE GREAT LITTLE TRAINS OF WALES
TRENAU BYCHAIN ENWOG CYMRU

Eight of the Welsh narrow gauge railways form this joint marketing panel. In order to commemorate the tenth anniversary of the panel a special stamp was issued by the five companies operating a letter service at that time: Talyllyn, Festiniog, Vale of Rheidol, Welshpool & Llanfair, and Llanberis Lake. The stamp was valid on any one of these lines and inter-company mail was carried on the first day of issue, where a connecting link was available via British Rail.

4/8/80. 10th Anniversary of the Joint Marketing Panel of Welsh Narrow Gauge Railways. Des: Anthony Daffern. Ptr: T. Stephenson & Sons Ltd., Prescot. Lithography in sheets of 8 (4 rows of 2, se-tenant horiz. 1+2), num. 1 - 2000. P11.

Dsgn: The logo of the Panel
1   15p Black and red (E)
2   15c Black and red (W)
          Se-tenant pair   £2.00
          Sheet of 8   £10.00

Nos: 8000 of each.

Note: These stamps will also be found catalogued in chronological sequence under the respective railways: Festiniog No.28+29; Llanberis Lake No.5+6; Talyllyn No.54+55; Vale of Rheidol No.13+14; Welshpool & Llanfair No.13+14.

GREAT WESTERN SOCIETY T.P.O. 814 GROUP

This society, based at Didcot Railway Centre, acquired a coach and ground apparatus from the Travelling Post Office service and in 1975 T.P.O. Brake Stowage Van 814 was brought to Didcot. From 1988 the vehicle underwent a major overhaul, and returned to service during the summer of 1994. Shortly afterwards the team of volunteers won the Scania Award for preservation and restoration work.

Mail that is carried on demonstration runs over the 300 metre long track and exchanged with the lineside equipment bear one or more special "Letter Exchange Fee" labels. The society's operations do not qualify them as signatories to the R.L.S. Agreement.

Enquiries to: Great Western Society, T.P.O. 814 Group, 51 Abingdon Road, Drayton, Abingdon, Oxfordshire OX14 4HW.

7/6/81. Great Western Society. Des: J. Tuck and C. J. Whitehead. Ptr: Triprint, Guildford. Offset lithography in sheets of 6 (2 rows of 3). R9.5.

Dsgn: Based on G.W.R. prepaid newspaper label c1880

L1	10p Rose red	.50
(L1)	Sheet of 6	£4.00
(L1Prf)	Sheet of 6 - canc. in blue	£35.00

Nos: L1) 6000; L1Prf) 132. The 22 proof sheets were each cancelled twice in the centre by a circular T.P.O. 814 handstamp, and are numbered 220001 onwards in the bottom right-hand corner. Single labels exist with a trial rubberstamped 'Specimen' in blue, and 'GWR150' or 'Specimen' typed black overprint in the lower panel.

27/3/82. 21st Anniversary of the Great Western Society. Des: J. Tuck and C. J. Whitehead. Ptr: Triprint. Offset lithography in sheets of 3 (1 row of 3). R9.5.

Dsgn: As L1, except inscribed "1961-1982"

L2	10p Olive green	.90
L2)	Sheet of 3	£3.00
(L2Sp)	Sheet of 3 - ovptd in black	£25.00

Nos: L2) 2100.

12/4/83. 50th Anniversary of the Great Western Railway Air Service. Des: J. Tuck and C. J. Whitehead. Ptr: Triprint. Offset lithography in sheets of 3 (1 row of 3). R9.5.

Dsgn: G.W.R. air mail aircraft and emblems

L3	15p Carmine-red	£1.00
(L3)	Sheet of 3	£3.00
(L3Sp)	Sheet of 3 - ovptd in black	£25.00

Nos: L3) 2100.

22/1/85. 150th Anniversary of the G.W.R. Des: C. J. Whitehead. Ptr: Phoenix Press, Guildford. Offset lithography in miniature sheets of 3 (1 row of 3, se-tenant horiz. L4+L5+L6). R4.75.

Dsgn: 4) G.W.R. 2-2-2 *Iron Duke*; 5) G.W.R. coat of arms, and inscribed "Didcot Railway Centre"; 6) G.W.R. "King" Class 4-6-0

L4	20p Olive green	
L5	20p Olive green	
L6	20p Olive green	
(L4-L6)	Sheet of 3	£2.50
(L4-L6)	Sheet of 9	£15.00
(L4Sp-L6Sp)	Sheet of 9 - ovptd in red	£35.00

Nos: L4-L6) 2500 of each, with 50 uncut sheets of 9 stamps (3 of each design). Colour proofs exist.

14/5/85. GWR150. Issued in Association with the Celebrations at the Didcot Railway Centre. Des: C. J. Whitehead. Ptr: Phoenix Press, Guildford. Offset lithography in miniature sheets of 3 (1 row of 3, se-tenant horiz. 7+8+9). R4.75.

Dsgn: As No.4-6

L7	20p Chocolate brown (4)
L8	20p Chocolate brown (5)
L9	20p Chocolate brown (6)

L1

L2

L3

L4-L6 & L7-L9

(L7-L9)	Sheet of 3	£2.50
(L7-L9)	Sheet of 9	£15.00
(L7Sp-L9Sp)	Sheet of 9 - ovptd in red	£35.00

Nos: L7-L9) 2500 of each, with 50 uncut sheets of 9 stamps (3 of each design). Colour proofs exist.

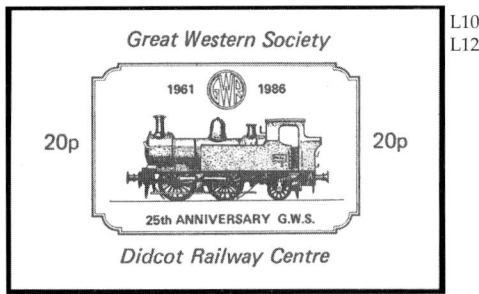

20/5/86. 25th Anniversary of the Great Western Society. Des: C. J. Whitehead. Ptr: Phoenix Press, Guildford. Single imperf labels.

Dsgn: G.W.R. 0-4-2T

L10	20p Red	.60
L10a	20p Red - with black cachet	£20.00
L10Sp	20p Red - ovptd in black	£10.00
L11	20p Green	.40
L11a	20p Green - with green cachet	£20.00
L11Sp	20p Green - ovptd in black	£10.00
L12	20p Blue	.60
L12a	20p Blue - with red cachet	£20.00
L12Sp	20p Blue - ovptd in black	£10.00

Nos: L10) 500; L10Sp) 30; L11) 700; L11Sp) 30; L12) 500; L12Sp) 30. A small number of stamps, L10a, L11a and L12a - perhaps 12 of each, (printed on paper approx. 100mm x 130mm) were distributed as publicity. Each had a small round "DIDCOT 25 G.W.S." cachet applied: black cachet below the red design, green below green, and red below blue. Colour proofs and trials exist.

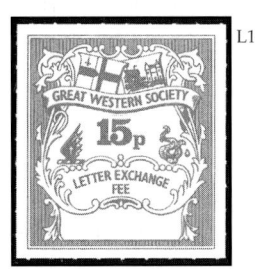
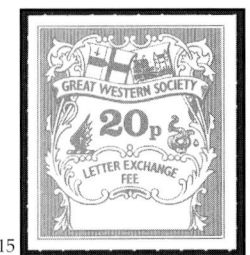

2/4/94. Return to Service of T.P.O. 814. Des: Adapted from L1. Ptr: Elsworthy & Son Ltd., Bristol. Offset lithography in sheets of 3 (1 row of 3). R4.75.

Dsgn: As L1 but with new values

L13	5p Yellow	.30
L14	15p Orange	.40
L15	20p Blue	.40
(L13)	Sheet of 3	£1.00
(L14)	Sheet of 3	£1.00
(L15)	Sheet of 3	£1.20

Nos: 3000 of each.

22/9/95. Mail By Rail Weekend. Des: Adapted from L1. Ptr: Elsworthy & Son Ltd., Bristol. Offset lithography in sheets of 3 (1 row of 3). R4.75.

Dsgn: As L1 but with new value

| L16 | 25p Purple-brown | .40 |
| | Sheet of 3 | £1.20 |

Nos: 1440.

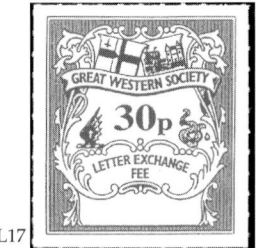

25/9/98. T.P.O. 814 Weekend. Des: Adapted from L1. Ptr: Rainbow Colour, Steventon, Oxon. Offset lithography in sheets of 3 (1 row of 3). R5.5.

Dsgn: As L1 but with new value and typeface

| L17 | 30p Brunswick green | .45 |
| | Sheet of 3 | £1.35 |

Nos: 3000.

ISLE OF MAN RAILWAY

The 3′ gauge line which runs westwards from Douglas to Port Erin across the south of the island, passes through stations at Port Soderick (3 miles), Santon (6), Ballasalla (8 1/3), Castletown (10), Ballabeg (11 1/2), Colby (12 3/4), and Port St. Mary (15). This 15 1/2 mile branch is the surviving arm of a steam hauled system which in earlier times covered much of the island. Opened in 1873, the railway has operated almost continuously since then and is one of the oldest preserved railways in Britain. Lack of finance for many years has meant it still retains much of its Edwardian atmosphere which is appreciated by the enthusiasts who are visiting the island in increasing numbers.

Labels were produced during 1971 which appear to have only been used on commemorative occasions (see pg 30). The railway issued official stamps in 1993 for the Year of Railways (the M.E.R. stamps, see pg 42, were also valid for use over the railway) and offered a full public letter service but found these operations a drain on resources. The Isle of Man Post Office, a postal authority independent of Royal Mail, took over responsibility for the service in 1998 and issued stamps the same year. Although these latter stamps are available from stations on the railway, and to an extent at the souvenir shop, the main stocks are held by the Post Office and drawn on from there as required.

The railway introduced plain circular station cancels, inscribed "Isle of Man" and "Railway Station" with moveable dates, when the railway letter service started on 14 August 1993, at Ballasalla, Castletown, Douglas, Port Erin, and Port St. Mary. These five were replaced on 2 May 1998, with similar "Isle of Man Steam Railway" / "Station" ones inscribed with the additional legend "Steam 125".

Enquiries to: Isle of Man Railways, Strathallan Crescent, Douglas, Isle of Man IM2 4NR [for No.1-4]; and Isle of Man Post Office Philatelic Bureau, P.O. Box IOM, Circular Road, Douglas, Isle of Man IM99 1PB [for No.5-8]

14/8/93. Centenary of the Isle of Man Railway. Des: Graham Warhurst. Ptr: The House of Questa. Offset lithography in miniature sheets of 4 (2 rows of 2), containing one example of each, num. A00001 - 12000. P13.2.

Dsgn: 1) Beyer Peacock 2-4-0T No.4 *Loch*; 2) Beyer Peacock 2-4-0T No.10 *G. H. Wood*; 3) Beyer Peacock 2-4-0T No.12 *Hutchinson*; 4) Beyer Peacock 2-4-0T No.11 *Maitland*

1	25p Multicoloured	
2	25p Multicoloured	
3	25p Multicoloured	
4	25p Multicoloured	
	Miniature sheet of 4	£2.00

Nos: 12000 of each.

2/5/98. Definitives. Des: Paul Ogden. Ptr: The House of Questa. Offset lithography in sheets of 8 (4 rows of 2, se-tenant horiz. 5+6), num. 00001 - 62500. P13.2.

Dsgn: 5) No.10 *G. H. Wood* departing from Douglas Station; 6) No.11 *Maitland* with train on the coast

5	25p Multicoloured	
6	25p Multicoloured	
	Se-tenant pair	.75
	Sheet of 8	£2.80

Nos: 50000 of each.

2/5/98. Definitives. Des: Paul Ogden. Ptr: The House of Questa. Offset lithography in sheets of 8 (4 rows of 2, se-tenant horiz. 7+8), num. 00001 - 62500. P13.2.

Dsgn: 7) No.4 *Loch* departing from Douglas Station; 8) No.12 *Hutchinson* with train at speed in the countryside

7	25p Multicoloured	
8	25p Multicoloured	
	Se-tenant pair	.75
	Sheet of 8	£2.80

Nos: 50000 of each.

LABELS

The labels produced during 1971, and used on commemorative occasions, are listed under Isle of Man Victorian Steam Railway on pg 30.

P.O. ONE-DAY POSTMARKS

2/5/98	Douglas - First Day of Issue Steam 125 [illus. ticket with names of stations inscribed along top and bottom]

On the fdi of the postage stamps to celebrate 125 years of Isle of Man Railways the P.O. used special cancels at the post offices closest to the railway stations along the line. Each was illustrated with the stylised drawing of a locomotive smokebox, chimney and bufferbeam:

2/5/98	Ballabeg Post Office Steam 125 First Day of Issue
2/5/98	Ballasalla Post Office Steam 125 First Day of Issue
2/5/98	Castletown Post Office Steam 125 First Day of Issue
2/5/98	Colby Post Office Steam 125 First Day of Issue
2/5/98	Port Erin Post Office Steam 125 First Day of Issue
2/5/98	Port St. Mary Post Office Steam 125 First Day of Issue
2/5/98	Regent Street [Douglas] Post Office Steam 125 First Day of Issue
2/5/98	Santon Post Office Steam 125 First Day of Issue
9/5/98	T.P.O. [illus. side view of typical I.o.M. 2-4-0T loco]

P.O. slogan postmarks were used to celebrate the "Year of Railways Isle of Man 1993" celebrations:

7/12/92	Douglas [White lettering on black]
20/1/93	Douglas [Black lettering on white]
25/1/93	Ramsey [Black lettering on white]

ISLE OF MAN VICTORIAN STEAM RAILWAY

These labels came into use in July 1971, for one season. Although items of mail were carried over the Isle of Man Railway's line for a period of weeks on commemorative occasions they do not appear to have been available for an on demand service. The proprietors of the I.o.M. Railway (see also pg 29) approached Gordon Quirk, who had run the island's strike mail earlier the same year with the approval of the island's postal authorities, to introduce a service as a means of raising funds. Labels were produced by Gordon Quirk who was responsible for a large number of printings, each with distinctive differences. Many of these were poorly produced in small quantities as required and colour shifts or missing colours are known. The basic designs are listed here for information:

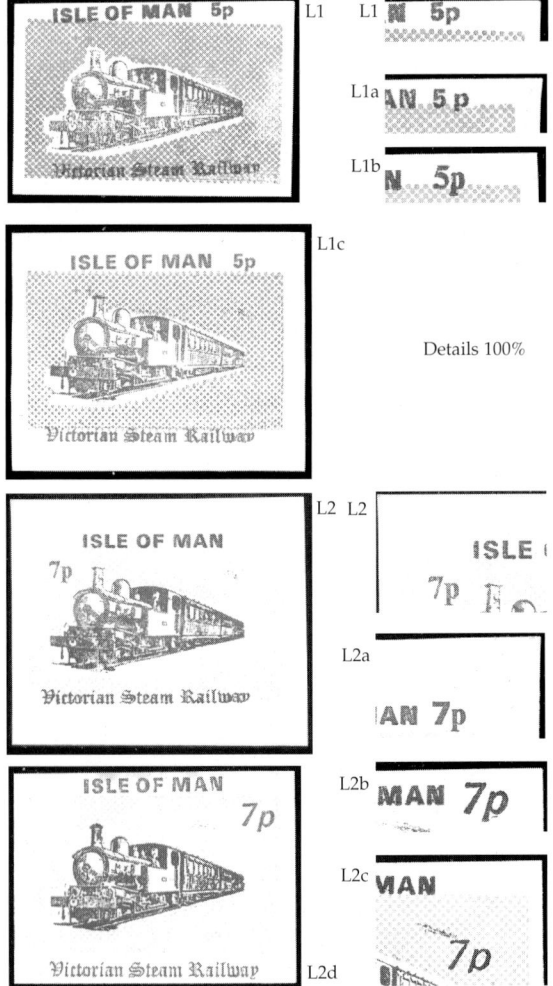

Details 100%

7/7/71 onwards. Definitives. Des and Ptr: Gordon Quirk. Letterpress, or offset lithography and letterpress, in sheets of 10 (2 rows of 5 tête-bêche). Imperf.

Dsgn: Beyer Peacock 2-4-0T locomotive and train

L1	5p Cornflower blue and grey (sans serif value)	£11.00
L1a	5p Cornflower blue and grey (sans serif value, gap between 5 and p)	£11.00
L1b	5p Bright blue and grey (serif value)	£8.00
L1c	5p Cornflower blue and grey (sans serif value, legend set wider)	£8.00
L2	7p Red, yellow and purple (serif value to left of loco chimney)	£11.00
L2a	7p Red, yellow and purple (value and serif 'p' in line with legend)	£11.00
L2b	7p Red, yellow and purple (italic sans serif value near top legend)	£11.00
L2c	7p Red, yellow and purple (italic sans serif value set lower)	£11.00
L2d	7p Red, yellow and purple (italic sans serif, legend set wider)	£8.00
L1/1a	Vert. tête-bêche se-tenant pair	£27.50
L1b/1c	Vert. tête-bêche se-tenant pair	£22.50
L2/2a/2b/2c	Vert. tête-bêche se-tenant pair	£27.50
L2d	Vert. tête-bêche se-tenant pair	£22.50
(L1/1a)	Sheet of 10	£150.00
(L1b/1c)	Sheet of 10	£125.00
(L2/2a/2b/2c)	Sheet of 10	£150.00
(L2d)	Sheet of 10	£125.00

Nos: L1) and L1a) 600 in total; L1b) 2000; 1c) a figure is not known for this variety. L2) 600; L2a) and L2b) 450 in total; L2c) 300; L2d) 4500. Most variations are the result of the separate printings produced as the need arose, but many colour shades exist. The only intentional change occurred when the supply of cornflower blue ink ran out and was replaced by a brighter blue. Most of the legends have their baselines set approx. 28mm apart. The wider set legends have baselines approx. 31mm apart which usually positions the lettering clear of the background colour. The position of each label's value can vary slightly within a printing batch because they were applied separately from the legend text. L2c and L2d are printed on pancake non-curl gummed paper which appears shiny on the reverse.

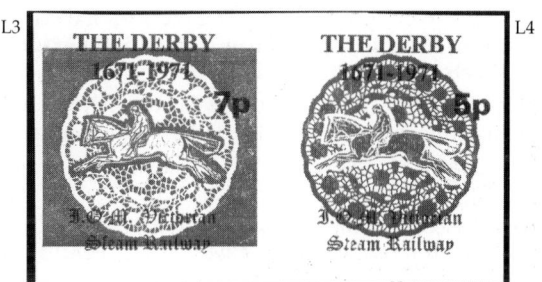

L3 / L4

L3   L3a   L4   L4a

Details 150%

Sfeam ailway

Examples of letterpress typographical errors e.g. "Sfeam ailway"

30/8/71. 300th Anniversary of The Derby. Des & Ptr: Gordon Quirk. Offset lithography in sheets of 12 (2 rows of 6, se-tenant horiz. L3+L4+L3+L4+L3+L4 (or L3a+L4a etc.) and tête-bêche creating vert. se-tenant pairs). Imperf.

Dsgn: Horse and jockey on lace doily

L3	7p Red and black - sans serif	£8.00
L3a	7p Red and black - gothic pen script	£25.00
L4	5p Red and black - sans serif	£8.00
L4a	5p Red and black - gothic pen script	£25.00
L3-L4	Horiz. se-tenant pair	£20.00
L3a-L4a	Horiz. se-tenant pair	-
L3-L4	Vert. tête-bêche se-tenant pair	£20.00
L3a-L4a	Vert. tête-bêche se-tenant pair	-
L3-L4	Tête-bêche block of 4	£40.00
L3a-L4a	Tête-bêche block of 4	-
(L3-L4)	Sheet of 12	£150.00
(L3a-L4a)	Sheet of 12	-

Nos: L3-L4 and L3a-L4a) 5000 of each value in total. There are several typographical errors in the legends which may have been corrected as and when they were discovered. Both styles of typefaces appear on first day covers. L3a-L4a appear to be very scarce.

L5

L5a

1/9/71. Parcel Label. Des & Ptr: Gordon Quirk. Letterpress and offset lithography in sheets of 8 (2 rows of 4 tête-bêche). Imperf.

Dsgn: Beyer Peacock 2-4-0T locomotive and train

L5	10p Red, yellow and black	
	- inscribed "PARCEL" in serif letters	£12.00
L5a	10p on 7p Red, yellow and black (2a)	
	- inscribed "Parcel Rate" in italic script	£80.00
L5	Tête-bêche se-tenant pair	£30.00
L5	Sheet of 8	£150.00

Nos: L5) 1500; L5a) 50. L5a was an early essay produced by surcharging L2a with the new value in italic sans serif font, adding the text in italic script, and overprinting the original value with a star. It was never issued so its status is 'prepared but not issued'. It is unlikely that complete sheets of the essay exist.

I.o.M. VICTORIAN STEAM RAILWAY CANCELLATIONS

1	7/7/71	Douglas [double ring cancel applied by letterpress on philatelic cards or by rubber stamp]
2	30/8/71	Derbyhaven - Derby Tercentenary 1671 - 1971 I.O.M.V.S.R. Site Excursion [illus. horse and jockey applied by rubber stamp in black or 'embossed' in gold]
3	1/9/71	Douglas [double ring cancel similar to No.1, but with "Parcel" added above the date]

KEIGHLEY & WORTH VALLEY RAILWAY

The railway is a 4¾ mile single track, standard gauge branch line built by the Midland Railway in 1867, running on a steep average gradient of 1 in 76, from a junction at Keighley, West Yorkshire. It serves stations at Ingrow (1¼), Damems (2), Oakworth (2¾), Haworth (3½), and Oxenhope. Haworth is world famous as the home of the Brontë family. The line was closed by British Railways in 1962, and the K.W.V.R. Preservation Society was formed the same year. Steady progress enabled the line to reopen to passengers in 1968.

Stamps are inscribed "Worth Valley", "Keighley & Worth Valley", or simply "KWVLR" and "KWVR". Instead of issuing a new stamp the railway introduced a "5p Rail Mail" handstamp on 27 September 1990, to make up the 25p letter rate which had been increased on 1st January 1990. The service, which was not known to operate a public service on a regular basis, ceased in the early 1990s with the retirement of the railway's postmaster.

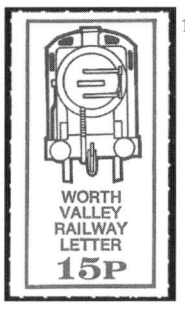
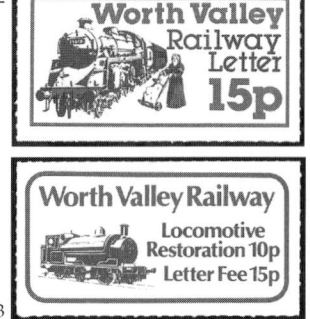

9/5/79. Definitive. Des: Walter Simms. Ptr: Guernsey Herald Ltd. Lithography in sheets of 15 (3 rows of 5). Coloured R5 (in black).

Dsgn: Front view of L.M.S. Class 4 0-6-0 locomotive

| 1 | 15p Black and red | .45 |
| | Sheet of 15 | £7.00 |

Nos: 10500. FDC: 1000

21/11/79. Christmas Issue. Des & Ptr: Larkfield Printing Co. Ltd., Brighouse, Leeds. Lithography in sheets of 10 (5 rows of 2). R10.

Dsgn: Santa Claus with platform barrow and perspective view of B.R. Class 4 4-6-0 locomotive

| 2 | 15p Black and red | .45 |
| | Sheet of 10 | £5.00 |

Nos: 6600. Examples are known with a significant upward shift of the red printing. FDC: 1000

The Railway Philatelic Group is the publisher of the following books of interest to the railway philatelist:

Travelling Post Offices of Great Britain & Ireland (Their history and postmarks with 41 photographs) -
by H.S. Wilson £21.00

Great Britain & Ireland T.P.O. Postmarks: A Guide & Catalogue -
by Frank J. Wilson £7.00

The Railway Sub Offices of Great Britain -
by A.M. Goodbody £3.00

Great Britain & Ireland Railway Letter Stamps 1957 - 1998
by Neill Oakley £10.00

Please add £4.00 postage and packing for the first book in the list and 50p each for the remainder. Available from:
H.S. Wilson, R.P.G. Publications Officer, 17 Heath Avenue, Littleover, Derby DE23 6DJ

12/3/80. Restoration Issue. Des & Ptr: Larkfield Printing Co. Ltd., from an idea by one of the railway's staff. Lithography in sheets of 10 (5 rows of 2). R10.

Dsgn: L.&Y.R. 0-6-0T No.752

3	15p + 10p charity surcharge	
	Black and red	£4.00
	Sheet of 10	£45.00

Nos: 6600; later an unknown number of stamps, up to 3000?, were surcharged for No.10-10b. FDC: 1000

Dsgn: Christmas carols at Keighley Station

5	20p Black and red	£1.00
	Sheet of 10	£12.00

Nos: 5000. FDC: 1000

 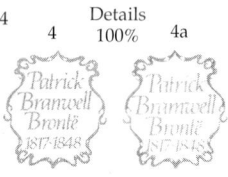

21/4/81. Bishop Eric Treacy Commemorative. Des: Robin Higgins. Ptr: Larkfield Printing Co. Ltd. Lithography in sheets of 20 (5 rows of 4, se-tenant horiz. 6+7+8+9). P11.

Dsgn: 6) L.M.S. "Patriot" Class 4-6-0 No.45525 hauling "The Merseyside Express" in Edge Hill cutting; 7) Keighley Parish Church; 8) B.R. Class 9F 2-10-0 No.92220 *Evening Star*; 9) Eric Treacy Memorial Hall, Wakefield Cathedral. All with portrait of Eric Treacy.

6	20p Purple and black	
7	20p Purple and black	
8	20p Purple and black	
9	20p Purple and black	
6-9	Se-tenant strip of 4	£3.00
6a-9a	Se-tenant strip of 4 - imperf	-
(6-9)	Sheet of 20	£15.00

9/7/80. Branwell Brontë Commemorative. Des: Robin Higgins; Illus: portrait by an unknown artist, the copyright of the Brontë Trust. Ptr: Larkfield Printing Co. Ltd. Lithography in sheets of 10 (5 rows of 2). R10.

Dsgn: Profile of Branwell Brontë

4	15p Black and dull green	.45
4a	15p Black and yellow green	
	- error, inscribed "Bramwell"	£32.50
4a	15p Black and yellow green	
	- "Bramwell" error (used on postcard)	£17.50
(4)	Sheet of 10	£5.00
(4a)	Sheet of 10 - "Bramwell" error	£300.00

Nos: 4) 6600; 4a) 250? No.4a was the original stamp but, when the spelling error was discovered shortly before the issue date, the printing was destroyed. The railway believed only about 140, which had already been distributed, remained from the print run of 6600 - 70 existing in mint condition and the others being used on R.M. PHQ cards prepared by a dealer - since the rest were supposed to have been destroyed in a locomotive firebox. From observation more must have survived, and although a total of 250 may exist they are still much sought after. No.4 was a hastily produced replacement. FDC: 1300

Nos: Two printings were made totalling approx 7000 stamps of each. Sheets from the first were mostly destroyed as sub-standard and a reprint was made. The paper used is either a creamy white or brilliant white, not necessarily from the two print runs. There are many varieties of No.6-9, including: perfs misplaced or double, colour shifts, and a number of sheets which had perfs omitted between the first and second, and second and third columns. Apparently at least one totally imperf sample sheet (No.6a-9a) was divided to provide publicity copies.
FDC: 1000

18/5/81. Centenary of No.752. Surcharged in black by Clemesha and Sons Ltd, Great Harwood, Lancs.

10	20p+10p on 15p+10p (3)	£5.00
10a	20p+10p on 15p+10p (3) (used on cover)	£5.00
10b	20p+10p on 15p+10p (3)	£5.00

19/11/80. Christmas Issue. Des: Robin Higgins. Ptr: Larkfield Printing Co. Ltd. Lithography in sheets of 10 (5 rows of 2). R10.

 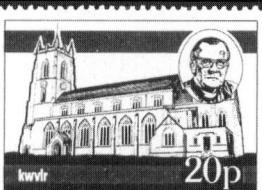  

Details 225%   10   10a   10b

(10)   Sheet of 10   £55.00
(10b)   Sheet of 10   £55.00

Nos: The numbers surcharged for each type are not known; perhaps up to 1000 of each type exist. The railway was unable to supply the printer with enough sheets of No.3 from one source to complete the print run required. After surcharging a batch delivered by hand the printer dismantled the forme by mistake before a second batch of sheets arrived by post. No.10b is thought to be the second printing. No explanation is known for the different block sizes on No.10 and 10a.

The three styles are identified as follows: No.10 and 10a have square fronted base to 2, thinner p - but No.10 has a patchy 'squarer' obliteration block (letterpress), and No.10a has a smaller rectangular block; No.10b has a round fronted base to 2, thicker p, a solid black rectangular obliteration block (lithography). All examples of No.10a were used on fdc.   FDC: 10a) 1000

19/9/82. Bluebell Railway and Keighley & Worth Valley Railway Joint Issue. For full details see pg 11.

11   20p Red, green and black

22/1/85. Famous Trains. Des: Robin Higgins. Ptr: Larkfield Printing Co. Ltd. Photo-lithography in sheets of 10 (5 rows of 2). P11.

Dsgn: S.R. "West Country" Class 4-6-2 No.34092 *City of Wells* hauling "Golden Arrow" train

12   20p Multicoloured   .40
12a   20p - imperf   -
(12)   Sheet of 10   £3.00
(12a) Sheet of 10 - imperf   -

Nos: 50000. Sheets with misaligned or missing rows of perforations are known. The imperf variety was used as press publicity copies.   FDC: 800

9/5/85. Locomotives for Victory. Des: John Holroyd. Ptr: Larkfield Printing Co. Ltd. Photo-lithography in sheets of 10 (5 rows of 2, se-tenant horiz. 13+14). P12.

Dsgn: 13) 0-6-0ST and 2-8-0 locos with British flags; 14) 0-6-0T and 2-8-0 locos with American flags

13   20p Pink, black, blue and red
14   20p Blue, black and red
       Se-tenant pair   .80
       Sheet of 10   £4.00

Nos: 10000 of each. On row 5, stamp 2 a black line descends towards the border from the dash which separates "USATC" and "40th".   FDC: 650

8/8/85. Naming of British Rail Class 47 Bo-Bo Locomotive No.47424 *The Brontës of Haworth*. Des: John Holroyd. Ptr: Larkfield Printing Co. Ltd. Photo-lithography in sheets of 10 (5 rows of 2). P11.

Dsgn: The Brontë sisters and B.R. Class 47 diesel

15   20p Blue, brown, yellow and red   .40
       Sheet of 10   £3.00

Nos: 5000. A sheet is reported imperf between the second and third rows.   FDC: 750

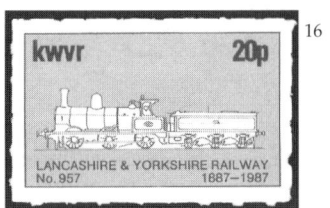

31/12/87. Barton Wright Locomotive Centenary. Des & Ptr: Crown Press, Keighley. Offset lithography in sheets of 10 (5 rows of 2). R3.5.

Dsgn: L.&Y.R. 0-6-0 No.957 (later B.R. No.52044)

16   20p Black and pink   .40
       Sheet of 10   £3.75

Nos: 5000. Constant flaws appear in row 3, stamp 1 (black dot under E of "Lancashire") and row 3, stamp 2 (black lines joining letters in the word "Yorkshire").   FDC: 500

22/7/89. Official Opening of Ingrow West Station. Des & Ptr: Lords Printers Ltd., Burnley. Offset lithography in sheets of 10 (5 rows of 2).

Dsgn: Ingrow West station building

17	20p Black and pink - P11	.40
17a	20p Black and pink - R9.5 (used on cover)	£2.50
(17)	Sheet of 10	£4.00

Nos: 17) 5000; 17a) 650. Two days before the station's official opening no stamps had arrived from the printers. The railway discovered that the stamps would not be ready in time because the perforating machine at the subcontracted firm had broken down and needed repairs. The printers arranged for sufficient sheets to be rouletted for the fdc so these could be prepared the night before they were carried. The perforated stamps were delivered four days late. All examples of the rouletted stamps (No.17a) were used on fdc, and only perforated examples (No.17) exist in mint condition.

FDC: 17a) 650

27/10/90. Welcome to Bahamas Locomotive Society. Des: Robin Higgins. Ptr: Lords Printers, Burnley. Offset lithography in sheets of 10 (5 rows of 2). R4.75.

Dsgn: L.M.S. Class 5 4-6-0 No.45596 *Bahamas*

18	25p Multicoloured	.40
	Sheet of 10	£3.50

Nos: 2000. FDC: 750

K.W.V.R. SPECIAL CANCELLATIONS

1	2/7/79	Haworth - First Day of Slogan Mark and 1979 Daily Services
2	21/11/79	Haworth - First Railway Christmas Stamp First Day
3	12/3/80	752 Stamp First Day
4	9/7/80	Branwell Brontë Stamp First Day The Brontë Country Line
5	19/11/80	Christmas First Day
6	21/4/81	Wakefield Cathedral Eric Treacy Memorial Hall [illus. cathedral coat of arms - undated]
7	21/4/81	Keighley - Eric Treacy Hall Project Inauguration
8	18/5/81	752 Centenary. First Day of Issue
9	29/8/81	Lion - Visits the Worth Valley 1981 [illus. side view of loco - undated]
10	29/8/91	Carried by Lion
11	18/11/81	Christmas Stamp Issue
12	19/9/82	Bulleid Centenary
13	22/1/85	Haworth - Famous Trains First Day of Issue
14	9/5/85	Locomotives for Victory First Day of Issue
15	9/5/85	V. 40th Anniversary [V shaped cancel]
16	27/7/85	Damems - Best Restored Station Plaque Unveiling Ceremony
17	8/8/85	Haworth - Naming of Class 47 Locomotive
	29/6/88	20th Anniversary of Reopening KWVRPS [illus. side view of 0-6-0T. Believed to have been sponsored by Benhams for their 'silk' covers only]
18	22/7/89	Ingrow West Station Official Opening

P.O. ONE-DAY POSTMARKS

1/7/78	Ten Years of Steam Trains
9/5/79	Haworth Station - First Day of Worth Valley Railway Letter Service
18/5/81	Centenary of Loco 752 [illus. loco]
29/6/88	Haworth - 20th Anniversary of Reopening of the Worth Valley Line [illus. 2-6-4T loco and train. Believed to have been sponsored by Benhams for their 'silk' covers only]

P.O. slogan postmarks have used to advertise the railway:

6/3/78	10 Yrs of Steam Trains
2/7/79	Daily Steam Trains July and August

KENT & EAST SUSSEX RAILWAY

This was the first standard gauge line opened under the Light Railway Act of 1896, and is typical of the country railways built with steep gradients and tight curves through sparsely populated areas. Built under the direction of Mr. (later Lt. Col.) H. F. Stephens, it was opened to goods traffic from Robertsbridge to Tenterden (at the station now called Rolvenden) on 26 March, and for passengers on 2 April 1900. The railway changed its original name, The Rother Valley Railway, to that now used in 1904, and was extended to Headcorn on 15 May 1905. The Company maintained its independence in 1923, but was nationalised in 1948. Passenger services were withdrawn in 1954 and the last British Railways goods train ran on 11 June 1961.

The Tenterden Railway Co. had use of the line on a rental basis between Tenterden Town Station and Bodiam since its inception in 1971, and purchased it in 1973. The running of trains between Tenterden and Rolvenden (1½ miles), commenced on 3 February 1974. The line has now been extended beyond Wittersham Road (4¼), currently terminating at Northiam (6¾) since 1990. The line will be extended to Bodiam (10) in the year 2000, and possibly to Robertsbridge (13½) at some future date.

The railway began its letter service in 1979, issuing cancellers to all three stations then operating. The service has been suspended in recent years except for special occasions. It is unlikely the railway will sign the 1998 Agreement. The definitive stamps and a few remaining covers are available from the railway.

Enquiries to: CSRE Ltd., Kent & East Sussex Railway, Tenterden, Kent, TN30 6HE.

11/7/79. Definitives. Des: Michael Seymour. Ptr: T. Stephenson & Sons Ltd, Prescot, Merseyside. Lithography in sheets of 10 (5 rows of 2, se-tenant horiz. 1+2, with large illustrated border which includes a column of 5 perforated stamp-size labels, one of which is numbered), num. 0001 - 4000 (see also No.3+4). P14.

Dsgn: 1) Hunslet 0-6-0ST No.23 *Holman F. Stephens*; 2) L.B.S.C.R. 0-6-0T No.10 *Sutton*

1	15p Black, blue-green and red	
2	15p Black, blue-green and red	
	Se-tenant pair	.75
(1-2)	Decor. sheet of 10	£3.75
(1Sp-2Sp)	Decor. sheet of 10 - ovptd in black across all 10 stamps	£25.00

Nos: 1-2) 20000 of each, later approx 2500 of each were surcharged for No.3-4, leaving an issue of approx 17500 of each. 1Sp-2Sp) 250 of each? Approx 50 unnumbered specimen sheets exist.   FDC: 4000

1/12/80. Provisionals. Surcharged in black by T. Stephenson & Sons Ltd., num. from 0301.

3	20p on 15p (1)	
4	20p on 15p (2)	
	Se-tenant pair	£3.50
	Decor. sheet of 10	£20.00

Nos: 2500 of each, approx. Sheets are known with numbering up to 853. A handful of examples are known with the overprint offset on the reverse.
FDC: 100

13/5/81. Definitives. Des: Michael Seymour. Ptr: Derek Smith, Gillingham, Kent. Lithography in sheets of 18 (6 rows of 3, se-tenant horiz. 5+6+7), num. 0001 - 2000. R5.

Dsgn: 5) Hawthorne Leslie 0-8-0T *Hecate*; 6) Royal Coach and portrait of H. F. Stephens; 7) Hawthorne Leslie 0-6-0T *Tenterden*

5	20p Blue and brown
6	10p Blue and brown
7	10p Blue and brown

	Se-tenant strip of 3	.80
	Decor. sheet of 18	£5.00

Nos: 12000 of each.

K.E.S.R. SPECIAL CANCELLATIONS

1	11/7/79	Wittersham Road - Official Opening of Railway Letter Service [The handstamp is dated 18/7/79, the proposed date of issue which was brought forward when the P.O. advanced the issue of their 'Year of the Child' stamps]
2	11/7/79	Tenterden Town - Official Opening of Railway Letter Service [see note above re. dates]
3	12/3/80	Tenterden - 80th Anniversary of Rother Railway [illus. 0-6-0T - miniature version of P.O. postmark]
4	24/5/81	Opening of Dixter Halt
5	9/6/82	The Lord Warden Carried on Inaugural Train [illus. coat of arms within headboard border]

P.O. ONE-DAY POSTMARKS

1/6/74	Tenterden - Re-opening
11/7/79	Tenterden - Children's Day
21/11/79	Tenterden - Father Christmas Special
12/3/80	Tenterden - 80th Anniversary of Rother Railway [illus. 0-6-0T - curved cancellation]
4/8/80	Tenterden - 80th Anniversary of Rother Railway [illus. line of 0-6-0T locos - rectangular cancellation]
4/6/90	Northiam Rye - Northiam Station Re-opening [illus. side view of L.B.S.C.R. 0-6-0T loco]

LLANBERIS LAKE RAILWAY
RHEILFFORDD LLYN PADARN

The 4' gauge Padarn Railway was opened in 1848, to connect the Dinorwic Slate Quarries at Llanberis, Gwynedd, with the coastal port of Velinheli (now Felinheli). The railway carried slates and general merchandise for the Dinorwic Estate and passenger trains were operated for the use of the quarrymen and estate employees. The line was closed in 1961, and road transport was then used until the final closure of the quarries in 1969.

The Llanberis Lake Railway was constructed as a 1'11½" gauge line on a two mile section of the Padarn Railway, opening to Cei Llydan in 1971, and through to Penllyn in 1972. Westbound trains do not stop at the intermediate station, but travel direct to Penllyn where passengers may not alight because of narrow clearances. Trains stop at Cei Llydan, a popular venue for lakeside picnics which is remote from any public road, on the return journey. Visitors can purchase postcards here and post them in the letterbox on each train. Mail is transferred by the Company to the post office at Llanberis for onward transmission to its destinations.

The Welsh stamps were initially inscribed "Rheilffordd Llyn Llanberis", but from No.3 were inscribed "Rheilffordd Llyn Padarn". Between the rate increase of 1 January 1978, and the issue of the 15p definitive No.3-4, 10p stamps were used plus a handstamp worded "Talwyd 5c / Ychwanegol / Addl. 5p Pd", in two layouts of text, to indicate the correct rate had been paid.

Enquiries to: Llanberis Lake Railway, Gilfach Ddu, Llanberis, Gwynedd LL55 4TY

4/8/76. Definitives. Des: Anthony Daffern. Ptr: T. Stephenson & Sons Ltd., Prescot. Lithography in sheets of 10 (5 rows of 2, se-tenant horiz. 1+2), num. 0001 - 1100. P14.

Dsgn: Hunslet 0-4-0ST No.3 *Dolbadarn*

1	10c Red and olive (W)	
2	10p Red and olive (E)	
	Se-tenant pair	£7.00
	Sheet of 10	£37.50

Nos: 5500 of each.

31/5/78. Definitives. Des: Anthony Daffern. Ptr: The Seal House Press Ltd, Liverpool. Lithography in sheets of 10 (5 rows of 2, se-tenant horiz., rows 1, 3 & 5: 3+4; rows 2 & 4: 4+3), num. 0001 - 2200. P11.

Dsgn: Hunslet 0-4-0ST No.1 *Elidir*

3	15c Red and brown (W)	
4	15p Red and brown (E)	
	Se-tenant pair.	£1.75
	Block of 4	£3.50
	Sheet of 10	£9.00

Nos: 15000 of each (sheets num. 0001 - 3000); later 4000 stamps (sheets num. 2201 - 3000) were surcharged for No.7-8, leaving an issue of 3) 12600; 4) 13400. A number of sheets have misaligned perfs or are imperf between the bottom pair of stamps and the margin.

4/8/80. Great Little Trains of Wales Joint Issue. For full details see pg 26.

5   15p Black and red (E)
6   15c Black and red (W)

?/10/80. Provisionals. The first column surcharged in black 5c or 5p, num. 2201 - 3000.

7	5c on 15c (W) (3)	
8	5p on 15p (E) (4)	
7+4	Se-tenant pair	£4.00
8+3	Se-tenant pair	£5.00
3+4+7+8	Block of 4	£9.00
(3+4+7+8)	Sheet of 10	£25.00

Nos: 7) 2400; 8) 1600. 800 sheets were surcharged. Sheets have been reported imperf between the bottom pair of stamps and the margin, or with double perfs down the centre of the sheet. Examples are also known with misaligned surcharges.
FDC: The Company did not fix an issue date for these provisionals; covers were serviced on 19/11/80, when the new rate was introduced, but envelopes also exist dated as early as 31/10/80, bearing only 5p or 5c stamps to make up the 15p rate. It is conceivable that they were used earlier.

19/7/81. 10th Anniversary. Des: Anthony Daffern. Ptr: T. Stephenson & Sons Ltd. Lithography in sheets of 10 (5 rows of 2, se-tenant horiz., rows 1, 3 & 5: 9+10; rows 2 & 4: 10+9), num. 1 - 500. As No.11+12, except overprinted in black "1971 Degfed Pen Blwydd 1981" or "1971 Tenth Anniversary 1981". P14.

Dsgn: Henschel 0-4-0T No.5 *Helen Kathryn*

9	20c Red (W)	
10	20p Red (E)	
	Se-tenant pair	£4.50
	Block of 4	£9.50
	Sheet of 10	£24.00

Nos: 2500 of each.

12/8/81. Definitives. Details as for No.9+10, except without overprint, num. 501 - 2000.

11	20c (W) (9)	
12	20p (E) (10)	
	Se-tenant pair	£3.00
	Block of 4	£6.00
	Sheet of 10	£17.50

Nos: 7500 of each.

7/3/89. Return to Steam of *Thomas Bach*. Des: Michael Seymour. Ptr: Faulwood & Herbert Ltd., Brighton. Offset lithography in sheets of 10 (5 rows of 2, se-tenant horiz. rows 1, 3 & 5: 13+14; rows 2 & 4: 14+13), num. 0001 - 0500. R4.75.

Dsgn: Hunslet 0-4-0ST *Wild Aster* (now *Thomas Bach*), inscribed "Return to Steam 1988" in W or E

13	20c Light blue, red and black (W)	
14	20p Light blue, red and black (E)	
	Se-tenant pair	£3.00
	Block of 4	£6.00
	Sheet of 10	£17.50

Nos: 2500 of each.

10/4/90. Centenary of *Elidir*. Des: Michael Seymour. Ptr: Faulwood & Herbert Ltd. Offset lithography in sheets of 10 (5 rows of 2, se-tenant horiz., rows 1, 3 & 5: 15+16; rows 2 & 4: 16+15), num. 0001 - 1000. R4.75.

Dsgn: Hunslet 0-4-0ST *Elidir*, inscribed "100 years old" in W or E

15	25c Grey, black and red (W)	
16	25p Grey, black and red (E)	
	Se-tenant pair	.75
	Block of 4	£1.50
	Sheet of 10	£4.00

Nos: 5000 of each.

16/6/92. 21st Anniversary of the Llanberis Lake Railway. Des: Michael Seymour. Ptr: Faulwood & Herbert Ltd. Offset lithography in sheets of 10 (5 rows of 2, se-tenant horiz. and vert., rows 1, 3 & 5: 17+18; rows 2 & 4: 19+20), num. 0001 - 1000. R14.

Dsgn: 17) and 19) Hunslet 0-4-0ST *Dolbadarn* in original condition at the Dinorwic Slate Quarries; 18) and 20) *Dolbadarn* as restored; all inscribed "21st Anniversary 1971 - 1992" in W or E

17	25c Blue, black, red and orange (W)	
18	25p Blue, black, red and orange (E)	
19	25p Blue, black, red and orange (E)	
20	25c Blue, black, red and orange (W)	
17+18	Se-tenant pair	.75
19+20	Se-tenant pair	£1.00
17-20	Se-tenant block of 4	£1.75
17-20	Sheet of 10	£4.00

Nos: 17 and 18) 1500 of each; 19 and 20) 1000 of each. A sheet is known with the red part of the design offset on the back.

L.L.R. SPECIAL CANCELLATIONS

1   1/5/93   Hunslet Hundred Steam Festival Visit by *Dolbadarn* [illus. loco]

P.O. ONE-DAY POSTMARK

10/6/72   Llanberis - Rheilffordd y llyn agoriad swyddogol [celebrating the opening of the line]

LLECHWEDD SLATE CAVERNS RAILWAY
RHEILFFORDD CEUDYLLAU LLECHWEDD

The railway network at Llechwedd (which now embraces the adjoining slate mines of Maenofferen, Votty & Bowydd, and Diphwys) dates back to 1825. It was linked to the F.R. in 1854; the Cambrian Railway, via Minffordd Exchange Sidings, in 1872; the L.N.W.R., via private sidings beside the Conwy Valley Line, in 1879 (this becoming part of the L.M.S. in 1923); and to the G.W.R.'s new central station in 1883.

An underground letter post was introduced on 30 August 1978, after full consultation with the Wales and the Marches Postal Board. Letters and cards bearing an additional company label could be posted in the underground letterboxes, which were cleared daily by company staff, handstamped "Posted underground at Llechwedd Slate Caverns", before collection each evening by a postman from Blaenau Ffestiniog post office. Letters not actually carried by rail, including stamped cards handed in on the surface and company mail, were cancelled with the company's undated circular logo inscribed bilingually: "Ceudwll Llechwedd Slate Caverns".

This was not a railway letter service under the terms of the Post Office Agreement but, because of its close association with other North Wales minor railways (including membership of the Great Little Trains of Wales), many collectors are interested in the Llechwedd issues. The original letterbox was at the end of the Miners' Tramway, along which passenger trains are hauled by $3^{1}/_{2}$ ton battery-electric locomotives. A second letterbox was installed in the Deep Mine, which passengers reach on a rope-hauled 24-seat vehicle on a 1 in 1.8 incline.

The company identified their designs by the code "LSCR" and a number, which also appeared in the sheet margin. These were used in early editions of this catalogue as the basis for the issue number, but increasing duplication and inconsistencies in the company's sequence means the labels are now listed here in strict chronological order. The company's "LSCR" code is appended in brackets after each label's description. In determining whether the English (E) or Welsh (W) design is given the lower catalogue number for each issue the stamps have been identified from left to right in row 1 of the sheet layout. The colour of the illustration is described before that of the legend. All issues are roulette 7.

Until 1986 all stamps were designed by Ivor Wynne

Jones, except the 'Incline' issue designed by I. W. Jones and Frank Gell, and the 'Engineering Achievements' issue designed by I. W. Jones and W. H. Brown. W. H. Brown designed the '150 Years of Slate Mining' issue of 1986. The labels were printed by The Craig-y-don Printing Works Ltd, Llandudno.

No new labels have been issued for more than ten years and they are not available for sale from the company. Posting boxes are no longer underground. Mail can be posted in the victorian pillarbox in the miner's village or handed to staff at the souvenir shop and are marked with one of two cachets, still worded "posted underground", introduced in 1993 to replace older rubber stamps.

30/8/78. BEV Locomotive and Train

L1	(5p) Red and black (LSCR-1)		.75
	Sheet of 40: Plate A		£30.00

Nos: 7200; 180 single panes.

11/7/79. Alice

L2	5p Black and purple (E) (LSCR-4)		
L3	5c Black and purple (W) (LSCR-5)		
	Se-tenant pair		£10.00
	Sheet of 20: Plate C		£100.00
L4	5p Black and blue (E) (LSCR-4)		
L5	5c Black and blue (W) (LSCR-5)		
	Se-tenant pair		£10.00
	Sheet of 20: Plate C		£100.00

Nos: L2-L5) 2000 of each; 200 sheets of 10 se-tenant pairs for each colour and design. The sheets are dated 18/7/79, the proposed date of issue, brought forward when the P.O. advanced the issue of their 'Year of the Child' stamps. Printed in double panes with L8-L9 and L6-L7 respectively; uncut sheets exist with both designs, Alice and Incline, printed in the same colours.

22/8/79. Incline

L6	5p Blue and black (E) (LSCR-2)
L7	5c Blue and black (W) (LSCR-3)
	Se-tenant pair £9.00
	Sheet of 20: Plate B £90.00

Nos: 2000 of each; 200 sheets of 10 se-tenant pairs. See footnote to L2-L5.

26/9/79. Incline

L8	5p Purple and black (E) (LSCR-2)
L9	5c Purple and black (W) (LSCR-3)
	Se-tenant pair £9.00
	Sheet of 20: Plate B £90.00

Nos: 2000 of each; 200 sheets of 10 se-tenant pairs. See footnote to L2-L5.

12/3/80. BEV Locomotive and Train

L10	5c Red and bright green (W) (LSCR-6)
L11	5p Red and bright green (E) (LSCR-7)
	Se-tenant pair £3.75
	Sheet of 20: Plate D or E £40.00

Nos: 5000 of each; 500 sheets of 10 se-tenant pairs, printed as double panes.

9/7/80. L10 and L11 overprinted "Gwobr Dyfrgi Arian 1980" (W), or "Silver Otter Award 1980" (E).

L12	5c (W) (L10) (LSCR-8)
L13	5p (E) (L11) (LSCR-9)
	Se-tenant pair £3.75
	Sheet of 20: Plate D or E £40.00

Nos: 5000 of each; 500 sheets of 10 se-tenant pairs, printed as double panes.

4/8/80. BEV Locomotive and Train (reprint)

L14	5c Deep red and dull green (W) (L10) (LSCR-6)
L15	5p Deep red and dull green (E) (L11) (LSCR-7)
	Se-tenant pair £2.00
	Sheet of 20: Plate D or E £22.50

Nos: 10000 of each; 1000 sheets of 10 se-tenant pairs, printed as double panes. Uncut sheets of paired panes exist. The reprints can be identified from the original issue by the figure 2 preceding the sheet's identification number.

10/9/80. Welsh Musicians

Dsgn: L16) David Francis, harpist; L17) Anne Edwards, soprano

L16　5c Black and purple (W) (LSCR-10)
L17　5p Black and purple (E) (LSCR-11)
　　　Se-tenant pair　　　　　　　　　£1.00
　　　Sheet of 20: Plate F or G　　　£10.00

Nos: 10000 of each; 1000 sheets of 10 se-tenant pairs, printed as double panes. Examples exist with the purple part of the design missing.

25/5/82. 150th Anniversary of Lewis Carroll's Birth

Dsgn: Alice Railway Scene

L18　5p Black and purple (E) (LSCR-12)
L19　5c Black and purple (W) (LSCR-13)
　　　Se-tenant pair　　　　　　　　　£4.00
　　　Sheet of 20: Plate H　　　　　　£45.00

Nos: 4000 of each; 400 sheets of 10 se-tenant pairs, printed in a single pane.

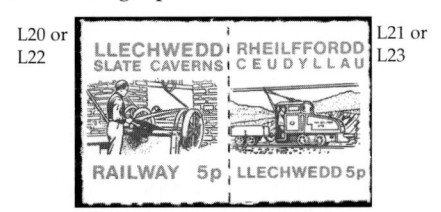

25/5/83. Engineering Achievements

Dsgn: L20) Electric Locomotive; L21) Slate Dressing Machine

L20　5p Blue and red (E) (LSCR-15/16)
L21　5p Blue and red (W) (LSCR-14/17)
　　　Se-tenant pair　　　　　　　　　.75
　　　Block of 4　　　　　　　　　　　£1.50
　　　Sheet of 20: Plate I　　　　　　£8.00

Nos: 4000 of each; 400 sheets of 10 se-tenant pairs, rows 1, 3 & 5: L20+L21+L20+L21, rows 2 & 4: L21+L20+L21+L20. Uncut sheets of paired panes of L20-L21 and L22-L23 exist.

6/7/83. Honouring the Regiments of Meirionnydd

Dsgn: As L20 and L21, except for margin inscription

L22　5p Red and blue (E) (L20) (LSCR-19/20)
L23　5p Red and blue (W) (L21) (LSCR-18/21)
　　　Se-tenant pair　　　　　　　　　.75
　　　Block of 4　　　　　　　　　　　£1.50
　　　Sheet of 20: Plate J　　　　　　£8.00

Nos: 4000 of each; 400 sheets of 10 se-tenant pairs, rows 1, 3 & 5: L22+L23+L22+L23, rows 2 & 4: L23+L22+L23+L22. See footnote to L20-L21.

30/5/85. Engineering Achievements

L24　5p Brown and green (E) (L20) (LSCR-15)
L25　5p Brown and green (W) (L21) (LSCR-14)
　　　Se-tenant pair　　　　　　　　　.75
　　　Block of 4　　　　　　　　　　　£1.50
　　　Sheet of 20: Plate I　　　　　　£8.00

Nos: 5000 of each; 500 sheets of 10 se-tenant pairs, rows 1, 3 & 5: L24+L25+L24+L25, rows 2 & 4: L25+L24+L25+L24.

18/4/86. 150 Years of Slate Mining 1836-1986

Dsgn: L26 and L28) Steam locomotive; L27 and L29) Horse-drawn slate wagons.

L26　10p Green and red (E) (LSCR-18)
L27　10c Green and red (W) (LSCR-16)
L28　10c Green and red (W) (LSCR-19)
L29　10p Green and red (E) (LSCR-17)
L26+L27　Se-tenant pair　　　　　　　.75
L28+L29　Se-tenant pair　　　　　　　£1.00
　　　Block of 4　　　　　　　　　　　£1.75
　　　Sheet of 20　　　　　　　　　　£10.00

Nos: L26 and L27) 4800 of each; L28 and L29) 3200 of each; 800 sheets with rows 1, 3 & 5: L26+L27+L26+L27, rows 2 & 4: L28+L29+L28+L29.

MANX ELECTRIC RAILWAY

This example of Victorian engineering and technology opened in 1893. The 3' gauge M.E.R. runs 18 miles along the eastern coast of the island giving passengers views of the beautiful coastline. Operated with a mixture of railway and tramway practice the line was a pioneer of electric traction and two of the original cars are still in service. In addition to many wayside stops the M.E.R. serves Douglas (Derby Castle), Groudle, Laxey (the start of the 3'6" gauge Snaefell Mountain Railway), Dhoon Glen, Ballaglass, and the northern terminus at Ramsey.

The first miniature sheet was issued by the Isle of Man Railway Company, but the service was taken over in 1998 by the Isle of Man Post Office who have latterly controlled procedures. Stamps issued for the Isle of Man Railway (see pg 29) are valid over this line.

The railway introduced plain circular station cancels, inscribed "Isle of Man" and "Railway Station" with moveable dates, when the railway letter service started on 14 August 1993, at Bungalow, Derby Castle, Laxey, Ramsey, and Summit. From 2 May 1998, similar ones, inscribed "Station", were used at Derby Castle, Laxey, Ramsey, and Snaefell Summit.

14/8/93. Centenary of Isle of Man Railway. Des: Alan Corlett. Ptr: The House of Questa. Offset lithography in miniature sheets of 4 (2 rows of 2), containing one example of each, num. B00001 - 120000. P13.2.

Dsgn: 1) Car No.1; 2) Car No.22; 3) Car No.5 and trailer; 4) Car No.3 on Snaefell

1	25p Multicoloured	
2	25p Multicoloured	
3	25p Multicoloured	
4	25p Multicoloured	
	Miniature sheet of 4	£2.00

Nos: 12000 of each.

MID-HANTS RAILWAY

The Alton, Alresford & Winchester Railway, which was renamed the Mid-Hants Railway even before it opened on 2 October 1865, provided a direct link between two L.S.W.R. lines. The latter acquired the railway's assets in June 1884, and it became part of the Southern Railway in 1923. When British Rail closed it in 1973 it was hoped to re-open the whole 17 miles, but it proved impossible to raise sufficient capital. Eventually enough money was raised to buy the 3 miles of track between Alresford and Ropley, and the 7 miles of formation between Ropley and Alton. In this form the line re-opened in 1977, but has now extended to Medstead & Four Marks (6), and Alton.

The railway issued five 10p labels in 1977 (see pg 46) but was not then a party to the railway letter agreement so they cannot be regarded as proper letter stamps. After becoming a signatory the introduction of the railway letter service, in March 1979, was unannounced and went almost unnoticed. At some unknown later date the stamps were quietly withdrawn and the railway letter service discontinued. After many years of dormancy a committee of railway volunteers relaunched the service in June 1990. The railway has signed the 1998 agreement.

Enquiries to: The Postal Co-ordinator, Mid-Hants Railway Letter Service, The Railway Station, Alresford, Hampshire SO24 9JG

24/3/79. Definitive. Des: J. Holder. Ptr: Itchen Press Ltd., Southampton. Lithography in sheets of 50 (10 rows of 5). R10.

Dsgn: S.R. Rebuilt "West Country" Class 4-6-2 No.34016 *Bodmin*

1	15p Red, green and black	£1.75
	Sheet of 50	£90.00

Nos: 5000. These stamps are likely to have been prepared as labels. When the railway signed the 1974 Agreement the inscription "Preservation Society Ltd" became inappropriate, since the railway itself was responsible for the letter service, and was obliterated before issue. Initially a thin horizontal line was used to cross through the heading which proved unsatisfactory, and so the operation was repeated with two thicker rules butted together above one another. Stamps exist with the thin rule showing because of the poor registration of the first overprint.

9/6/90. Definitive. Des: Ian Cooper. Ptr: William Sessions Ltd., York. Offset lithography in sheets of 6 (2 rows of 3). R4.75.

Dsgn: S.R. locomotive standing at signal

2	25p Green, red and black	.40
	Sheet of 6	£2.40

Nos: 12000. Two perforated sheets are known with a trial zig-zag separation.   FDC: 750 rail only

30/6/90. 125th Anniversary of the Opening of the Mid-Hants Railway. Des: Ian Cooper. Ptr: William Sessions Ltd. Offset lithography in sheets of 6 (2 rows of 3). R4.75.

Dsgn: Mid-Hants 125 logo

3	25p Crimson, brown and yellow	.40
	Sheet of 6	£2.40

Nos: 9000; later 3600 were destroyed leaving an issue of 5400.   FDC: 700 rail only

3/2/91. Railway Letter Service Centenary. Des: Ian Cooper. Ptr: William Sessions Ltd. Offset lithography in sheets of 6 (2 rows of 3). R4.75.

Dsgn: Booking office counter with covers and canceller, and L.S.W.R. Class T3 4-4-0 No.563

4	25p Black, green and red	.40
	Sheet of 6	£2.40

Nos: 6000; later 900 stamps were destroyed leaving an issue of 5100. FDC: 250 rail & post; 500 rail only

29/3/91. Locomotive Series. Des: Ian Cooper. Ptr: William Sessions Ltd. Offset lithography on sheets of 6 (2 rows of 3). R4.75.

Dsgn: S.R. Class S15 4-6-0 No.506

5	25p Black, green and red	.40
	Sheet of 6	£2.40

Nos: 6000.   FDC: 200 rail & post; 300 rail only cards

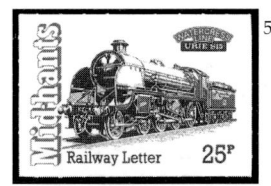

5/9/91. Locomotive Series. Des: Ian Cooper. Ptr: William Sessions Ltd. Offset lithography in sheets of 6 (2 rows of 3). R4.75.

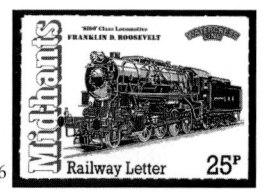

Dsgn: U.S.A. Class S160 2-8-0 No.701 *Franklin D. Roosevelt*

6	25p Black, blue and red	.40
	Decor. sheet of 6	£2.40

Nos: 6000. On perhaps fewer than 12 sheets, a dry print of the black colour occurred on the bottom row of 2 stamps, giving the loco a grey appearance.
FDC: 150 covers and 250 postcards rail & post; 300 covers and 250 postcards rail only.

17/4/92. Locomotive Series. Des: Ian Cooper. Ptr: Faulwood & Herbert Ltd. Offset lithography in sheets of 6 (3 rows of 2). R14.

Dsgn: B.R. Standard Class 4 2-6-0 No.76017

7	25p Black, red and beige	.40
	Decor. sheet of 6	£2.40

Nos: 5500. A flaw was discovered in the print run of 6000 stamps and 500 were destroyed.
FDC: 150 covers and 250 postcards rail & post; 300 covers and 250 postcards rail only

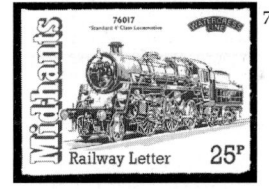

6/9/92. Locomotive Series. Des: Ian Cooper. Ptr: Faulwood & Herbert Ltd. Offset lithography in sheets of 6 (3 rows of 2). R14.

Dsgn: S.R. "West Country" Class 4-6-2 No.34105 *Swanage*

8	25p Black, green and red	.40
(8)	Decor. sheet of 6	£2.40
(8Sp)	Decor. sheet of 6 - imperf and ovptd in black	£35.00

Nos: 8) 6000; 8Sp) 150. The wrong Pantone colour, which was a yellower green, was specified to the printer for the first printing of this issue. Apart from two proofs on card and a handful of perforated sheets the entire printing was destroyed. A constant red line flaw on the streamline casing of the locomotive exists on stamp 1 in rows 2 and 3 of the issued stamps. 25 untrimmed and imperf sheets were numbered and signed by the designer, the Locomotive Superintendent and the Acting General

Manager of the M.H.R.. Each of these sheets received one vertical "Specimen" overprint.
FDC: 200 covers and 250 postcards rail & post; 150 covers and 250 postcards rail only.

3/7/93. 20th Anniversary of the Mid-Hants Preservation Society. Des: Ian Cooper. Ptr: Faulwood & Herbert Ltd. Offset lithography in sheets of 6 (3 rows of 2). R14.

Dsgn: S.R. Class S15 No.506, in the style of a S.R. poster

9	25p Red, green, black and yellow	.40
	Decor. sheet of 6	£2.40

Nos: 6000; later 900 stamps were destroyed leaving an issue of 5100. FDC: 200 covers and 250 postcards rail and post; 150 covers and 250 postcards rail only.

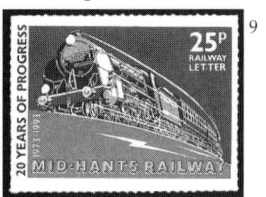

27/11/93. Christmas Stamp. Des: Ian Cooper. Ptr: Faulwood & Herbert Ltd. Offset lithography in sheets of 6 (2 rows of 3). R14.

Dsgn: Snowman dressed as guard holding green flag with S.R. 4-6-0 loco in background

10	25p Black, green and red	.40
	Decor. sheet of 6	£2.40

Nos: 6000.
FDC: 250 rail and post and 250 rail only postcards.

6/6/94. 50th Anniversary of D-Day. Des: Ian Cooper. Ptr: SJC Colour Printers, Guiseley. Offset lithography in sheets of 6 (3 rows of 2). R9.5.

Dsgn: U.S.A.T.C. S160 2-8-0 *Franklin D. Roosevelt* and goods train inscribed "D-Day 50th Anniversary"

11	25p Black, red and yellow ochre	.40
	Decor. sheet of 6	£2.40

Nos: 6000; later 1500 stamps were destroyed leaving an issue of 4500. FDC: 200 covers and 250 postcards rail & post; 300 covers and 250 postcards rail only.

3/9/94. Locomotive Series. Des: Ian Cooper. Ptr: SJC Colour Printers Ltd. Guiseley. Offset lithography in sheets of 6 (3 rows of 2). R9.5.

Dsgn: B.R. Standard Class 5 4-6-0 No.73096 restored as No.73080 *Merlin*

12	25p Black, red and yellow ochre	.40
	Decor. sheet of 6	£2.40

Nos: 6000.   FDC: 200 rail & post; 300 rail only.

27/5/95. 10th Anniversary of Operating Trains to Alton. Des: Ian Cooper. Ptr: SJC Colour Printers Ltd. Offset lithography in sheets of 6 (3 rows of 2). R9.5.

Dsgn: B.R. Network SouthEast electric multiple unit and S.R. Class U 2-6-0 No.31806 at Alton Station, inscribed "10th Anniversary of the return to Alton"

13	25p Black, red, blue and yellow	.40
	Decor. sheet of 6	£2.40

Nos: 6000.   FDC: 200 rail & post; 100 rail only.

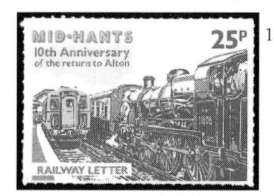

2/9/95. Locomotive Series. Des: Ian Cooper. Ptr: SJC Colour Printers Ltd. Offset lithography in sheets of 6 (3 rows of 2). R9.5.

Dsgn: S.R. Class N 2-6-0 No.31874

14	25p Black, red, and yellow ochre	.40
	Decor. sheet of 6	£2.40

Nos: 6000.   FDC: 150 rail & post; 100 rail only.

6/4/96. Definitive. Des: Neill Oakley; Illus: Kenneth Hankin (oil painting). Ptr: Walsall Security Printers. Offset lithography in sheets of 9 (3 rows of 3). P14.

Dsgn: S.R. Class M7 0-4-4T No.30480 at Alresford Station

15	25p Multicoloured	.40
(15)	Sheet of 9	£3.50
(15a)	Sheet of 9 - imperf.	£30.00

Nos: 15) 6000; 15a) 540. The 60 imperf sheets were signed by the Managing Director, Chief Executive and the designer. FDC: 100 covers and 250 postcards rail & post; 150 covers and 200 postcards rail only.

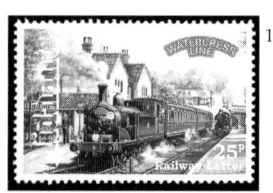

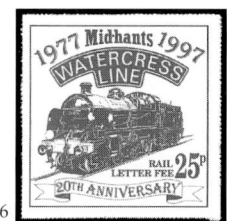

3/5/97. 20th Anniversary of the Re-opening of the Mid-Hants Railway. Des: Neill Oakley; Illus: Ian Cooper (drawing). Ptr: SJC Colour Printers. Offset lithography in sheets of 9 (3 rows of 3). R26.

Dsgn: An adapted anniversary logo and S.R. Class U 2-6-0 No.31674

16	25p Dark green	.40
(16)	Decor. sheet of 9	£3.50
(16a)	Decor. sheet of 9 - imperf.	£27.50

Nos: 6000. FDC: 125 covers and 125 postcards rail & post; 125 covers and 125 postcards rail only.

5/7/97. 30th Anniversary of the End of Steam on the Southern Railway. Des: Neill Oakley; Illus: Tony Genever (photo). Ptr: SJC Colour Printers Ltd. Offset lithography in sheets of 9 (3 rows of 3). R26.

Dsgn: S.R. "Merchant Navy" Class 4-6-2 No.35005 *Canadian Pacific*

17	25p Multicoloured	.40
	Sheet of 9	£3.50

Nos: 6000. FDC: 125 covers and 125 postcards rail & post; 125 covers and 125 postcards rail only.

13/9/97. Definitive. Des: Neill Oakley; Illus: Jim Swift (photo). Ptr: SJC Colour Printers Ltd. Offset lithography in sheets of 9 (3 rows of 3). R26.

Dsgn: S.R. "Battle of Britain" Class 4-6-2 No.34067 *Tangmere*

18	25p Multicoloured	.40
	Sheet of 9	£3.50

Nos: 18) 6000. FDC: 75 covers rail & post; 140 covers rail only. Some rail only covers signed and flown, or signed only, by Sqdn. Ldr. Neville Duke.

16/5/98. Definitive. Des: Neill Oakley; Illus: Cedric Johns (photo). Ptr: SJC Colour Printers Ltd. Offset lithography in sheets of 9 (3 rows of 3). R26.

Dsgn: S.R. Class U 2-6-0 No.31625 at Alresford

19	25p Multicoloured	.40
(19)	Sheet of 9	£3.50
(19a)	Sheet of 9 - imperf	£10.00

Nos: 19) 6000; 19a) 450. FDC: 100 covers and 50 postcards rail & post; 100 covers and 50 postcards rail only.

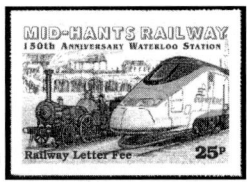

11/7/98. 150th Anniversary of the Opening of Waterloo Station. Des: Neill Oakley. Ptr: SJC Colour Printers Ltd. Offset lithography in sheets of 9 (3 rows of 3). R26.

Dsgn: Early L.S.W.R. loco alongside Eurostar powercar with etching of Waterloo Station, c1848, in background

20	25p Multicoloured	.40
(20)	Decor. sheet of 9	£3.50
(20a)	Decor. sheet of 9 - imperf.	£10.00

Nos: 20) 6000; 20a) 450. 50 imperf sheets were numbered and signed by the designer.
FDC: 125 covers and 100 postcards rail & post ; 175 covers and 100 postcards rail only, of which 50 covers were carried to Waterloo by courier and later signed by Sir Robert Horton, Chairman of Railtrack.

M.H.R. SPECIAL CANCELLATIONS

1	30/4/77	First Anniversary of the Watercress Line [Used for L1-L4 - before the letter service started]
2	25/3/78	Rededication of Austerity 0-6-0ST No.196 *Errol Lonsdale* [Used for S1. See also above]
3	8/5/94	Alresford - Alton *Britannia* [illus. side view of locomotive and nameplate]
4	6/6/94	Alresford - U.S. 47th Infantry Regiment D-Day 1944 [illus. crest of regiment]
5	10/9/94	Alresford - War on the Line [illus. loco crew in cab in front of tarpaulined goods wagon]
6	4/2/95	Alresford - *Union of South Africa* visits the Mid-Hants [illus. a stylised drawing of the loco]
7	15/7/95	Alresford - S15 1920-1995 [illus. engineering drawing and view of loco]
8	2/3/96	Alresford - *Sir Nigel Gresley* [illus. picture of locomotive at speed]
9	14/8/96	Alresford - The Light Railways Act [illus. Royal crest from Act of Parliament]
10	30/11/96	Alresford - Merry Christmas [illus. 0-4-4T loco with Santa on the footplate - red]
11	5/7/97	Alresford - End of Steam on the Southern [illus. original B.R. lion on wheel totem]
12	1/1/98	Alresford - SR75 BR50 [illus. B.R. 'hotdog' totem]

13	11/7/98	Alresford - 1848 L.&S.W.R. Waterloo to Alresford Third Class - M.H.R./ S.W.T. Alresford to Waterloo Standard Class 1998 [ticket design]
14	11/7/98	Alton - 1848 L.&S.W.R. Waterloo to Alresford Third Class - M.H.R./ S.W.T. Alresford to Waterloo Standard Class 1998 [ticket design]

LABELS

30/4/77. Railway Labels. R9.5.

Dsgn: L1) Steam locomotive and footplate crew; L2) Side view of 2-6-0 locomotive; L3) Signal, signalbox and bridge; L4) Train passing under bridge. All labels are inscribed "Mid-Hants Railway Preservation Society Ltd"

L1	10p Blue	£7.50
L2	10p Brown	£7.50
L3	10p Green	£7.50
L4	10p Vermilion	£7.50

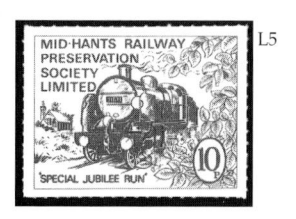

7/6/77. Special Jubilee Run. R9.5.

Dsgn: S.R. Class N 2-6-0 No.31874, foliage and signalbox

L5	10p Black and red	£7.50

STATIONERY ENVELOPE

25/3/78. Re-Dedication of Austerity 0-6-0ST *Errol Lonsdale*.

Dsgn: Austerity 0-6-0ST No.196 *Errol Lonsdale*

S1	15p Black, blue and red	£5.00

A good range of G.B. Railway Letter Stamps (old and modern issues) including cover material always in stock.

Please let me have details of your requirements and I will do my best to help.

ROGER HUDSON

**P.O. Box 172,
COVENTRY CV6 6NF
Tel: (01203) 686613
Fax: (01203) 667428**

MIDLAND RAILWAY CENTRE

"More than just a railway" would seem an accurate publicity description of the 57 acre museum site and 35 acre country park near Ripley in Derbyshire. Recreating the atmosphere of the Midland Railway the 3½ mile standard gauge line runs from Butterley to Swanwick Junction, home of the large Matthew Kirtley Museum which houses much of their historic collection, where the completion of a short branch line has added to the authentic atmosphere.

The Trust made enquiries to start their railway letter service at the time Royal Mail was negotiating a new agreement with other railways. As a result the Trust made a temporary agreement to launch the service. With a lack of funding the service effectively ceased towards the end of 1998, and the Centre did not feel able to sign the new 1998 Agreement.

20/9/97. Definitive. Des: Arthur Weaver; Illus: Alan Caladine (photo). Ptr: William Sessions Ltd., York. Offset lithography in sheets of 6 (3 rows of 2). R4.75.

Dsgn: M.R. locomotives at Butterley Station

1	25p Multicoloured with black surcharge and "Railway Letter" overprint	.40
1a	26p Multicoloured (see footnote)	-
(1)	Sheet of 6	£2.40

Nos: 1) 18000; 1a) up to 200.   FDC: Not known.

Due to a misinterpretation of the text of the draft agreement, by which the letter service was operated, the stamps were printed with a 26p value equal to the first class Royal Mail rate. A number of these stamps were affixed to envelopes and cancelled as publicity examples. It was then decided that all the remainder should be overprinted with the correct 25p value and an indication they were railway letter stamps. A sheet missing the cyan and black colours, but having the 25p overprint, is known.

NENE VALLEY RAILWAY

The first passenger train ran on this line, then part of the Northampton & Peterborough Railway, in June 1845. Train services to Rugby operated over this portion of line after 1879, making it an important cross country route. But road competition increased after World War II and passenger trains were withdrawn in 1964 with freight services ceasing seven years later.

The first 5½ miles to be preserved reopened in June 1977. Since then the line has achieved a unique position among British preserved railways by its operation of 4'8½" gauge locomotives and rolling stock from all over Europe, particularly Scandinavia, by extending the loading gauge to the 'Berne' standard. At first trains operated from Wansford, through Ferry Meadows, to Orton Mere, but the line returned to Peterborough in 1986 when its 1½ mile extension to the new terminus of Peterborough N.V.R. was opened. A further one mile of track, to the west of Wansford, takes passengers through Wansford Tunnel to Yarwell Junction.

Railway Letter Service volunteers are now also involved in the restoration of a T.P.O. vehicle, No.M30272M, which they hope to return to active service on the N.V.R. The railway signed the 1998 agreement.

Enquiries to: Nene Valley Railway Ltd, Railway Letter Service, Wansford Station, Stibbington, Peterborough, PE8 6LR.

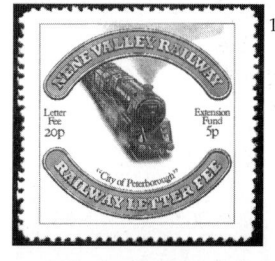

4/6/86. Peterborough Extension. Des: Ed Roberts. Ptr: Fisherprint, Peterborough. Lithography in sheets of 12 (3 rows of 4), num. 0001 - 0800. P11.

Dsgn: B.R. Class 5MT 4-6-0 No.73050 *City of Peterborough* in steam, inscribed "Extension Fund 5p"

1	20p + 5p extension surcharge Multicoloured	.60
(1)	Sheet of 12	£7.50
(1a)	Sheet of 12 - imperf	£70.00

Nos: 1) 9600; 1a) 180. 15 imperf proof sheets were prepared and signed by Keith Fisher, director of the printing firm. FDC: 975 rail & post, 25 of which were transferred to a local T.P.O.; 30 rail only.

1/6/87. 10th Anniversary of Opening. Des: Ed Roberts. Ptr: Fisherprint. Lithography in sheets of 9 (3 rows of 3, se-tenant horiz. 2+3+4), num. 0001 - 1500. P14.

Dsgn: 2) Swedish Class S 2-6-2T No.1178; 3) French Nord Class 3500 4-6-0 No.3.628; 4) B.R. "Battle of Britain" Class 4-6-2 *92 Squadron*

2	20p Multicoloured	
3	20p Multicoloured	
4	20p Multicoloured	
	Se-tenant strip of 3	£2.00
(2-4)	Sheet of 9	£7.00
(2a-4a)	Sheet of 9 - imperf	£45.00

Nos: 2-4) 4500 of each; 2a-4a) 225. 25 imperf proof sheets were prepared and signed by the designer. FDC: 1000 rail & post, some of which were transferred to the two local T.P.O.s; 40 rail only.

10/5/88. 150th Anniversary of the First Travelling Post Office. Des: Ed Roberts and Paul Way. Ptr: Fisherprint. Lithography in sheets of 12 (3 rows of 4), num. 001 - 500. P11.

Dsgn: Illustration as No.1, but inscribed "TPO 150" and "1838 1988"

5	20p Multicoloured	.90
(5)	Sheet of 12	£12.00
(5a)	Sheet of 12 - imperf	£50.00

Nos: 5) 6000; 5a) 240. 20 imperf proof sheets were prepared and signed. FDC: 1400 rail & post, plus 100 transferred to the two local T.P.O.s; 100 rail only.

14/11/89. Locomotive No.1800 *Thomas*. Des: Tony Theobald. Ptr: Fisherprint. Lithography in sheets of 9 (3 rows of 3), num. 0001 - 2500. P14.

Dsgn: British Sugar Corporation 0-6-0T No.1800 *Thomas* running light at Wansford Station

6	25p Multicoloured	.40
(6)	Sheet of 9	£3.60
(6a)	Sheet of 9 - imperf	£40.00

Nos: 6) 22500; 6a) 288. 32 imperf proof sheets were prepared, and of these 30 were numbered and signed by the designer. With an imminent increase in the letter fee on 1/1/90, the railway issued the stamp with a 25p value although the rate at the time of issue was still 20p. FDC: 1380 rail & post, including 35 each on two local T.P.O.s; 120 rail only.

1/1/90. Definitive. Des: Ed Roberts and Paul Way. Ptr: Fisherprint. Offset lithography in sheets of 12 (3 rows of 4), num. 0001 - 0300. P11.

Dsgn: As No.1 but valued 25p

7	25p Multicoloured	.75
(7)	Sheet of 12	£10.00
(7a)	Sheet of 12 - imperf	£45.00

Nos: 7) 3600; 7a) 420. 35 imperf sheets were prepared, and signed by Rt. Hon. John Major M.P. FDC: 300 rail & post, including 25 each on two local T.P.O.s; 50 rail only.

17/7/91. Railway Letter Service Centenary. Des: Paul Way; Illus: David Weston (oil painting). Ptr: Fisherprint. Offset lithography in sheets of 9 (3 rows of 3), num. 0001 - 2000. P14.

Dsgn: L.M.S. "Black 5" 4-6-0 No. 5231, inscribed "Railway Letter Service 1891 - 1991"

8	25p Multicoloured	.40
(8)	Sheet of 9	£3.50
(8a)	Sheet of 9 - imperf	£28.00

Nos: 18000; later approx. 1800 were overprinted for No.22, leaving an issue of 8) approx. 16200; 8a) 540. 60 imperf proof sheets were numbered and signed by the designer.

FDC: 2000 rail & post, plus 100 approx were transferred to local T.P.O.s; 200 rail only.

7/4/92. 150 Years of Polish Railways. Des: David Weston. Ptr: Fisherprint. Offset lithography in sheets of 9 (3 rows of 3), num. 0001 - 2000. P14.

Dsgn: Polish Railways "Krieglok" Type 2 2-10-0 No.7173

9	25p Multicoloured	.40
(9)	Sheet of 9	£3.50
(9a)	Sheet of 9 - imperf	£28.00

Nos: 9) 18000; 9a) 540. 60 imperf proof sheets were prepared, numbered in manuscript, and signed by the designer.

FDC: 1000 rail & post, plus a few rail & post covers transferred to three local T.P.O.s; 150 rail only.

14/9/93. Definitive. Des: Brian White; Illus: (artwork). Ptr: Fisherprint. Offset lithography in sheets of 9 (3 rows of 3), num. 0001 - 2000. R9.5.

Dsgn: 2d L.N.W.R railway letter stamp of 1891 beside 25p N.V.R. version in the same style

10	25p Green, pink and black	.40
(10)	Sheet of 9	£3.50
(10Prf)	Sheet of 9 - imperf	£25.00

Nos: 10) 18000; 10a) 540. 60 imperf proof sheets were prepared, numbered in manuscript, and signed by Richard Paten, owner of B.R. Standard Class 5 4-6-0 No.73050 which arrived in Peterborough 25 years before. Of these 20 were trimmed to the size of the perf sheets in error.

3/5/94. Definitive. Des: Stuart Hudson; Illus: Laurie Manns (photo). Ptr: St. Ives Quickprint. Offset lithography in sheets of 9 (3 rows of 3). R9.5.

Dsgn: Swedish Class B 4-6-0 No.101A

11	25p Multicoloured	.40
(11)	Sheet of 9	£3.50
(11a)	Sheet of 9 - imperf	£20.00
(11Prf)	Sheet of 9 - imperf	£28.00

Nos: 11) 18000; 11a) 540. 60 imperf proof sheets were prepared, numbered in manuscript, and signed by the photographer. Of the perf sheets No.77 is known imperf and No.80 has misaligned perfs.

FDC: 650 rail & post, plus 400 covers transferred to four local T.P.O.s; 50 rail only.

1/11/94. *Thomas*. Des: Brian White. Ptr: St. Ives Quickprint Ltd. Offset lithography in sheets of 9 (3 rows of 3), num. 0001 - 2000. R10.

Dsgn: British Sugar Corporation 0-6-0T *Thomas* at an automatic level crossing

12	25p Multicoloured	.40
(12)	Sheet of 9	£3.50
(12a)	Sheet of 9 - imperf	£28.00

Nos: 12) 18000; 12a) 540. 60 imperf proof sheets were prepared.

14/3/95. 150th Anniversary Year of Railways in Peterborough. Des: Michael Scott. Ptr: Fisherprint. Offset lithography in sheets of 9 (3 rows of 3), num. 0001 - 2000. P14.

Dsgn: B.R. Standard Class5MT 4-6-0 No.73050 *City of Peterborough*

13	25p Multicoloured	.40
(13)	Sheet of 9	£3.50
(13a)	Sheet of 9 - imperf	£28.00

Nos: 13) 18000; 13a) 540. 60 imperf proof sheets were prepared, numbered in manuscript, and signed by the artist.

2/5/95. N.V.R. Locomotives. Des: The Moors Studio; Illus: David Weston. Ptr: Walsall Security Printers. Offset lithography in sheets of 9 (3 rows of 3, se-tenant horiz. row 1: 14+15+16; row 2: 14a+15+16a; row 3: 14b+15+16b), num. 0001 - 2000. P14.

Dsgn: Panorama of locomotives outside Wansford engine shed showing: 14, 14a and 14b) B.R. Class 14 0-6-0DH diesel D9516, and B.R. Class 5MT 4-6-0 No.73050 *City of Peterborough*; 15) B.R. Class 40 1Co-Co1 D306 *Atlantic Conveyor*, Hunslet Clarke 0-6-0T *Thomas*, diesel, and D.B. Class 52 2-10-0 No.7173; 16, 16a and 16b) G.W.R. 4-6-0 No.7819 *Hinton Manor*; and diesel

49

14 detail    14a   15   16a    16b detail

14	25p Multicoloured	
14a	25p Multicoloured	
14b	25p Multicoloured	
15	25p Multicoloured	
16	25p Multicoloured	
16a	25p Multicoloured	
16b	25p Multicoloured	
(14+15+16)	Se-tenant strip of 3	£1.20
(14a+15+16a)	Se-tenant strip of 3	£1.20
(14b+15+16b)	Se-tenant strip of 3	£1.20
(14-16b)	Sheet of 9	£3.50
(14Prf-16b Prf)	Sheet of 9 - imperf	£28.00

Nos: 14-14b and 16-16b) 2000 of each; 15) 6000; 14Prf-16bPrf) 55 or 165 of each. 55 imperf proof sheets were numbered and signed by the artist. The complications in cataloguing this issue are due to the colour of the vertical bands on the stamps in the left and right columns. At the top of the sheet these start dark green but gradually fade to white at the bottom. A complete sheet is therefore required to collect all the varieties of the design. Specific se-tenant strips were used on each version of fdc to minimise the number of permutations.

30/10/95. Santa Specials. Des: Ann Pick, Phil Jones and Michael Scott. Ptr: Walsall Security Printers. Offset lithography in sheets of 8 (4 rows of 2), num. 0001 - 2000. P14.

Dsgn: Santa, shouldering a sack of presents, in front of a Christmas tree

17	25p Multicoloured	.40
(17)	Sheet of 8	£3.50
(17a)	Sheet of 8 - imperf	£28.00

Nos: 17) 16000; 17a) 480. 60 imperf proof sheets were numbered in manuscript.

17   18

6/8/96. Definitive. Des: Stuart Hudson; Illus: Laurie Manns (photo). Ptr: St. Ives Quickprint. Offset lithography in sheets of 9 (3 rows of 3), num. 0001 - 2500. R9.5.

Dsgn: Danish 0-6-0T No.656 *Tinkerbell*

18	25p Multicoloured	.40
(18)	Sheet of 9	£3.50
(18a)	Sheet of 9 - imperf	£25.00

Nos: 18) 22500; 18a) 540. 60 imperf proof sheets numbered in manuscript were prepared.
FDC: 650 rail & post; plus 400 rail & post covers transferred to four local T.P.O.s; 50 rail only.

28/10/96. Christmas 1996. Overprinted vert. "1996" in black by W. F. Grant, num. 1500 - 1900.

19	25p Multicoloured (17)	.75
(19)	Sheet of 8	£7.50
(19a)	Sheet of 8 - imperf	£28.00

Nos: 19) 3208. A limited number of proof sheets were issued. One perf sheet is known with two 'ghost' images of the overprint across the lowest pair of stamps and the bottom margin.

10/6/97. Definitive. Des: Stuart Black. Ptr: Walsall Security Printers. Offset lithography in sheets of 9 (3 rows of 3), num. 0001 - 2000. P14.

Dsgn: S.R. "Battle of Britain" Class 4-6-2 No. 34081 *92 Squadron*

20	25p Multicoloured	.40
(20)	Sheet of 9	£3.50
(20a)	Sheet of 9 - imperf	£28.00

Nos: 20) 18000; later 1800 were overprinted for No.25 leaving an issue of 20) 16200; 20a) 540. The 60 imperf proof sheets were numbered and signed by Sqdn. Ldr. Neville Duke.

20   21

12/8/97. T.P.O. Restoration Scheme. Des: Stuart Hudson. Ptr: Walsall Security Printers. Offset lithography in sheets of 9 (3 rows of 3), num. 0001 - 2000. P14.

Dsgn: T.P.O. carriage M30272M

21	25p Multicoloured	.40
(21)	Sheet of 9	£3.50
(21a)	Sheet of 9 - imperf	£28.00

Nos: 21) 18000; 21a) 540. The 60 imperf proof sheets were numbered and signed by the designer.

27/10/97. Santa Specials. Overprinted "Xmas Santa Specials 1997" in blue by W. F. Grant, num. various.

22	25p Multicoloured (8)	.40
	Sheet of 9	£3.50

Nos: Approx. 1800. Some sheets were destroyed after an ink spillage at the printers and an uncertain number of sheets were sent to replace those that were damaged. One sheet of nine stamps, separated and affixed on fdc, appears to have missed the overprint.

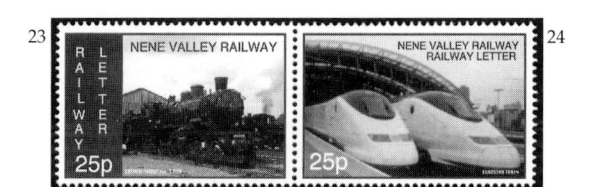

23/6/98. 21st Anniversary of the Nene Valley Railway. Des: Brian White; Illus: 23) Chris Randall; 24) Phil Marsh (photos). Ptr: Walsall Security Printers. Offset lithography in sheets of 8 (4 rows of 2, se-tenant horiz.), num. 0001 - 2000. P14.

Dsgn: 23) French Nord Class No.3.628; 24) Eurostar trains at Waterloo International Station, London

23	25p Multicoloured	
24	25p Multicoloured	
(23+24)	Se-tenant pair	.75
(23-24)	Sheet of 8	£3.25
(23a-24a)	Sheet of 8 - imperf	£28.00

Nos: 23-24) 8000 of each; 23a-24a) 240 of each. 60 imperf and unnumbered sheets were issued.

12/9/98. 50th Anniversary of No.3408192 *Squadron*. Overprinted "50th Anniversary 1948-1998 34081" in black by W.F. Grant, num. various.

25	25p Multicoloured (20)	£1.00
	Sheet of 9	£12.00

Nos: 1800.
FDC: 100 covers were signed by Oliver Butler.

2/11/98. International Scene on the N.V.R. Des: Brian White; Illus: P. Bason (photos). Ptr: Walsall Security Printers. Offset lithography in sheets of 9 (3 rows of 3, se-tenant horiz. 26+27+28), num. 0001 - 2000. P14.

Dsgn: 26)L.N.E.R. Class B1 4-6-0 No.1306 *Mayflower* outside Wansford shed; 27) B.R. Class 37 Co-Co diesel No.306 *Atlantic Conveyor* and goods train passing Wansford signalbox; 28) French Nord 4-6-0 No.3.628 at Wansford Station

26	25p Multicoloured	.40
27	25p Multicoloured	.40
28	25p Multicoloured	.40
26-28	Se-tenant strip of 3	£1.20
(26-28)	Sheet of 9	£3.60
(26a-28a)	Sheet of 9 - imperf	£28.00

Nos: 26-28) 6000 of each.

N.V.R. SPECIAL CANCELLATIONS

1	30/6/86	Peterborough Extension Royal Opening [illus. chalice and rail keys]
2	22/7/86	Wansford Station - A S [Royal Wedding of Andrew and Sarah; illus. bells and ribbon bow]
3	1/6/87	10 Anniversary [decagon border]
4	10/5/88	TPO S.4920 [double ring cancel]
5	3/7/88	Mallard 50 Anniversary Steam Speed Record
6	14/11/89	Wansford Station [illus. the face of *Thomas*]
7	1/1/90	Minor Railways Letter Fee - 25p First Day of Issue
8	17/9/91	Railway Letter Service Centenary 1891 - 1991 [illus. letter stamp design]
9	27/9/91	Wansford Station - Last Day of TPO Services between Peterborough, Crewe and Lincoln [illus. T.P.O. carriage]
10	30/9/91	Wansford Station - First Day of TPO Services between Peterborough and Carlisle [illus. T.P.O. carriage]
11	7/4/92	Wansford - Polish Railways 1842-1992 [illus. heraldic eagle]
12	26/6/92	*Thomas* 21st Birthday [illus. picture of *Thomas*]
13	9/12/92	Wansford Station - *Thomas* in Steam [oval moveable date cancel]

14	14/9/93	Nene Valley Railway [frame 57 x 32mm and date lettering in capitals illus. side view of B.R. Class 5 4-6-0]
15	14/9/93	Nene Valley Railway [frame 57 x 20mm and date lettering in lower case, illus. as above]
16	23/3/94	Opening of Second Platform at Orton Mere Naming of B.R. Class 31 Diesel *Nene Valley Railway*
17	3/5/94	Euro Tunnel Opening Folkestone to Calais [illus. stylised cross section of Channel with Tunnel below]
18	29/10/94	Nene Valley Railway visit by *Union of South Africa*
19	30/10/94	[As above, redated]
20	1/11/94	Nene Valley Railway - Santa [illus. Santa aboard cartoon 0-4-4T loco]
21	25/3/95	Wansford - Railway Letter Service Seminar
22	2/5/95	Nene Valley Railway R·L·S [inverted triangle]
23	2/6/95	N.V.R. R.L.S. Peterborough Rail 150 [B.R. 'hotdog' totem frame]
24	6/6/95	Royal Visit - H.R.H. Duke of Gloucester R·L·S· N·V·R· [illus. signal arm]
25	30/10/95	Wansford - Christmas Greetings
26	12/4/96	Wansford - 2nd RLS Seminar at NYMR Pickering
27	11/5/96	Freight Fest '96
28	31/5/96	Peterborough - Carlisle T.P.O. Carlisle - Peterborough T.P.O. Last Day of Service
29	6/8/96	Nurse Edith Cavell 1865-1915
30	28/10/96	N.V.R. R.L.S. - Christmas 1996
31	10/6/97	Wansford - *92 Squadron* [see also cancel 40]
32	12/8/97	Wansford [illus. a parcel tied with string - see also cancel 39]
33	12/8/97	Wansford - GPO [illus. G.P.O mailbag tied with label tag. Used for N.V.R. R.L.S. Friends of T.P.O. M30272M covers]
34	27/10/97	Wansford - Nene Valley Railway Santa Specials
35	3/2/98	Nene Valley Railway Letter Service Queen of Hearts [illus. memorial ribbon]
36	23/6/98	NVR 21 Anniversary [decagon border]
37	3/7/98	Wansford - 60th Anniversary of the World Speed Record for Steam 4468 *Mallard* [illus. side view of loco and carriage - see also N.Y.M.R. cancel 130]
38	12/9/98	Wansford - *92 Squadron* [oval frame]
39	17/10/98	Wansford - "Rail Mail Weekend" [illus. parcel tied with string - see also cancel 32]
40	12/9/98	Wansford - *92 Squadron* [See also cancel 31]
41	2/11/98	Nene Valley Railway Letter Service [illus. Christmas tree with presents beneath]

P.O. ONE-DAY POSTMARKS

3/6/80	Peterborough - Third Anniversary Nene Valley International Steam Railway Commencement of Public Service [Used before letter service started]
20/9/80	Wansford - Nene Valley Railway Eurosteam [Used before letter service started]
4/6/86	Peterborough - Introduction of Letter Service [illus. chalice and rail keys]
1/6/87	Peterborough - 10th Anniversary [illus. French Nord loco]
10/5/88	Peterborough - TPO 150 Anniversary 1838 - 1988 [illus. background of netting]
3/7/88	Peterborough - 50th Anniversary *Mallard's* World Speed Record for Steam Traction [illus. L.N.E.R. Class A4 loco]
14/11/89	Peterborough - *Thomas* Invites You to Nene Valley Railway's 'Santa Specials' 2-24 Dec 1989 [illus. face of *Thomas* and holly]
17/9/91	Peterborough - Visit the Nene Valley Railway [illus. Ordnance Survey map showing Wansford Station]
7/4/92	Peterborough - City of Europe [illus. crossed keys and E.U. stars]
29/10/94	Wansford-in-England Peterborough - Nene Valley Railway
2/5/95	Peterborough - Rail 150 [illus. Peterborough's "612" postal postmark]
6/8/96	Peterborough - Nurse Edith Cavell 1865 1915
10/6/97	Peterborough - Return to Steam *92 Squadron* [illus. the loco]
12/8/97	Peterborough - TPO Travelling Post Office Restoration Scheme [illus. T.P.O. pick-up equipment and satchel]
27/10/97	Peterborough - Santa Specials [illus. 0-6-0 loco and holly]
3/2/98	Peterborough - Queen of Hearts [illus. memorial ribbon]
23/6/98	Peterborough - Nene Valley Railway 21 Years 1977-1998 [lettering in oval with screws]
12/9/98	Peterborough - Nene Valley Railway Golden Jubilee *92 Squadron* [illus. "Battle of Britain" loco]

NORTH YORKSHIRE MOORS RAILWAY

The success of the Stockton & Darlington Railway, opened in 1825, prompted the inhabitants of Whitby to consult George Stephenson, with the result that an Act of Parliament for his proposed 23¾ mile line to Pickering received the Royal Assent in 1833. Designed for operation by horses, rope-haulage and gravity, the line opened in 1835-6, and was converted for steam working when purchased by the York & North Midland Railway. It passed in turn to the North Eastern, the L.N.E.R., and British Railways, and later the line was threatened by the Beeching cuts. The first 5¾ miles from Whitby to Grosmont were reprieved as part of the route to Middlesborough, and the remainder was closed on 6 March 1965.

The Preservation Society was formed in 1967, which reopened the railway to the public on 22 April 1973. From Grosmont trains climb a 1 in 49 gradient, and after Goathland (3¾), they serve Newtondale (8½), Levisham (12¼), and Pickering (18 miles). Generally the rights and privileges of the previous owners passed to the Society, which became the North York Moors Historical Railway Trust Limited, and on this basis the case for the continuing right to operate a railway letter service was being pressed with the Post Office. The N.Y.M.R. signed the agreement on 13 August 1976, but was unable to introduce the service before 1981.

During the early years of the N.Y.M.R. letter service the railway used Whitby Town (B.R.) parcel labels to denote payment of the B.R. fee when covers were sent over the main line system. To commemorate the 150th anniversary of the commencement of the public service from Whitby to Tunnel (later Grosmont) on 8 June 1985, arrangements were made to revive the letter service over B.R. metals. It is not known whether they were official, but suitable adhesive labels which were promised by B.R. did not materialise. An emergency label was prepared locally by rubber stamping B.R. "To be called for" labels, which were readily available, with the inscription "BR Fee £2.08" on the bottom left corner.

Enquiries to: N.Y.M.R. R.L.S., Pickering Station, North Yorkshire YO18 7AJ.

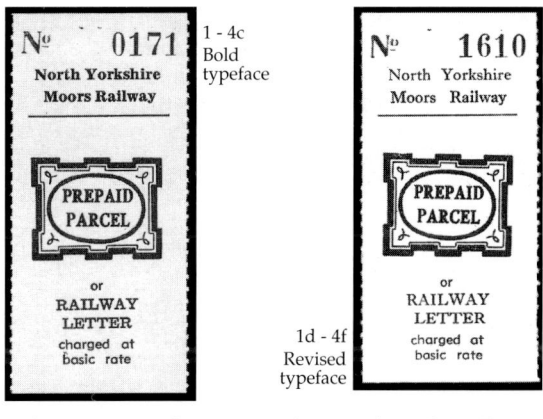

22/4/81 onwards. General Parcel and Railway Letter Stamps. Des: David Calvert. Ptr: Abbey Press, Whitby. Letterpress single copies, attached to other documentation. Imperf x R9.5. No.1-4, a, aa, and b, have Coloured R (in black).

Dsgn: Decorative border suggested by Welsh Highland Railway parcel stamps. The background colour resembles the 'official colour' of the station of issue.

1	(20p)	Green (Grosmont) Bold typeface	
		- Num. 0000 - 0499 (22/4/81)	£5.00
1a	(20p)	- Num. 0500 - 0649	£6.50
1b	(20p)	- Num. 0650 - 0799	£8.00
1c	(20p)	- Num. 0800 - 1299	£6.50
1d	(20p)	Revised typeface	
		- Num. 1300 - 1699 (22/1/85)	£5.00
1e	(20p)	- Num. 1700 - 1899	£6.50
1ee	(20p)	- Num. 1700 - 1899	-
1f	(20p)	- Num. 1900 - 2999	£1.50
1f	(20p)	ditto with documentation	£3.00
2	(20p)	Pink (Pickering) Bold typeface	
		- Num. 0000 - 0499 (22/4/81)	£5.00
2a	(20p)	- Num. 0500 - 0649	£6.50
2b	(20p)	- Num. 0650 - 0799	£8.00
2c	(20p)	- Num. 0800 - 1299	£6.50
2d	(20p)	Revised typeface	
		- Num. 1300 - 1699 (22/1/85)	£5.00
2e	(20p)	- Num. 1700 - 1899	£6.50
2ee	(20p)	- Num. 1700 - 1899	-
2f	(20p)	- Num. 1900 - 2999	£1.50
2f	(20p)	ditto with documentation	£3.00
3	(20p)	Yellow (gold - Goathland) Bold typeface	
		- Num. 0000 - 0249 (4/5/81)	£6.50
3aa	(20p)	- Num. 0250 - 0284, 05?? - 0649	£10.00
3a	(20p)	- Num. 0285 - 05??	£7.50
3b	(20p)	- Num. 0650 - 0799	£8.00
3c	(20p)	- Num. 0800 - 1299	£6.50
3d	(20p)	Revised typeface	
		- Num. 1300 - 1699 (22/1/85)	£5.00
3e	(20p)	- Num. 1700 - 1899	£6.50
3ee	(20p)	- Num. 1700 - 1899	-

3f	(20p)	- Num. 1900 - 2999	£1.50
3f	(20p)	ditto with documentation	£3.00
4	(20p)	Blue (lilac - Levisham) Bold typeface	
		- Num. 0000 - 0249 (4/5/81)	£6.50
4a	(20p)	- Num. 0250 - 0649	£5.00
4b	(20p)	- Num. 0650 - 0799	£8.00
4c	(20p)	- Num. 0800 - 1299	£6.50
4d	(20p)	Revised typeface	
		- Num. 1300 - 1699 (22/1/85)	£5.00
4e	(20p)	- Num. 1700 - 1899	£6.50
4ee	(20p)	- Num. 1700 - 1899	-
4f	(20p)	- Num. 1900 - 2999	£1.50
4f	(20p)	ditto with documentation	£3.00

Nos: As indicated for each style.
FDC: 1-4) 10 of each; 1d-4d) 200 of each

These general stamps were undenominated and could continue in use if the rates increased, so provisional issues were unlikely to be required. No.1-4 were originally issued as a trial, on the dates noted above, before being placed on general sale on 22/7/81. Most of the styles are caused by changes of numbering machine resulting in different forms of "No." for each batch of stamps. The change of typeface (from d onwards) shows the railway's name in plain weighted letters in contrast to the earlier batches which were bold. Most of the stamps of style ee were destroyed because they were considered unsatisfactory, only about 20 of each colour exist in a pre-cancelled mint state, and were replaced by style e. Style f results from the printing being set lower on the paper, although a few examples are positioned correctly. A yellow Goathland label, No.529, is thought to show a type 3b style of "No.".

On 31/8/90, the stamps were withdrawn from use, because of the time required to complete the documentation of counterfoil and receipt attached to the stamp itself. A set of parcel labels was issued for this particular traffic on 1/9/90, (see pg 66). After withdrawal and their invalidation for use a limited number of stamps of style f, complete and attached to their documentation, were sold to collectors.

22/7/81. Definitive. Des: David Calvert; Illus: Nigel Trotter (photo). Ptr: Walsall Security Printers Ltd. Photo-lithography in sheets of 12 (4 rows of 3), num. 0000 - 0799. P14 x 13.75.

Dsgn: L.H.&J.C. 0-6-2T No.29 and train at Beckhole

5	20(p) Multicoloured		£1.50
(5)	Sheet of 12		£20.00

Nos: 12000; later 2400 were overprinted for No.20, leaving an issue of 9600. A small blue patch appears on the green boiler where it meets the locomotive's smokebox on row 3, stamp 1 on some stamps. A green spot appears in the grass above the second A of "Railway" on row 3, stamp 3, for a proportion of the sheets. FDC: 400

29/7/81. Royal Wedding, and 30 Years of the Talyllyn Railway and the Railway Preservation Movement. Des: Steve Reed, from a sketch by David Calvert. Ptr: Abbey Press. Letterpress in sheets of 4 (2 rows of 2, se-tenant horiz. 6+7). R9.5.

Dsgn: 6) L.H.&J.C. 0-6-2T No.29; 7) L.H.&J.C. 0-6-2T No.5. Both with the Prince of Wales' feathers, and a Talyllyn train in the smoke

6	20(p) Black and chrome yellow		
7	20(p) Black and chrome yellow		
6+7	Se-tenant pair		£20.00
(6-7)	Sheet of 4		£45.00

Nos: 1900 of each. Approx 700 of No.7 show a black mark to the rear of the loco's bunker. A wide range of shades exist. FDC: 350

5/7/82. 150th Anniversary of George Stephenson's Report on the Railway from Whitby. Des: David Calvert; Illus: F. M. Sutcliffe (photo). Ptr: Stephenson Print for Abbey Press. Letterpress in sheets of 4 (2 rows of 2), num. 0000 - 1974. R9.5.

Dsgn: Photograph entitled "Whitby from the Railway" c1882, showing the Angel Inn

8	20(p) Gold, black, red and white		.90
	Sheet of 4		£4.00

Nos: 7900; later 2000 (500 sheets) were overprinted for No.24-25, leaving an issue of 5900. There are a number of varieties, several constant, many of these due to the way the photograph was trimmed to fit each stamp. FDC: 600

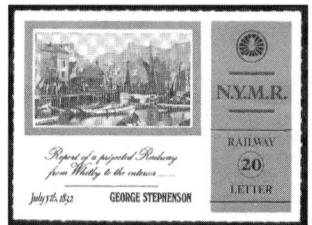

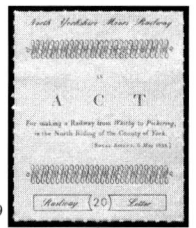

1/5/83. 150th Anniversary of the Royal Assent to the Whitby & Pickering Railway Act. Des: David Calvert. Ptr: Abbey Press. Letterpress in sheets of 6 (2 rows of 3), num. 0000 - 0999. R9.5.

Dsgn: The introduction to an original copy of the Act of Parliament

9	20(p) Blue on silver	£1.75
	Sheet of 6	£12.00

Nos: 6000; later 2700 were overprinted for No.21, leaving an issue of 3300. Colour trials exist. FDC: 600

8/6/85. 150th Anniversary of Commencement of Public Service Whitby - "Tunnel" (Grosmont). Des: David Calvert. Ptr: Larkfield Printing Co. Ltd., Brighouse. Photo-lithography in sheets of 12 (2 panes of 6, containing one example of each, each block being separated by a horiz. gutter margin), num. 0000 - 1999. P11.

Dsgn: 10) Grosmont c1847; 11) Grosmont Junction and Ironworks c1880; 12) Grosmont Station and tunnel c1960; 13) Grosmont Station and staff c1900; 14) Grosmont Station c1960; 15) L.N.E.R. Class P3 0-6-0 leaving Grosmont Station c1975

10	10(p) Black, red and gold	
11	10(p) Black, red and gold	
12	10(p) Black, red and gold	
13	5(p) Black, red and gold	
14	5(p) Black, red and gold	
15	20(p) Black, red and gold	
	Block of 6	£2.00
	Sheet of 12	£4.50

Nos: 4000 of each. Most sheets have rough perfs. The quality of the gold printing is poor and liable to damage.
FDC: 10, 13 & 14) 450; 11 & 12) 450; 15 & 16, see below) 450. Other combinations exist.

8/6/85. Telephone Stamp. Des: David Calvert. Ptr: Abbey Press. Letterpress in sheets of 5 (5 rows of 1) with selvedge at top and bottom, stamps num. 000000 - 004999. R4.5 x imperf.

Dsgn: N.Y.M.R. badge

16	10(p) Maroon and green	.45
	Sheet of 5	£2.50

Nos: 5000. When items sent endorsed "to be called for" and bearing this stamp arrived at the destination station the addressee was informed by telephone. This service is no longer available and the stamps have sold out. Both the background green and the maroon design vary in intensity. A few examples exist with the roulette perfs bisecting the stamp numbering.
FDC: 16 x 3) 180, includes telephone fee (also 15 & 16, as above).

26/5/86. 150th Anniversary of the Whitby & Pickering Railway. Des: David Calvert; Illus: 17) Connie Shepherd (watercolour), 18) Whitby Town Council (adapted from official logo), 19) M. Hutchinson (oil painting). Ptr: Larkfield Printing Co. Photo-lithography in sheets of 9 (3 rows of 3, se-tenant horiz. 17+18+19), num. 0000 - 1999. R20.

Dsgn: 17) Horsedrawn train leaving Grosmont c1836; 18) N.Y.M.R./W.&P.R. 150 logo; 19) L.M.S. Class 5 4-6-0 No.4767 *George Stephenson* arriving at Pickering

17	10(p) Multicoloured	
18	20(p) Red, black, gold and green	
19	10(p) Multicoloured	
	Se-tenant strip of 3	£1.25
	Sheet of 9	£3.75

Nos: 6000 of each. There are a number of varieties. Imperf proofs exist on glossy paper.

17   18   19

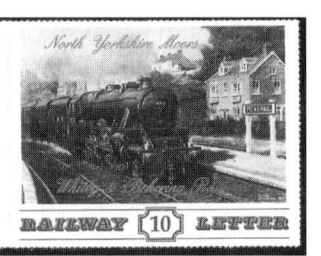

FDC: 17 and 19) 500; 18) 200; 300 cards containing the W.&P.R. medallion, rail only; 280 'historical covers' bearing No.17-20 and seven other railway letter stamps; 20 other covers: a total of 800 covers for each design.

26/5/86. 150th Anniversary of the Whitby & Pickering Railway. Overprinted "W.&P.R.150" and "1836-1986" in red by Abbey Press, num. 0000 - 0199.

20	20(p) Multicoloured (5)	£3.50
	Sheet of 12	£45.00

Nos: 2400. Over half the bottom margin was cut off to remove the original sheet numbers as part of the overprinting, and the sheets were renumbered in the right-hand margin. Approx 25 stamps exist with a significant shift of the letterpress overprint.

FDC: 700, plus 280 'historical covers' (see above) and 20 other assorted covers (above): a total of 1000 covers for this design.

22/4/87. Anniversary of Second W.&P.R. Act. Des: David Calvert; Illus: Connie Shepherd (drawing from a contemporary picture). Overprinted "2nd W.&P.R. Act / 5.V.1837" in maroon by Abbey Press, num. 0000 - 0449.

Dsgn: A typical W.&P.R. horse-drawn train

21	20(p) Maroon ovptd on (9)	£3.50
	Sheet of 6	£25.00

Nos: 2700. Six sheets received experimental colour trials in maroon, brown or vermilion, with the date expressed as "5.5.1837". A second trial in maroon involved two or three sheets with the date expressed as "5.v.1837" (small v). An example of each colour trial is known on cover.   FDC: 800

10/5/88. Definitive. Des: David Calvert; Illus: Nigel Trotter (photo). Ptr: Walsall Security Printers. Photo-lithography in sheets of 6 (2 rows of 3), num. see below. P14 x 13.75.

Dsgn: L.N.E.R. Class K1 2-6-0 No.2005 and train passing Beckhole

22	20(p) Multicoloured	£1.00
	Sheet of 6	£6.00

Nos: 6000. Some sheets had margin numbering, probably in the sequence 0001 - 0300.   FDC: 500

22   23

20/8/88. Definitive. Des: David Calvert; Illus: Nigel Trotter (photo). Ptr: Walsall Security Printers. Photo-lithography in sheets of 6 (2 rows of 3). P14 x 13.75.

Dsgn: B.R. Class J72 0-6-0T No.69023 *Joem* and train

23	20(p) Multicoloured [NYMR 25]	.40
	Sheet of 6	£2.40

Nos: 6000. This issue was announced and numbered 25 by the N.Y.M.R. in advance publicity, but hurriedly released before the "Feasibility Study" stamps (see below) when stocks of definitives ran low. Since the administration of the letter service was also being transferred at this time the railway was unable to prepare any fdc.

8/10/88. Feasibility Study. Surcharged "10"(p) in red, with No.25 overprinted " 'Feasibility Study 1988' " in red, and obliteration block in black, by Abbey Press, se-tenant horiz. 24+25, num. as below.

24   10(p) on 20(p) (8) [NYMR 23]
25   10(p) on 20(p) (8) [NYMR 24]

Se-tenant pair	£6.00
Sheet of 4: Num. between 1000 - 1299 and 1600 - 1899	£12.00
Sheet of 4: Num. obliterated	£15.00

Nos: 1000 of each. When the consignment was overprinted some of the sheets had the numbers at the bottom right-hand corner of the margin obliterated with a black rectangular block in error. A handful of sheets exist with sheet numbers outside the sequence stated above. The N.Y.M.R. officially numbers these stamps as No.23 and 24 as detailed in their pre-publicised issue programme.   FDC: 350

2/2/89. 20th Anniversary of the First N.Y.M.R. Engine Movement. Des: Geoff and Margaret Atkins; Illus: Chris Reattig (photo). Ptr: Faulwood & Herbert Ltd., Brighton. Offset lithography in sheets of 6 (3 rows of 2). R4.75.

Dsgn: 0-4-0ST *Mirvale* in snow near Goathland

26	20p Multicoloured	.40
	Sheet of 6	£2.40

Nos: 12000; later 3600 were surcharged for No.44, leaving an issue of 8400. A number of flaws appear on various stamps in the sheet including a green spot on the left edge of row 2 stamp 1, on part of the printing. FDC: 750

22/4/89. Diesel Day. Des: Geoff and Margaret Atkins. Ptr: Faulwood & Herbert Ltd. Offset lithography in sheets of 6 (3 rows of 2). R4.75.

Dsgn: B.R. Class 25 Bo-Bo diesel locomotive

27	20p Black on pale green	.50
	Sheet of 6	£3.00

Nos: 12000; later 4800 were surcharged for No.49, leaving an issue of 7200. FDC: 200

6/6/89. Definitive. Des: David Calvert; Illus: Nigel Trotter (photo). Ptr: Walsall Security Printers. Photo-lithography in sheets of 6 (2 rows of 3). P14 x 13.75.

Dsgn: L.H.&J.C. 0-6-2T No.5 climbing the 1 in 49 gradient between Grosmont and Goathland in evening sunshine

28	20(p) Multicoloured	£1.00
	Sheet of 6	£6.00

Nos: 6000 FDC: 500

16/8/89. 10 Years of Dining on the N.Y.M.R. Des: Stuart Hudson. Ptr: Wayzgoose, Sleaford. Offset lithography in sheets of 12 (3 rows of 4). R9.5.

Dsgn: "The North Yorkshireman" Dining Train logo

29	20p Burgundy and cream	.40
	Sheet of 12	£4.80

Nos: 12000; later 7200 were surcharged for No.36, leaving an issue of 4800. The stamps received from the printer were substandard and the railway considered they could not be used. After keeping examples for their records the remainder were destroyed. Wayzgoose quickly supplied a second printing which was issued. FDC: 600

9/9/89. Definitive. Des: David Calvert; Illus: Nigel Trotter (photo). Ptr: Walsall Security Printers. Photo-lithography in sheets of 6 (2 rows of 3). P14 x 13.75.

Dsgn: N.E.R. Class T2 0-8-0 No.2238 hauling "The Moorlander" dining train at Esk Valley, near Grosmont

30	20(p) Multicoloured	£1.00
	Sheet of 6	£6.00

Nos: 6000; later 3000 were surcharged for No.37, leaving an issue of 3000. FDC: 400

1/4/90. Definitives. Des: Geoff and Margaret Atkins, and Stuart Hudson. Ptr: William Sessions Ltd. Offset lithography in sheets of 6 (3 rows of 2) R4.75.

Dsgn: B.R. Standard Class 4MT 2-6-4T No.80135

31	25p Black, green and red	.40
	Sheet of 6	£2.40

Nos: 12000. FDC: 500

3/5/90. Definitive. Des: Geoff and Margaret Atkins, and Stuart Hudson. Ptr: William Sessions Ltd. Offset lithography in sheets of 6 (3 rows of 2). R4.75.

Dsgn: S.R. "Schools" Class 4-4-0 No.30926 *Repton*

32	25p Black, yellow and red	.40
	Sheet of 6	£2.40

Nos: 12000. FDC: 700

24/5/90. 15th Anniversary of N.Y.M.R. Using Pickering Station. Des: Geoff and Margaret Atkins; Illus: 33) Whitby Museum; 35) Margaret Atkins (photos). Ptr: Faulwood & Herbert Ltd. Offset lithography in sheets of 9 (3 rows of 3, se-tenant horiz. 33+34+35), num. 000001 - 001500. R4.75.

Dsgn: 33) Pickering Station, with overall roof, in the 1880s; 34) N.Y.M.R. logo; 35) W.D. No.3672 *Dame Vera Lynn* at Pickering Station in 1989

33	10p Sepia, green, red and black	
34	15p Red, green and black	
35	25p Multicoloured	
	Se-tenant strip of 3	.90
	Sheet of 9	£2.75

Nos: 4500 of each. Three se-tenant strips which are imperf vertically have been found in the £7.50 book of stamps (see pg 65). FDC: 33+34) 500; 35) 500

23/6/90. "Royal Mail Pullman". Surcharged in black by Kitts of London.

36	25p on 20p (29)	.60
	Sheet of 12	£7.50

Nos: 7200. FDC: 500

1/7/90. 125th Anniversary of Goathland Station and Deviation Line. Surcharged and overprinted "Deviation Opened 1 July 1865" in black by Kitts of London.

37	25p on 20(p) (30)	£2.00
	Sheet of 6	£15.00

Nos: 3000. FDC: 650 transferred to NE Night Up T.P.O. at York.

1/2/91. Railway Letter Service Centenary. Des: Neill Oakley and Geoff and Margaret Atkins; Illus: Stuart Hudson (drawings and artwork). Ptr: William Sessions Ltd. Offset lithography in sheets of 8 (1st row of 2 stamps, with design between; 2nd & 3rd rows have 3 stamps). R4.75.

Dsgn: N.E.R. Class P3 0-6-0 No.2392, and N.E.R. 2d railway letter stamp

38	25p Multicoloured	.40
	Sheet of 8	£3.20

Nos: 12000. FDC: 500

1/2/91. Railway Letter Service Centenary. Des: Geoff and Margaret Atkins; Illus: Stuart Hudson (drawings and artwork). Ptr: William Sessions Ltd. Offset lithography in sheets of 8 (1st row of 2 stamps, with design between; 2nd & 3rd rows have 3 stamps). R4.75.

Dsgn: N.E.R. Class Q7 0-8-0 No.63460, with N.E.R. crest and N.Y.M.R. wheel logo

39	25p Multicoloured	.40
	Sheet of 8	£3.20

Nos: 12000. FDC: 400 rail only

24/4/91. 10th Anniversary of the N.Y.M.R. Railway Letter Service. Des: Geoff and Margaret Atkins; Illus: Stuart Hudson (drawing). Ptr: William Sessions Ltd. Offset lithography in sheets of 6 (2 rows of 3) R4.75.

Dsgn: G.W.R. Class 56XX 0-6-2T No.6619 at Grosmont Station, within frame resembling original N.E.R. letter stamp design

40	25p Brown, green and red	.40
	Sheet of 6	£3.20

Nos: 9000; later approx. 4500 were surcharged for No.53, and approx 2000 destroyed, leaving an issue of approx. 2500. FDC: 500

15/6/91. 10th Anniversary of the Opening of Newtondale Halt. Des: Geoff and Margaret Atkins and Bernard Parkinson; Illus: Don Smith (photo). Ptr: William Sessions Ltd. Offset lithography in sheets of 6 (2 rows of 3). R4.75.

Dsgn: B.R. 2-6-4T No.80135, within band and buckle frame

41	25p Multicoloured	.50
	Sheet of 6	£3.00

Nos: 9000.   FDC: 650 transferred to T.P.O.

15/9/91. Bulleid Pacific Locomotives. Des: Geoff and Margaret Atkins and Stuart Hudson. Offset lithography in sheets of 8 (4 rows of 2, se-tenant horiz. 42+43). R4.75.

Dsgn: 42) S.R. Rebuilt "West Country" Class 4-6-2 No.34027 *Taw Valley*; 43) S.R. "Battle of Britain" Class 4-6-2 No.34072 *257 Squadron*

42	25p Black, green and red	
43	25p Black, green and red	
	Se-tenant pair	£1.00
	Sheet of 8	£4.00

Nos: 6000 of each.
FDC: 650 covers plus 100 postcards.

7/12/91. 15th Anniversary of Santa Specials on the N.Y.M.R. Surcharged in scarlet red by Faulwood & Herbert Ltd.

44	25p on 20p (26)	.40
	Sheet of 6	£2.40

Nos: 3600.   FDC: 480

6/2/92. 40th Anniversary of the Accession of Queen Elizabeth II. Des: Geoff and Margaret Atkins, and Stuart Hudson. Ptr: William Sessions Ltd. Offset lithography in sheets of 6 (3 rows of 2). R4.75.

Dsgn: W.D. 2-10-0 No.3672 *Dame Vera Lynn*

45	25p Black, purple and red	.40
	Sheet of 6	£2.40

Nos: 9000; later 4800 were overprinted for No.50, leaving an issue of 4200.   FDC: 750

3/6/92. 25th Anniversary of the N.Y.M.R.'s First Founders' Meeting. Des: Stuart Hudson. Ptr: Eastwood Press, Rotherham. Offset lithography in sheets of 6 (2 rows of 3), num. 0001 - 1500. R7.25.

Dsgn: L.H.&J.C. 0-6-2T No.29, inscribed "25th Anniversary N.Y.M.R. Founders Meeting 3rd June 1967"

46	25p Reflex blue and silver	.40
(46)	Sheet of 6	£2.40
(46Sp)	Sheet of 6 - ovptd in black	£35.00

Nos: 46) 9000; 46Sp) 300. The 50 'specimen' sheets were signed by the six remaining founder members and certified with the signature of Margaret Atkins.
FDC: 700 covers and 150 postcards

21/7/92. Definitive. Des: Geoff and Margaret Atkins, and Dave Collier Graphics; Illus: Don Smith (photo). Ptr: Walsall Security Printers. Offset lithography in sheets of 6 (2 rows of 3), num. 0001 - 2200. P14 x 13.75.

Dsgn: L.M.S. Class 5 No.44767 *George Stephenson*

47	25p Multicoloured	.40
	Sheet of 6	£2.40

Nos: 13200. FDC: 750 rail & post covers transferred to T.P.O.; 100 covers and 150 postcards rail & post.

18/9/92. *Blue Peter's* Return to Steam. Des: Geoff and Margaret Atkins, and Bernard Parkinson; Illus: Don Smith (photo). Ptr: Walsall Security Printers. Offset lithography in sheets of 6 (2 rows of 3), num. 0001 - 2000. P14 x 13.75.

Dsgn: L.N.E.R. "Peppercorn" Class A2 4-6-2 No. 60532 *Blue Peter*, within a brown band and buckle frame

48	25p Multicoloured	.40
	Sheet of 6	£2.40

Nos: 12000.   FDC: 1000 transferred to T.P.O.

20/9/92. First York - Pickering Through Train Since 1951. Surcharged "25p" in black and red, and overprinted "Silver Jubilee" in black and "Special Train" in red, by Eastwood Press.

49	25p on 20p (27)	.40
	Sheet of 6	£2.40

Nos: 4800. A handful of examples are known with the black part of the overprint missing.   FDC: 750

31/10/92. Wartime Weekend. Overprinted "31 Oct 1 Nov 1992 Wartime Weekend" in green by William Sessions Ltd.

50	25p (45)	.40
	Sheet of 6	£2.40

Nos: 4800.   FDC: 775

1/5/93. 20th Anniversary of the Royal Opening. Des: Geoff and Margaret Atkins, and Dave Collier Graphics, York; Illus: Margaret Atkins (photo). Ptr: Walsall Security Printers. Offset lithography in sheets of 6 (3 rows of 2), num. 0001 - 2200. P13.7 x 13.9.

Dsgn: N.E.R. Class P3 0-6-0 No.2392 light engine near Goathland water tower

51	25p Multicoloured	.40
	Sheet of 6	£2.40

Nos: 13200. FDC: 870 covers and 150 postcards. 70 covers were signed by three N.Y.M.R. founders and the Chief Executive of the plc.

2/6/93. 40th Anniversary of the Coronation of Queen Elizabeth II. Des: Geoff and Margaret Atkins, and Dave Collier Graphics, York; Illus: Margaret Atkins (photo). Ptr: Walsall Security Printers. Offset lithography in sheets of 6 (3 rows of 2), num. 0001 - 2200. P13.7 x 13.9.

Dsgn: SR Class S15 No.30841 approaching the north end of Goathland Station

52	25p Multicoloured	.40
	Sheet of 6	£2.40

Nos: 13200. FDC: 800 covers and 150 postcards transferred to T.P.O.

2/10/93. Arrival of U.S.A.T.C. S160 No.2253. Overprinted "Arrival S160 No.2253", and an illustration of the locomotive by Stuart Hudson, in black by Eastwood Press, Rotherham.

53	25p Multicoloured (40)	.40
	Sheet of 6	£2.40

Nos: 4500; later approx. 1500 destroyed, leaving an issue of 3000.   FDC: 500 covers and a few postcards

10/11/93. Silver Jubilee of the First Working Party and Voluntary Work on the N.Y.M.R. Des: Geoff and Margaret Atkins; Illus: David Idle (photo). Ptr: The House of Questa. Offset lithography in sheets of 8 (2 panes of 4, each 2 rows of 2, separated by a horiz. gutter margin). P14.

Dsgn: L.H.&J.C. 0-6-2T No.29

54	25p Multicoloured	.40
	Sheet of 8	£3.20

Nos: 20000.   FDC: 500.

18/1/94. "Age of Steam" Des: Geoff and Margaret Atkins; Illus: David Idle (photos). Ptr: The House of Questa. Offset lithography in sheets of 8 (2 panes of 4, containing one example of each, separated by a horiz. gutter margin). P14.

Dsgn: 55) S.R. 4-6-0 No.30841; 56) L.N.E.R. 0-8-0 No.901; 57) L.M.S. 4-6-0 No.44767 *George Stephenson*; 58) G.W.R. 0-6-2T No.6619

55	25p Multicoloured	
56	25p Multicoloured	
57	25p Multicoloured	
58	25p Multicoloured	
	Pane of 4	£1.60
	Sheet of 8	£3.20

Nos: 4000 of each. FDC: 900 covers and 200 postcards. 800 Covercraft covers were also officially prepared and carried (200 sets of 4).

22/4/94. 21st Anniversary of the First Public Train. Des: Geoff and Margaret Atkins, and Neill Oakley; Illus. Stuart Hudson, The Moors Studio (paintings). Ptr: The House of Questa. Offset lithography in sheets of 10 (2 rows of 5, in two rows se-tenant horiz. 59+60+61+62+63). P14.

Dsgn: 59) L.N.E.R. Class P3 0-6-0 No.2392 entering Grosmont Tunnel; 60) B.R. TSO coach at Goathland; 61) B.R. FK coach at Newtondale; 62) B.R. BSO coach at Levisham; 63) L.H.&J.C. 0-6-2T No.29 at Pickering

59	25p Multicoloured	
60	25p Multicoloured	
61	25p Multicoloured	
62	25p Multicoloured	
63	25p Multicoloured	
	Se-tenant strip of 5	£2.00
	Sheet of 10	£4.00

Nos: 4000 of each.
FDC: 900 covers and 200 postcards.

3/5/94. 60th Anniversary of the Building of S.R. No.30926 *Repton*. Des: Geoff and Margaret Atkins, and Stuart Hudson; Illus: Tony Hart (photo). Ptr: The House of Questa. Offset lithography in sheets of 8 (2 panes of 4, each 2 rows of 2, separated by a vert. gutter margin). P14.

Dsgn: S.R. "Schools" Class 4-6-0 No.30926 *Repton* with train

64	25p Multicoloured	.40
	Pane of 4	£1.45
	Sheet of 8	£2.75

Nos: 16000. FDC: 650 covers and 150 postcards transferred to T.P.O.

6/6/94. 50th Anniversary of D-Day. Des: Geoff and Margaret Atkins; Illus: David Idle (photo). Ptr: The House of Questa. Offset lithography in sheets of 8 (2 panes of 4, each 2 rows of 2, separated by a horiz. gutter margin). P14.

Dsgn: W.D. 2-10-0 No.3672 *Dame Vera Lynn* passing under Green End Bridge near Goathland

65	25p Multicoloured	.40
	Pane of 4	£1.60
	Sheet of 8	£3.20

Nos: 16000; later 4000 were destroyed leaving an issue of 12000. FDC: 800 covers and 200 postcards.

4/7/94. 150th Anniversary of the Act of Parliament for the Building of the York to Pickering Railway. Des: Stuart Hudson; Illus: David Idle (photo). Ptr: The House of Questa. Offset lithography in sheets of 8 (2 panes of 4, each 2 rows of 2, separated by a horiz. gutter margin). P14.

Dsgn: L.N.E.R. Class K1 2-6-0 No.2005 and train by the signal and watertower at Goathland Station

66	25p Multicoloured	.40
	Pane of 4	£1.60
	Sheet of 8	£3.20

Nos: 16000. FDC: 600 covers and 175 postcards transferred to T.P.O.

1/9/94. 75th Anniversary of N.E.R. No.901. Des: Geoff and Margaret Atkins; Illus: Peter Doel (photo). Ptr: The House of Questa. Offset lithography in sheets of 10 (2 rows of 5). P14.5.

Dsgn: N.E.R. Class Q7 0-6-0 No.901 at the head of a passenger train

| 67 | 25p Multicoloured | .40 |

	Sheet of 10	£4.00
Nos: 20000.	FDC: 800 covers and 175 postcards	

8/10/94. 21st Anniversary of Steam Galas and the Completion of the Rebuilding of B.R. No.75014. Des: Stuart Hudson. Ptr: The House of Questa. Offset lithography in sheets of 8 (2 panes of 4, each 2 rows of 2, separated by a horiz. gutter margin). P14.

Dsgn: B.R. Standard Class 4 4-6-0 No.75014

68	25p Multicoloured	.40
	Pane of 4	£1.60
	Sheet of 8	£3.20
Nos: 16000.	FDC: 775 covers and 175 postcards	

30/12/94. Anniversary of the Act of Parliament for the Whitby & Pickering Railway. For full details see pg 65.

N1-N2   25p Multicoloured

24/3/95. First Railway Letter Service Seminar. Des: Martyn Fry and The Moors Studio; Illus: Peter Doel (photo). Ptr: Walsall Security Printers. Offset lithography in sheets of 8 (4 rows of 2), num. 0001 - 2500. P14.

Dsgn: S.R. 'Schools' Class 4-6-0 No.30926 *Repton*

69	25p Multicoloured	.40
	Sheet of 8	£3.20
Nos: 20000.	FDC: 575 covers and 175 postcards	

2/5/95. 50th Anniversary of V. E. Day. Des: Stuart Hudson. Ptr: Walsall Security Printers. Offset lithography in sheets of 8 (4 rows of 2), num. 0001 - 2000. P14.

Dsgn: W.D. 2-10-0 No.90775 on the turntable with Pickering Castle in background, and a pale blue flag and Union Flag at bottom left

70	25p Multicoloured	.40
	Sheet of 8	£3.20

Nos: 16000; later 4000 were overprinted for No.82, leaving an issue of 12000.
FDC: 750 covers and 175 postcards

7/7/95. 150th Anniversary of the York to Pickering Railway. Des: Geoff and Margaret Atkins; Illus: Maurice Burns (photos). Ptr: Walsall Security Printers. Offset lithography in sheets of 8 (2 panes of 4, each 2 rows of 2, se-tenant horiz. 71+72, separated by a horiz. gutter margin). P14.

Dsgn: 71) G.N.R. Stirling Single 4-2-2 No.1; 72) B.R. Class 9F 2-10-0 No.92220 *Evening Star*; both stamp designs sharing a diagramatic map of stations on the York to Whitby railway route

71	25p Multicoloured	
72	25p Multicoloured	
	Se-tenant pair	.80
	Pane of 4	£1.75
	Sheet of 8	£3.20

Nos: 10000 of each.
FDC: 660 covers and 175 postcards

5/9/95. Rebuilding of No.45428 *Eric Treacy*. Des: The Moors Studio; Illus: Peter Doel (photo). Ptr: Walsall Security Printers. Offset lithography in sheets of 9 (3 rows of 3), num. P14.

Dsgn: L.M.S. Class 5 4-6-0 No.45428 *Eric Treacy* and maroon coaches at Esk Valley

73	25p Multicoloured	.40
(73)	Sheet of 9	£3.60
(73a)	Sheet of 9 - imperf	£25.00

Nos: Approx. 10000; later approx. 4000 were overprinted for No.87, and approx. 3500 were destroyed, leaving an issue of approx. 2500; 73a) 540.
FDC: 500 covers and 125 postcards

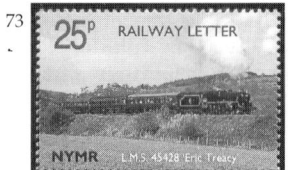

6/10/95. Rebuilding of No.34027 *Taw Valley*. Des: Kevin McGee; Illus: John Hunt (photo). Ptr: Walsall Security Printers. Offset lithography in sheets of 8 (4 rows of 2), num. 0001-2500. P14.

Dsgn: S.R. "West Country" 4-6-2 No.34027 *Taw Valley*

74	25p Multicoloured	.40
(74)	Sheet of 8	£3.20
(74a)	Sheet of 8 - imperf	£20.00

Nos: 74) 10000; 74a) 540. FDC: 500 covers and

postcards. A few fdc were autographed by the locomotive's owner Bert Hitchen.

12/4/96. Second Railway Letter Service Seminar. Des: Geoff and Margaret Atkins; Illus: Margaret Atkins (photo). Ptr: Walsall Security Printers. Offset lithography in sheets of 8 (4 rows of 2), num. 0001 - 2000. P14.

Dsgn: W.D. *Dame Vera Lynn* bringing "The Moorlander" Pullman train into Pickering Station

75	25p Multicoloured	.40
	Sheet of 8	£3.20

Nos: 16000.   FDC: 500 covers and 150 postcards

26/5/96. Building of New Grosmont Crossing Signalbox. Des: Geoff and Margaret Atkins; Illus: Geoff Atkins (photo). Ptr: Walsall Security Printers. Offset lithography in sheets of 8 (4 rows of 2), num. 0001 - 2000. P14.

Dsgn: U.S.A.T.C. Class S160 2-8-0 No.2253 and train passing Grosmont Crossing Signalbox

76	25p Multicoloured	.40
	Sheet of 8	£3.20

Nos: 16000.   FDC: 500 covers and 150 postcards

20/7/96. N.Y.M.R. Vintage Vehicle Weekend. Des: Geoff and Margaret Atkins; Illus: Stuart Hudson (watercolour). Ptr: Walsall Security Printers. Offset lithography in sheets of 8 (4 rows of 2), num. 0001 - 2000. P14.

Dsgn: 77) L.N.E.R. Class K1, with Bedford lorry; 78) MG saloon car, Leyland single-deck bus and B.R. Standard Class 4MT 2-6-4T No.80135

77	25p Multicoloured	
78	25p Multicoloured	
(77+78)	Se-tenant pair	.80
(77-78)	Sheet of 8	£3.20
(77a-78a)	Sheet of 8 - imperf	£22.50

Nos: 77-78) 8000 of each; 77a-78a) 200 of each. FDC: 500 covers and 150 postcards. 50 imperf sheets were issued as a limited edition set, each paired with a sheet of No.79, and signed by Roger Heath, Chairman of the N.Y.M.H.R.T., and Stuart Hudson.

23/8/96. Visit to the N.Y.M.R. of *Sir Nigel Gresley*. Des: Geoff and Margaret Atkins; Illus: Stuart Hudson (watercolour). Ptr: Walsall Security Printers. Offset lithography in sheets of 8 (4 rows of 2), num. 0001 - 2000. P14.

Dsgn: L.N.E.R. Class A4 4-6-2 No.60007 *Sir Nigel Gresley* passing signals at Goathland

79	25p Multicoloured	.40
(79)	Sheet of 8	£3.20
(79a)	Sheet of 8 - imperf	£22.50

Nos: 79) 16000; 79a) 400. FDC: 800 covers and 150 postcards. 50 imperf sheets were issued as a limited edition set, each paired with a sheet of No.77-78, and signed by Roger Heath and Stuart Hudson.

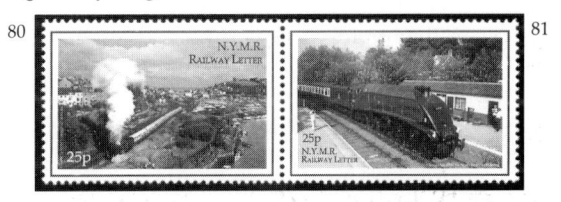

19/4/97. 150th Anniversary of Steam on the Whitby - Pickering Railway. Des: Geoff and Margaret Atkins; Illus: 80) Peter Doel; 81) Margaret Atkins (photos). Ptr: Walsall Security Printers. Offset lithography in sheets of 8 (4 rows of 2), num. 0001 - 2000. P14.

Dsgn: 80) Aerial view of B.R. 2-10-0 No.92000 *Evening Star* leaving Whitby; 81) L.N.E.R. 4-6-2 No.60007 *Sir Nigel Gresley* entering Pickering Station

80	25p Multicoloured	
81	25p Multicoloured	
80+81	Se-tenant pair	.80
(80-81)	Sheet of 8	£3.20
(80a-81a)	Sheet of 8 - imperf	£25.00

Nos: 80-81) 8000 of each; (81a-81a) 200 of each. 50 imperf sheets were issued as a limited edition set, each paired with a sheet of No.83-86.

FDC: 800 covers and 150 postcards

21/4/97. Golden Wedding Anniversary of H.M. Queen Elizabeth II and Prince Philip. Overprinted "Royal Golden Wedding 1997" in gold by Intoprint, Rotherham, num. various.

82	25p Multicoloured (70)	.40
	Sheet of 8	£3.20

Nos: 4000.   FDC: 500 covers and 125 postcards

6/6/97. 30th Anniversary of the Formation of the N.Y.M.R. Des: Geoff and Margaret Atkins; Illus: Stuart Hudson (paintings). Ptr: Walsall Security Printers. Offset lithography in sheets of 8 (2 miniature panes of 4, containing one example of each, separated by a horiz. gutter margin), num. 0001-2000. P14.

Dsgn: 83) L.N.E.R. 0-6-0T No.69023 *Joem* at the watertower at Grosmont Station; 84) Bedford OB coach on the approach to Goathland Station with L.M.S. 4-6-0 No.45428 *Eric Treacy* in the distance; 85) L.H.&J.C. 0-6-2T No.29 at Levisham Station; 86) L.N.E.R. 2-6-0 No.2005 in snow at Pickering Station with overall roof

83	25p Multicoloured	
84	25p Multicoloured	
85	25p Multicoloured	
86	25p Multicoloured	
(83-86)	Pane of 4	£1.60
(83-86)	Sheet of 8	£3.20
(83a-86a)	Sheet of 8 - imperf	£25.00

Nos: 83-86) 10000 of each; 83a-86a) 200 of each. 50 imperf sheets were issued as a limited edition set, each paired with a sheet of No.80-81. FDC: 500

12/8/97. 60th Birthday of Locomotive No.45428. Overprinted "45428 Diamond Jubilee" in silver by Intoprint.

87	25p Multicoloured (73)	.40
	Sheet of 9	£3.60

Nos: Approx. 4000; later approx. 1000 were destroyed, leaving an issue of approx. 3000. FDC: 500

1/5/98. 25th Anniversary of the Royal Opening. Des: Margaret Atkins; Illus: Stuart Hudson (painting). Ptr: Walsall Security Printers. Offset lithography in sheets of 8 (4 rows of 2), num. 0001-2500. P14.

Dsgn: 88) Grosmont Station platform; 89) L.N.E.R. Class P3 No.2392 and L.H.&J.C. No.29 hauling Royal Train

88	25p Black, but multicoloured at right edge	
89	25p Multicoloured	
88+89	Se-tenant pair	.80
(88-89)	Sheet of 8	£3.20
(88a-89a)	Sheet of 8 - imperf	£25.00

Nos: 88-89) 10000 of each; 88a-89a) 240 of each. 60 unnumbered imperf sheets were issued as a limited edition set, each paired with a sheet of No.94.
FDC: 700 covers and 150 postcards

2/7/98. Anniversary Pullman. Des: Geoff and Margaret Atkins; Illus: Stuart Hudson (artwork), Maurice Burns (photo). Ptr: Walsall Security Printers. Offset lithography in sheets of 8 (4 rows of 2), num. 0001-2500. P14.

Dsgn: L.N.E.R. Class K1 2-6-0 No.2005 and Pullman train at Levisham

90	25p Multicoloured	.40
	Sheet of 8	£3.20

Nos: 20000. FDC: 700 covers and 150 postcards

3/10/98. 25th Anniversary Steam Gala Weekend. Des: Margaret Atkins; Illus: Stuart Hudson (painting). Ptr: Walsall Security Printers. Offset lithography in sheets of 9 (3 rows of 3, se-tenant horiz. 91+92+93), num. 0001-2000. P14.

Dsgn: 91) L.N.E.R. 4-6-2 No.60007 *Sir Nigel Gresley* and L.M.S. 4-6-0 No.45428 *Eric Treacy*; 92) L.N.E.R. 2-6-0 No.2005 and W.D. 2-10-0 No.3672 *Dame Vera*

Lynn; 93) S.R. 4-4-0 No.926 *Repton* under the coaling plant at Grosmont Shed

91	25p Apricot, brown, green and black	
92	25p Apricot, brown, green and black	
93	25p Apricot, brown, green and black	
	Se-tenant strip of 3	£1.10
	Sheet of 9	£3.60

Nos: 7500 of each. FDC: 700 covers and 125 postcards The artwork for these designs was in full colour and sent to print as such. During a visit to the printers, to see the job on the machine, the plates were being set up with four special inks (see catalogue entry) from the previous print job with a startling and attractive result. After the order had been printed as the full colour version it was decided the job should be run again in the 'set up' colours and these stamps were issued first. The multicoloured (cyan, magenta, yellow and black four colour process) stamps may be issued in 1999.

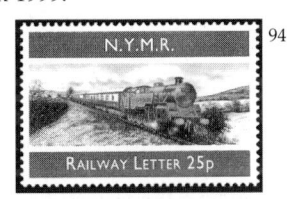

12/11/98. Rebuilding of Standard Tank No.80135. Des: Derek Miller. Ptr: Walsall Security Printers. Offset lithography in sheets of 8 (4 rows of 2), num. 0001-2500. P14.

Dsgn: B.R. Standard Class 4MT 2-6-4T No.80135 and train passing Moorgates, near Goathland

94	25p Multicoloured	.40
(94)	Sheet of 8	£3.20
(94a)	Sheet of 8 - imperf	£25.00

Nos: 94) 20000; 94a) 480. FDC: 700 covers and 125 postcards. 60 imperf sheets were issued, numbered in manuscript and signed by the designer.

STAMP BOOKS

1986. £5 Book of Stamps. 150th Anniversary of the Whitby & Pickering Railway.

In late 1986, the railway produced an 8¼" x 7¼" book containing five of their stamp issues commemorating the 150th Anniversary of the Whitby & Pickering Railway: 1 sheet No.8; 1 sheet No.9; 1 pane No.10-15; 1 sheet No.17-19; and ½ sheet No.20. In addition to the £5 face value of the stamps, which are held in transparent envelopes, the book has a one-page philatelic introduction to the stamps and twelve pages reproducing original documents from 1836.

Complete book	£100.00

Nos: 100.

1991. £7.50 Book of Stamps. An Illustrated History of the N.Y.M.R. and its Railway Letter Service.

To commemorate the letter service's 10th anniversary the railway published a 7½" x 7" book on 22 April 1991. It included stamps to a face value of £7.50 with individual stamps, blocks and sheets held in protective mounts: 2 x No.23; 1 sheet No.26; 1 sheet No.27; 1 sheet No.28; 2 x No.31; 1 x No.32; 1 se-tenant strip No.33-35; 4 x 36; top se-tenant strip No.38; ditto No.39; 1 x No.40. In addition about 35 pages on the history of the line from Whitby to Pickering from 1836 to date, and a further 9 on the N.Y.M.R. railway letter service were included. The publication was accompanied in its plastic sleeve by a certificate of authenticity signed by Margaret Atkins.

Complete book	£30.00

Nos: 500.

PREPARED BUT NOT ISSUED R.L.S.

30/12/94. Anniversary of the Act of Parliament for the Whitby & Pickering Railway. Des: Geoff and Margaret Atkins; Illus: Maurice Burns (photos). Offset lithography in sheets of 8 (2 panes of 4, each 2 rows of 2, se-tenant horiz N1+N2, separated by a horiz. gutter margin). P14.

Dsgn: N1) G.N.R. Stirling Single 4-2-2 No.1 - with error "Sterling"; N2) B.R. Class 4 2-6-4T No.80135 crossing bridge

N1	25p Multicoloured	
N2	25p Multicoloured	
	Pane of 4 (upper) - canc in black	£7.00
	Pane of 4 (lower) - canc in black	£7.00
	Sheet of 8 - canc in black	£14.00

Nos: 2000 of each. Only after the stamps were delivered from the printers, and a few panes and sheets had been sent out as publicity to dealers, was it noticed that the designer's name on the left-hand stamp had been spelt "Sterling" (as in monetary pounds) in error. Although the railway contacted those concerned promptly, before the original date planned for issue, and asked them not to release any of these stamps one sheet, split into pairs, appeared on the market. Other collectors heard of the error and wanted their own examples to complete their collections and the railway letter service came in for some unfair criticism. Eventually the Railway decided to release a quantity of the stamps as complete sheets, or separated into panes of four stamps. 500 of the 2000 sheets printed were cancelled in the centre of each block by the Grosmont Booking Office cancel dated "30 DEC 1994". Although the stamps retained their original gum the railway pre-cancelled them to indicate they are not valid for use as railway letter postage. The remaining sheets held by the railway were destroyed, leaving a handful of uncancelled sheets, distributed before the date of issue, in existence.

LABELS

[Illustration of parcel label: N.Y.M.R. PARCEL, DATE, FEE PAID, ISSUED SUBJECT TO THE COMPANY'S REGULATIONS, TO BE CALLED FOR AT, No 0067 STATION] — L1-L4

1/9/90. Parcel Labels. Des: Geoff and Margaret Atkins, and Stuart Hudson. Offset lithography in single imperf labels.

L1	Green	£1.00
L2	Red ('pink')	£1.00
L3	Orange ('gold')	£1.00
L4	Purple ('lilac')	£1.00

Nos: 1000 of each.
Following the withdrawal of the original design of general parcel and railway letter stamps (see pg 55) the railway issued these parcel labels. The shades chosen were approximations of the 'official colours' of the four stations: Grosmont (green), Pickering (pink), Goathland (gold), Levisham (lilac). A limited number of labels were carried on the first day and sold, on piece, to collectors. They were withdrawn from use on 1/12/98, with the impending cessation of heavier weight bands on the introduction of the 1998 Agreement.

N.Y.M.R. SPECIAL CANCELLATIONS

1	22/7/81	First Day
2	29/7/81	Royal Wedding [red]
3	19/9/81	80135 Brighton Works 1956 [red or black - undated. See also cancel 23]
4	31/10/81	Diesel Day [illus. Class 25 diesel - green]
5	6/12/81	North Yorkshire Pullman
6	6/12/81	Pullman Centenary 1881-1981 [illus. end of Pullman carriage - purple - undated]
7	6/12/81	Seasons Greetings [illus. Santa emerging from loco chimney with sack of toys - red - undated]
8	2/6/82	Eric Treacy 2nd June 1907 - 13th May 1978 [illus. loco nameplate - purple, green or black - undated]
9	3/6/82	15th Anniversary Inaugural Founders Meeting [lozenge border]
10	3/6/82	[illus. 0-4-0T *Mirvale* - undated]
11	21/8/82	Welcome to the "Deltics" 55009 *Alycidon* and 55019 *Royal Highland Fusilier* [border in shape of headboard - undated]
12	1/5/83	First Day of Issue
13	10/9/83	W.P.R. Work Begins
14	22/1/85	First Day of Issue [i) L.N.E.R. 4-6-2 *Flying Scotsman* - green; ii) G.W.R. "Castle" Class 4-6-0 - brown; iii) L.M.S. "Black 5" 4-6-0 - red; iv) L.B.S.C.R. 0-4-2T - yellow ochre. A set of four cancels illus. loco drawings - all undated]
15	22/1/85	1835 GWR 1985 [G.W.R. logo - brown - undated]
16	8/6/85	Whitby & Pickering Railway Whitby - Tunnel Public Service Commenced June 8th 1835 [purple, blue or black - undated]
17	8/6/85	W.&P.R. Whitby - Tunnel 1835 June 8th 1985 [black, green or red]
18	8/6/85	First Day of Issue [purple - undated]
19	26/5/86	W&PR NYMR 150 1836-1986 Tunnel to Pickering Pickering to Grosmont First Class [ticket design - brown]
20	26/5/86	[Pictorial cancel showing P.O. letterbox, sheep and N.Y.M.R. train - olive]
21	26/5/86	[Pictorial cancel of L.H.&J.C. No.29 - illus. drawing of loco from RLS No.6 - purple]
22	23/7/86	Royal Wedding [red]
23	20/10/86	80135 Brighton Works 1956 30 [black with "30" superimposed in green. See also cancel 3]
24	22/4/87	The Goathland Plough Stots English Long-sword Dancers Folk Festival April 24th - 26th [illus. ring of dancers tossing "rose" of swords]
25	22/4/87	Goathland Station - [illus. "rose" of crossed dance swords]
26	5/5/87	Whitby & Pickering Railway Acts of Parliament [green - undated]
27	3/6/87	Inaugural Meeting of NYMR Preservation Society at the Home of Mr T. Salmon 3/6/67 [See also cancel 36]
28	3/6/87	20th Anniversary 3.VI.87 N.Y.M.R.P.S.
29	11/10/87	Whitby Pickering Pickering Whitby

#	Date	Description
		[commemorating the first N.Y.M.R. through train - red]
30	22/11/87	Grosmont - 120 The Methodist Church Consecrated on the Feast of St Cecilia 1867 [black with "120" superimposed in red]
31	22/11/87	North Yorkshire Moors Railway Year 20 [double ring design with "Year 20" in centre]
32	22/4/88	First Public Train - April 22nd 1973 Royal Opening - May 1st 1973 NYMR 15 [green]
33	1/5/88	[As 32 above - but red]
34	10/5/88	Goathland - 88 First Day of Issue [illus. "88" with horse-drawn coach, loco, wayside cross, and early warning station within each 'circle']
35	24/5/88	John Wesley First Visit to Whitby: 1761 He Preached on the Abbey Plain Octagon Chapel 1762/4 Wesley Chapel 1788 [red - undated]
36	3/6/88	[As 27 above, red with the figures "21" superimposed in purple]
37	18/6/88	Royal Mail Pullman [headboard design - red]
38	18/6/88	N.Y.M.R. North Yorkshire Pullman [red]
39	8/10/88	Feasibility Study Pickering - Whitby [red - undated]
40	2/2/89	First Day of Issue [illus. *Mirvale* in steam - undated]
41	7/3/89	Goathland - History of Farming 1989 [illus. N.E.R. loco and cattle trucks passing fields - green - undated]
42	23/4/89	Naming of Class 25 Locomotives Diesel Day April 1989 [blue - undated]
43	6/6/89	*Dame Vera Lynn* Return to Traffic 3672 1944 D. Day 1989 [red]
44	10/6/89	NELPG NYMR 40th Birthday K1 2005 [green]
45	9/9/89	Evacuation of Children by Whitby to Pickering Railway 1939 50 1989
46	7/10/89	Centenary Regulation of Railways Act 1889-1989 N.E.R. - N.Y.M.R.
47	3/5/90	Restoration of *Repton* / 150th Anniversary of Penny Black Stamp [illus. nameplate]
48	24/5/90	Pickering Station 15 Years of NYMR Use [black or red]
49	8/6/90	R·E·U·N·I·O·N No.6 Group Headquarters Royal Canadian Air Force [illus. R.C.A.F. crest - blue]
50	23/6/90	Royal Mail Pullman [headboard design - red]
51	2/8/90	To Celebrate the 90th Birthday of Her Majesty Queen Elizabeth the Queen Mother on August 4th 1990 [illus. crown - purple]
52	1/2/91	Grosmont - Centenary of Railway Letter Service 1891-1991 [oval cancellation]
53	1/2/91	Centenary of Railway Letter Service 1891 N.E.R.-N.Y.M.R. 1991 [round cancellation]
54	22/4/91	Grosmont - 10th Anniversary NYMR Railway Letter Service First Day of Issue
55	23/5/91	Grosmont - North Eastern Weekend
56	15/6/91	10th Anniversary of Opening of Newtondale Halt N.Y.M.R. [illus. 2-6-4T No.80135]
57	16/7/91	Grosmont - Visit of *257 Squadron* and *Taw Valley*
58	7/12/91	Grosmont - 15th Anniversary of Santa Specials [illus. Santa in loco cab - red]
59	6/2/92	Grosmont - God Save the Queen 40th Anniversary of the Accession [illus. crown]
60	3/6/92	Grosmont - 25th Anniversary Inaugural Founders Meeting of the N.Y.M.R. First Day of Issue [red]
61	27/6/92	Pickering - N.Y.M.R. Silver Jubilee Gala [blue]
62	21/7/92	Grosmont - Return to Traffic of 44767 *George Stephenson* First Day of Issue [illus. side view of loco]
63	18/9/92	Grosmont - To Celebrate the Restoration of 60532 *Blue Peter* [illus. side view of front of loco - green]
64	19/9/92	Grosmont - The Silver Jubilee Special Train [headboard design]
65	31/10/92	Pickering - Wartime Weekend [illus. L.N.E.R. tin helmet]
66	2/6/93	40th Anniversary of the Coronation [illus. royal orb - blue]
67	14/9/93	Grosmont - 70th Anniversary The Building of Loco P3 No.2392
68	10/11/93	Grosmont - 25th Anniversary of First N.Y.M.R. Working Party [illus. N.Y.M.R. wheel logo]
69	12/4/94	Goathland - N.Y.M.R. Celebrates the Centenary of Pictorial Postcards [border similar to frames around R.M. stamps]
70	22/4/94	Grosmont - First day of Issue [illus. length of track]
71	3/5/94	Grosmont - 60th Birthday & Anniversary of the Building of Loco 30926 '*Repton*' First Day of Issue [illus. notice on easel]
72	6/6/94	Grosmont - NYMR Commemorates D-Day [illus. side view of W.D. 2-10-0 in front of symbolic ship within a flag-shaped frame]
73	4/7/94	Grosmont - 4th July 1994 is the 150th Anniversary of the Act of Parliament for the Building of the York to Pickering

#	Date	Description
		Railway [scroll design]
74	1/9/94	Grosmont - 75th Anniversary Building Loco 901 London & North Eastern Rly Darlington Works 1919 [illus. oval builder's plate]
75	8/10/94	Grosmont - 21st Anniversary Steam Galas and Restoration of BR Standard 4 No.75014 [illus. stylised front view of loco and steam]
76	24/3/95	Goathland - Railway Letter Service Seminar at The Great Northern Railway Hotel, Peterborough [border of perforations and illus. front view of loco]
77	2/5/95	Grosmont - The North Yorkshire Moors Railway Celebrates the 50th Anniversary of V.E. Day [illus. Union Flag]
78	16/5/95	Grosmont - Centenary of the Birth of R. J. Mitchell [illus. Spitfire]
79	7/7/95	Grosmont - 150th Anniversary of the Opening of the York to Pickering Railway [illus. portrait of George Hudson]
	7/7/95	Grosmont - 150th Anniversary of the Opening of the York to Pickering Railway [illus. Pickering Station's old overall roof. Sponsored by Benhams and used on their 'silk' covers only]
80	5/9/95	Grosmont - Rebuilding of 45428 *Eric Treacy* & Bi centenary of Sir Roland [sic] Hill [red - the date 15/9 is incorrect]
81	6/10/95	Grosmont - Record Rebuild '34027 *Taw Valley*' [illus. Golden Arrow motif]
82	26/12/95	Grosmont - Christmas Trains N.Y.M.R. [illus. loco, Christmas tree, Santa and wrapped parcels]
83	25/1/96	Levisham - 1759-1796 The NYMR Celebrates the Life of Robert Burns [illus. outline profile of poet and open book]
84	26/2/96	Levisham - Greetings from the NYMR [illus. loco and tender]
85	12/3/96	Levisham - *Bittern* Wildfowl and Wetlands [illus. bittern in flight and *Bittern* nameplate]
86	12/4/96	Grosmont - 1996 Seminar [illus. N.Y.M.R. Railway Letter Service stamp logo]
87	13/4/96	Pickering - Pullman to Celebrate the RLS Pullman [illus. stylised Pullman table lamp and curtains]
88	16/4/96	Grosmont - NYMR Celebrates 100 Years of Cinematography 1896-1996 [illus. cinema ticket outline]
	16/4/96	[illus. loco and train design similar to RLS No.67. Sponsored by Benhams and used on their 'silk' covers only]
89	21/4/96	Goathland - 70th Birthday of HM Queen Elizabeth II [illus. gates]
90	14/5/96	Grosmont - NYMR Celebrates European Football [illus. headboard with football]
91	26/5/96	Grosmont - Opening of New Signalbox [illus. signal arm and section token]
92	31/5/96	Grosmont - NYMR Marks the Last Run of the Carlisle / Peterborough T.P.O. [illus. T.P.O. carriage - red]
93	25/6/96	Grosmont - First Use of New Royal Mail Definitive Stamps
94	9/7/96	Grosmont - Olympic Games [illus. flag, torch and Olympic rings]
95	20/7/96	Pickering - Vintage Vehicle Weekend [illus. vintage van in N.Y.M.R. livery]
96	6/8/96	Grosmont - First Day of Suspension of Royal Mail Letters Monopoly
97	6/8/96	Grosmont - Dame Vera Lynn Women of Achievement [illus. nameplate]
98	23/8/96	Grosmont - Visit of *Sir Nigel Gresley* No.60007 to the NYMR [illus. with side view of streamlined front]
99	31/8/96	Grosmont - North Eastern Railway Weekend [illus. group of five locos]
100	3/9/96	Grosmont - NYMR Celebrates Childrens' TV (illus. nameplate, tv set and open book]
101	1/10/96	Grosmont - Classic Cars [illus. loco wheel and stylised wings]
102	28/10/96	Grosmont - Xmas Greetings from the NYMR [illus. Christmas tree, loco headboard and Santa hat]
103	6/1/97	Greetings from the NYMR [illus. Tudor rose]
104	21/1/97	Grosmont - 450th Anniversary of the Death of Henry VIII [illus. King's portrait]
105	11/3/97	Grosmont - Eric Treacy Missions of Faith [illus. loco nameplate and bishop's mitre]
106	18/3/97	Grosmont - N.Y.M.R. Marks the Launch of the First British Self Adhesive Stamps in Rolls [illus. border of stamp perforations]
107	19/4/97	Grosmont - 150th Anniversary of Steam on the Whitby - Pickering Railway [illus. 0-8-0 loco in steam]
108	21/4/97	Grosmont - Congratulations from the NYMR Queen's Golden Wedding [illus. bells and ribbon]
109	13/5/97	Goathland - Tales & Legends [illus. facade of Whitby Abbey and clouds]
110	6/6/97	Grosmont - 30th Anniversary of the Formation of the N.Y.M.R. [illus. No.65894 leaving a tunnel]
111	10/6/97	Grosmont - A Tribute to Aircraft Designers from the NYMR [illus. R.A.F. roundel and bomber]
112	30/6/97	Grosmont - The N.Y.M.R. Marks the Return of Hong Kong to Chinese Rule

113	8/7/97	[illus. side view of Chinese 4-6-4T loco] Grosmont - The Queen's Horses [illus. a horse-drawn railway carriage]
114	12/8/97	Grosmont - Centenary of Sub-Post Offices [illus. post office building next to Grosmont Station]
115	12/8/97	Grosmont - 60th Birthday of 60007 *Sir Nigel Gresley* 45428 *Eric Treacy* [illus. belt and buckle border]
116	9/9/97	Grosmont - NYMR Celebrates the Centenary of Enid Blyton [illus. loco with the number 5 on the side tank within frame in shape of book]
117	27/10/97	Grosmont - Merry Christmas from the NYMR [illus. loco exploding out of a cracker]
118	13/11/97	Grosmont - Royal Golden Wedding [illus. facade of Westminster Abbey]
119	13/11/97	Grosmont - Royal Golden Wedding [illus. 0-6-0 loco in steam]
120	20/1/98	Grosmont - Endangered Species [illus. front of loco and mouse]
121	3/2/98	Pickering - England's Rose [illus. roses]
122	24/2/98	Grosmont - The Queen's Heraldic Beasts [illus. Loco No.29 within band and buckle border]
123	10/3/98	Grosmont - Prestige Stamp Book Dorothy Wilding's Portrait of Queen Elizabeth II [illus. Wilding stamp frame designs and border]
124	24/3/98	Grosmont - NYMR Celebrates the 300th Anniversary of the Eddystone Lighthouse [illus. front view of loco with beam from smokebox lamp]
125	23/4/98	Grosmont - Comedians [illus. mask on locomotive smokebox]
126	1/5/98	Grosmont - NYMR 25 Years Recreating History [illus. anniversary logo]
127	2/6/98	Grosmont - 3672 *Dame Vera Lynn* 100,000 Miles in Preservation [illus. side view of loco]
128	23/6/98	Grosmont - Health [illus. cross on shield]
129	2/7/98	Grosmont - Anniversary Pullman [illus. side view of Pullman carriage]
130	3/7/98	Grosmont - 60th Anniversary of the World Speed Record for Steam 4468 *Mallard* [illus. side view of loco and carriage. See also N.V.R. cancel 37]
131	21/7/98	Grosmont - Magical Worlds [illus. face on loco smokebox with steam]
132	3/10/98	Pickering - 25th Anniversary Steam Gala Weekend [illus. front view of loco]
133	12/11/98	Pickering - Rebuilding of Standard Tank 80135 [illus. side view of front of loco]
134	22/11/98	Pickering - Captain Cook Pullman [loco headboard design]

P.O. ONE-DAY POSTMARKS

30/8/70	Grosmont - NYMRPS Open Weekend [illus. W.&P.R. crest. Used before letter service]
31/8/70	[As above but with different date]
29/5/72	Grosmont - Steam Gala [illus. side view of stylised 0-6-2T loco. Pre- RLS service]
1/5/73	Grosmont - Official [Royal] Opening North Yorkshire Moors Railway [Pre- RLS service]
10/11/73	Grosmont - 50th Anniversary Special Train Locomotive No.2392 [Pre- RLS service]
22/1/85	York - Rail Riders World, York Station, A Magical World of Trains [Rail Riders World and B.R. logos]
10/5/88	York - *Mallard* '88. National Railway Museum, 50th Anniversary of the World Speed Record for Steam [illus. Royal crest and *Mallard* nameplate]
1/5/93	Pickering - 20th Anniversary NYMR Royal Opening [illus. side view of 0-6-2T No.29]
18/1/94	York - NYMR Celebrates the Age of Steam [illus. N.Y.M.R. wheel logo]
22/4/94	Pickering - 21st Anniversary First Public Train [illus. side view of 0-6-2T No.29]
27/9/94	York Post Shop [illus. *Mallard* and train. Idea and artwork for the design supplied by NYMR/RLS]
7/7/95	Pickering [illus. three N.Y.M.R. locos]
12/4/96	Pickering [illus. locomotive and "50H" shed plate]
20/7/96	Grosmont · Whitby - Vintage Vehicles Weekend [illus. vehicles as RLS No.77+78]
31/8/96	Pickering - NYMR · NER Weekend [illus. L.N.E.R. Class A4 loco]
19/4/97	Pickering - 150th Anniversary of Steam on the Whitby - Pickering Railway [illus. 0-8-0 loco in steam]
6/6/97	Goathland Whitby - 30th Anniversary of the Formation of the N.Y.M.R. [illus. No.65894 leaving Grosmont Tunnel]
3/2/98	England's Rose [illus. rose]
1/5/98	Pickering - NYMR 25 Years Recreating History [illus. anniversary logo]
2/6/98	Pickering - 3672 *Dame Vera Lynn* 100,000 Miles in Preservation [illus. side view of loco]
2/7/98	Pickering - Anniversary Pullman Train [illus. Pullman crest]
3/10/98	Pickering - 25th Anniversary Steam Gala Weekend
22/11/98	Whitby - Captain Cook Pullman Train [illus. ship's wheel]

A P.O. slogan postmark has been used to advertise the railway:

3/6/92	North Yorkshire Moors Railway 25 Years 1967 - 1992 [illus. side view of W.D. No.3672 *Dame Vera Lynn*]

RAILWAY PRESERVATION SOCIETY OF IRELAND

CUMANN CAOMHNAITHE IARNRÓID NA H-ÉIRANN

The society, formed in 1964 to preserve steam operations in Ireland, has restored ten engines to working order, some over 100 years old. Based at Whitehead Excursion Station (built by the L.M.S.(N.C.C.) in 1903, to cope with the day trip traffic from Belfast) they operate several main line rail tours each year. With the co-operation of Northern Ireland Railways and Coras Iompair Eireann, the society has access to all railway routes in Ireland, north and south of the border.

On 12-13, and 19 April 1980, the society carried covers which bore a rectangular blue cachet on the reverse. The inscription read: "Railway Letter Service / 40p Fee Paid / Railway Preservation Society of Ireland". In May 1981, they became party to the agreement with the British Post Office for the carriage of railway letters and issued their first stamps on 13 May 1981. As they regularly operate in the Republic of Ireland the appropriate issues are surcharged in Irish punts. From 17 March 1986, a "T.P.O. Fee Paid" circular cancellation was used on covers for that year.

13/5/81. Definitives. Des & Ptr: Format Security Printers, London; Illus: R.P.S.I. (photos). Offset lithography in sheets of 9 (3 rows of 3, se-tenant horiz. 1+2+3). P14.

Dsgn: 1) G.N.R.(I.) S-Class 4-4-0 No.171 *Slieve Gullion*; 2) G.S.&W.R. J-15 Class 0-6-0 No.186; 3) L.M.S.(N.C.C.) 2-6-4T No.4

1	20p Multicoloured	
2	20p Multicoloured	
3	20p Multicoloured	
	Se-tenant strip of 3	£5.00
	Sheet of 9	£14.00

Nos: 12600 of each; later 8238 were surcharged or overprinted for No.4-15, leaving an issue of 4362 of each. Two proof sheets, which have the total face value printed in the lower margin, exist. Five sets of progressive proofs for the complete sheets of 9 are known. FDC: 1000

12/12/81. Irish Republic Surcharges. Surcharged in red by M.M.T. Printers, Belfast.

4	IR£O.33 on 20p (1)	
5	IR£O.33 on 20p (2)	
6	IR£O.33 on 20p (3)	
	Se-tenant strip of 3	£9.00
	Sheet of 9	£25.00

Nos: 4350 of each. Inverted surcharges exist. Three trial proof sheets exist surcharged in black. FDC: 300

21/8/82. "Portrush Flyer" Overprint. Overprinted in black by M.M.T. Printers.

7	22p on 20p (1)	
8	22p on 20p (2)	
9	22p on 20p (3)	
	Se-tenant strip of 3	£4.00
	Sheet of 9	£10.00

Nos: 1500 of each. Inverted overprints exist. FDC: 260

4/9/82. "Steam Enterprise" Overprint. Overprinted in black by M.M.T. Printers.

10	22p on 20p (1)	
11	22p on 20p (2)	
12	22p on 20p (3)	
	Se-tenant strip of 3	£4.00
	Sheet of 9	£10.00

Nos: 1500 of each. Inverted overprints exist. FDC: 265

1/9/84. Emergency Surcharges. Surcharged in black by M & G Printers, Cookstown, Co. Tyrone.

13	IR£1.00 on 20p (1)	
14	IR£1.00 on 20p (2)	
15	IR£1.00 on 20p (3)	
	Se-tenant strip of 3	£9.00
	Sheet of 9	£27.50

Nos: 888 of each. This was an emergency issue when the authorities required railway letters to be franked at the same rate as the official railway company (C.I.E.). FDC: 600 of each

1-3

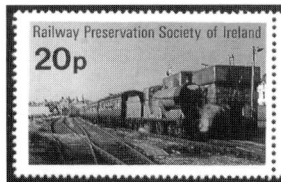

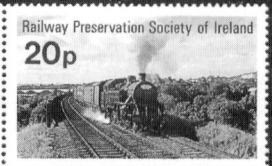

10/5/85. Sterling Currency Definitives. Des & Ptr: Dollco Printing and Banknote Co., Ottawa, Canada; Illus: Messrs. McBride, Kitts, and McCorkell (photos). Offset lithography in miniature sheets of 8 (2 rows of 4), containing one example of each. P13 x 13.4.

Dsgn: 16) No.171 *Slieve Gullion*; 17) No.171 *Slieve Gullion* on bridge; 18) No.186; 19) No.171 *Slieve Gullion* and No.4; 20) No.171 *Slieve Gullion* in station; 21) No.186 with train; 22) No.4 and "Portrush Flyer"; 23) Avonside 0-6-0ST No.3 *R. H. Smythe*

16	20p Multicoloured	
17	20p Multicoloured	
18	20p Multicoloured	
19	20p Multicoloured	
20	20p Multicoloured	
21	20p Multicoloured	
22	20p Multicoloured	
23	20p Multicoloured	
	Sheet of 8	£7.00

Nos: 4500 of each; later 1200 of each were overprinted for No.36-67, leaving an issue of 3300 of each. This issue was produced in conjunction with Stangib (Canada). A quantity of sheets were sold to an Australian stamp dealer and were subsequently overprinted "AUS STEAM '88" in green; these items are outside the scope of this catalogue.

FDC: 200 of each

11/5/85. Irish Currency Definitives. Des & Ptr: Dollco Printing and Banknote Co.; Illus: Messrs. McBride, Kitts, and McCorkell (photos). Offset lithography in miniature sheets of 4 (2 rows of 2), containing one example of each. P13 x 13.4.

Dsgn: 24) No.3 *R. H. Smythe* with coach; 25) No.186 in station; 26) No.171 *Slieve Gullion* with train; 27) No.4 approaching station

24	IR£1.23 Multicoloured	
25	IR£1.23 Multicoloured	
26	IR£1.23 Multicoloured	
27	IR£1.23 Multicoloured	
	Sheet of 4	£10.00

Nos: 4476 of each; later 900 of each were surcharged or overprinted for No.28-31, 32-35 and 68-71, leaving an issue of 3576 of each. This issue was produced in conjunction with Stangib (Canada). Some sheets were later overprinted "AUS STEAM '88" and "IR£1.10" in green; see footnote to No. 16-23.

FDC: 200 of each

17/3/86. Change in Irish Republic Letter Rate. Surcharged in black by Brough, Cox and Dunn, Belfast.

28	IR£1.10 on IR£1.23 (24)	
29	IR£1.10 on IR£1.23 (25)	
30	IR£1.10 on IR£1.23 (26)	
31	IR£1.10 on IR£1.23 (27)	
	Sheet of 4	£25.00

Nos: 300 of each. FDC: 100 of each

11/5/86. "1986 Western Tour" Overprint. Overprinted in black by Brough, Cox and Dunn.

32	IR£1.10 on IR£1.23 (24)	
33	IR£1.10 on IR£1.23 (25)	
34	IR£1.10 on IR£1.23 (26)	
35	IR£1.10 on IR£1.23 (27)	
	Sheet of 4	£25.00

Nos: 300 of each. FDC: 100 of each

12/5/86. "Rail Tour 1986" Overprint. Overprinted in black by Brough, Cox and Dunn.

36	20p Multicoloured (16)
37	20p Multicoloured (17)
38	20p Multicoloured (18)
39	20p Multicoloured (19)
40	20p Multicoloured (20)
41	20p Multicoloured (21)
42	20p Multicoloured (22)
43	20p Multicoloured (23)
	Sheet of 8 £22.50

Nos: 300 of each. One sheet is known with the overprint inverted. FDC: 100 of each

19/7/86. "Portrush Flyer" Overprints. Overprinted in black by Brough, Cox and Dunn.

44	20p Multicoloured (16)
45	20p Multicoloured (17)
46	20p Multicoloured (18)
47	20p Multicoloured (19)
48	20p Multicoloured (20)
49	20p Multicoloured (21)
50	20p Multicoloured (22)
51	20p Multicoloured (23)
	Sheet of 8 £22.50

Nos: 300 of each. One sheet and a set of covers are known having stamps with an uninked impression of the letterpress overprint. FDC: 100 of each

25/8/86. "Bangor Belle" Overprint. Overprinted in black by Brough, Cox and Dunn.

52	20p Multicoloured (16)
53	20p Multicoloured (17)
54	20p Multicoloured (18)
55	20p Multicoloured (19)
56	20p Multicoloured (20)
57	20p Multicoloured (21)
58	20p Multicoloured (22)
59	20p Multicoloured (23)
	Sheet of 8 £22.50

Nos: 300 of each. FDC: 100 of each

6/9/86. "Steam Enterprise" Northern Ireland Overprint. Overprinted in black by Brough, Cox and Dunn.

60	20p Multicoloured (16)
61	20p Multicoloured (17)
62	20p Multicoloured (18)
63	20p Multicoloured (19)
64	20p Multicoloured (20)
65	20p Multicoloured (21)
66	20p Multicoloured (22)
67	20p Multicoloured (23)
	Sheet of 8 £22.50

Nos: 300 of each. FDC: 100 of each

20/9/86. "Steam Enterprise" Irish Republic Overprint. Overprinted in black by Brough, Cox and Dunn.

68	IR£1.10 on IR£1.23 (24)
69	IR£1.10 on IR£1.23 (25)
70	IR£1.10 on IR£1.23 (26)
71	IR£1.10 on IR£1.23 (27)
	Sheet of 4 £22.50

Nos: 300 of each. FDC: 100 of each

17/8/91. "Portrush Flyer". Des: Peter McBride. Ptr: The House of Questa, London. Offset lithography in miniature sheets of 6 (2 rows of 3, se-tenant horiz. and vert., row 1: 72+73+72; row 2: 73+72+73). P14.1.

Dsgn: 72) G.N.R.(I.) 4-4-0 No.85; 73) D.&S.E.R. 2-6-0 No.461

72	25p Multicoloured
73	25p Multicoloured
	Se-tenant pair .80
	Se-tenant block of 4 £1.60
	Sheet of 6 £2.50

Nos: 15000 of each; later 500 of each were overprinted for No.94-97, leaving an issue of 14500. Five imperf proofs exist. FDC: 250 of each

17/8/91. "Castlerock Link". Des: Peter McBride. Ptr: The House of Questa. Offset lithography in miniature sheets of 6 (2 rows of 3, se-tenant horiz. and vert., row 1: 74+75+74; row 2: 75+74+75). P14.1.

Dsgn: 74) No.186; 75) No.171 *Slieve Gullion*

74	25p Multicoloured
75	25p Multicoloured
	Se-tenant pair .80
	Se-tenant block of 4 £1.60
	Sheet of 6 £2.50

Nos: 15000 of each; later 500 of each were overprinted for No.86-89, leaving an issue of 14500. Five imperf proofs exist. FDC: 250 of each

17/8/91. R.P.S.I. and D.&A.R. Joint Railway Operation Definitives. For full details see pg 74.

76   50p Multicoloured
77   50p Multicoloured

7/9/91. "The Rosslare Special". Des: Peter McBride. Ptr: The House of Questa. Offset lithography in miniature sheets of 6 (2 rows of 3, se-tenant horiz. and vert., row 1: 78+79+78; row 2: 79+78+79). P14.1.

Dsgn: 78) No.4; 79) No.171 *Slieve Gullion*

78   55p Multicoloured
79   55p Multicoloured

Se-tenant pair	£2.00
Se-tenant block of 4	£4.00
Sheet of 6	£6.00

Nos: 15000 of each; later 500 of each were overprinted for No.90-93, leaving an issue of 14500. Five imperf proofs exist.   FDC: 250

7/9/91. "Limerick 300". Des: Peter McBride. Ptr: The House of Questa. Offset lithography in miniature sheets of 6 (2 rows of 3, se-tenant horiz. and vert., row 1: 80+81+80; row 2: 81+80+81). P14.1.

Dsgn: 80) No.186; 81) No.4

80   55p Multicoloured
81   55p Multicoloured

Se-tenant pair	£2.00
Se-tenant block of 4	£4.00
Sheet of 6	£6.00

Nos: 15000 of each; later 500 of each were overprinted for No.82-85, leaving an issue of 14500. Five imperf proofs exist.   FDC: 250

4/7/93. "Baile Atha Claithe [Dublin] - Baile Atha Luain [Athlone] - Beal Atha na Sluaighe [Ballinasloe]" Overprint. Overprinted in black (2 rows of 3, se-tenant horiz. and vert., row 1: 82+83+84; row 2: 83+84+85).

82   55p "Baile Atha Cliath" (80)
83   55p "Baile Atha Luain" (81)
84   55p "Beal Atha na Sluaigh" (80)
85   55p "Baile Atha Cliath" (81)
      Sheet of 6   £6.50

Nos: 82 and 85) 500 of each; 83 and 84) 1000 of each.

17/7/93. "Belfast - Portrush - Castlerock" Overprint. Overprinted in black (2 rows of 3, se-tenant horiz. and vert., row 1: 86+87+88; row 2: 87+88+89).

86   25p "Belfast" (74)
87   25p "Portrush" (75)
88   25p "Castlerock" (74)
89   25p "Belfast" (75)
      Sheet of 6   £4.00

Nos: 86 and 89) 500 of each; 87 and 88) 1000 of each.

24/7/93. "Baile Atha Claithe [Dublin] - Loch Garman [Wexford] - Calafort Ros Lair [Rosslare]" Overprint. Overprinted in black (2 rows of 3, se-tenant horiz. and vert., row 1: 90+91+92; row 2: 91+92+93).

90   55p "Baile Atha Cliath" (78)
91   55p "Loch Garman" (79)
92   55p "Calafort Ros Lair" (78)
93   55p "Baile Atha Cliath" (79)
      Sheet of 6   £6.50

Nos: 90 and 93) 500 of each; 91 and 92) 1000 of each.

31/7/93. "Belfast - Coleraine" Overprint. Overprinted in black (2 rows of 3, se-tenant horiz. and vert., row 1: 94+95+94; row 2: 96+97+96).

94   25p "Belfast" (72)
95   25p "Coleraine" (73)
96   25p "Belfast" (73)
97   25p "Coleraine" (72)
      Sheet of 6   £3.50

Nos: 94 and 96) 1000 of each; 95 and 97) 500 of each.

Until contacted during the compiling of this catalogue the society was not aware that stamps No.82-97 had been issued by their agent. Their status will be reviewed before the publication of the next edition.

R.P.S.I. SPECIAL CANCELLATIONS

1	16/5/81	Dublin - "Ben Bulben" Railtour
2	12/12/81	Santa Special 1981
3	10/5/85	Belfast - First Day of Issue Posted on Train
4	11/5/85	Dublin - First Day of Issue Posted on Train
5	25/8/86	Belfast - "Bangor Belle"
6	6/9/86	"Steam Enterprise" [undated]
7	17/8/91	"Portrush Flyer"
8	17/8/91	"Castlerock Link"
9	7/9/91	Greystones - First Day of Issue

10	7/9/91	Dublin - First Day of Issue
11	4/7/93	First Day of Issue Dublin Athlone Ballinasloe Posted on Board Train
12	17/7/93	First Day of Issue Belfast Portrush Castlerock Posted on Board Train
13	24/7/93	First Day of Issue Dublin - Wexford - Rosslare Harbour Posted on Board Train
14	31/7/93	First Day of Issue Belfast Coleraine

RAILWAY PRESERVATION SOCIETY OF IRELAND AND DOWNPATRICK & ARDGLASS RAILWAY JOINT RAILWAY OPERATION

Although these stamps appeared on first day covers carried on R.P.S.I. or D.&A.R. trains neither the Society nor the Railway have seen or had knowledge of these stamps before they were contacted as part of the compilation of this catalogue. There have never been joint operations. Both organisations are 70 miles apart with no rail connection, although some rail specials have been bused from the national network to the preserved line. The status of these stamps will be reviewed before the next edition of this catalogue.

17/8/91. Definitives. Des: Peter McBride; Illus: 1) Charles Friel; 2) Colin Holliday (photos). Ptr: The House of Questa, London. Offset lithography in miniature sheets of 6 (2 rows of 3, se-tenant horiz. and vert., row 1: 1+2+1; row 2: 2+1+2). P14.1.

Dsgn: L1) G.N.R.(I) 4-4-0 No.85 and train; L2) Hudswell Clarke 0-4-0ST No.3BG *Guinness* and train, with Down Cathedral in background

1   50p Multicoloured
2   50p Multicoloured
    Se-tenant pair   £1.50
    Se-tenant block of 4   £3.00
    Sheet of 6   £4.50

Nos: 15000 of each.   FDC: 250 of each

The sheets are inscribed "Joint Railway Operation" in the upper margin. Five imperf proof sheets exist. The photographs which appear on these R.P.S.I. and D.&A.R. sheets originally bore the legend "Downpatrick & Ardglass Railway Co." on the proof sheets, with the upper margin inscribed "Railway Preservation Society of Ireland", the lower margin inscribed "Railway Letter Stamp", and each stamp with a 25p value (see pg 14). Until contacted during the compiling of this catalogue the railways were not aware that these stamps had been issued. Their status will be reviewed before the publication of the next edition.

Note: These stamps will also be found catalogued in chronological sequence under the respective railways: Downpatrick & Ardglass No.3+4; Railway Preservation Society of Ireland No.76+77.

RAVENGLASS & ESKDALE RAILWAY

The railway originated in 1873, when powers were obtained to construct a 3' gauge line from the coast at Ravenglass to ore workings near Boot. The original company went into liquidation but in 1915 the line was taken over, converted to 15" gauge, and provided with equipment that enabled it to continue carrying ore and passengers until quarrying ceased in 1953. The quarry company, which owned the line, ran the passenger service until 1960, when it put the railway up for sale. A buyer was found and, supported by enthusiasts, the passenger traffic has developed to make the railway an important tourist attraction in the area.

From Ravenglass there are stations at Muncaster Mill (1), Irton Road (4¼), The Green (4¾), Beckfoot (6½), and Eskdale (Dalegarth) the present terminus, 7 miles up the valley.

Although the railway carried the Royal Mails for many years it was not until 1969 that the company became party to the agreement of 1891. The service commenced on 1 July of that year. Rather than scrap the prepared 1s2d stamp, when the 1s3d rate was announced, the company decided to apply a "1d surcharge paid" rubber handstamp showing that the extra fee had been paid. For the rates to Douglas, Isle of Man, and to Northern Ireland, a 4d rubber stamp was applied. A "9d surcharge paid" handstamp was used shortly after the rate increased to 2s. When the rate rose from 15p to 16p, the handstamp was used with 1p inserted in manuscript. On 7 April 1973, V.A.T. was introduced making the rate 16p+2p. The customer, however, was not charged the tax, the extra cost being borne by the company.

In the early 1960s a parcel service was operated by the railway, and a package label issued in the mid-1970s, see pg 78. This line used British Railways newspaper stamps to denote payment of the B.R. fee when covers were sent over the main line system; this facility was little used. The railway achieved continuity of operation by signing both the 1974 and, after a slight delay, the 1998 Agreements.

Enquiries to: Ravenglass & Eskdale Railway Co. Ltd., Ravenglass, Cumbria CA18 1SW

1/7/69. Definitive. Des: P. Williams. Ptr: R. H. Bethwaite, Cleator Moor, Cumbria. Lithography in single stamps with selvedge at left, made up into booklets of 50 stamps. R5 at left of stamp, other edges imperf.

Dsgn: Clarkson 2-8-2 *River Mite*

1	1s2d White on black background	£25.00
1a	1s2d White on dull black	£25.00
1b	1s2d White on glossy black	£25.00
1c	1s2d - error, imperfectly printed	-
	Booklets of 50:	
(1)	Buff covers	-
(1a)	White covers	-
(1b)	Red covers	-

Nos: 1) 1000 copies, and 1a) 2000, were issued concurrently, the majority being used on first day covers. A third printing, issued in 8/69, produced 1000 copies indistinguishable from No.1a; and a fourth (1b) was for 1000 copies. The error (1c) was a printing of 2000 which produced stamps with a slight brownish tinge, further identifiable by the missing rail between the leading wheels and the patchy appearance of most horizontal lines; after 30 had been issued it was decided to scrap those remaining because of their poor appearance. One copy was kept for record purposes. FDC: 2176

3/6/70. William Wordsworth Bicentenary. Des & Ptr: T. Stephenson & Sons Ltd., Prescot, after a sketch by Douglas Ferreira. Lithography in sheets of 12 (4 rows of 3), num. 0001 - 0600. P11.2.

Dsgn: Heywood 0-8-0T *Muriel* (now 0-8-2 *River Irt*) and daffodils

2	1s3d Red, yellow, green and black on pale green	£3.00
	Sheet of 12	£40.00

Nos: 12000; later 4800 were surcharged for No.3, leaving an issue of 7200. A very limited number were surcharged as a temporary measure - see below.

?/9/70. Temporary Provisional. Surcharged in violet by the Railway.

*	2/- on 1s3d (2)	-

This overprint came to light early in 1993. The railway has confirmed their authenticity but have no record of how many were surcharged in this style.

75

Only very few could have been issued since it appears they were prepared as an emergency measure when the letter fee was increased on 27/9/70, until the "9d Surcharge Paid" rubber stamp was introduced in 11/70. Examples are handstamped, having a solid shape partially covering the original value, with the "2/-" value to the right of it.

15/2/71. Provisional. Surcharged in black by R. H. Bethwaite, num. 0601 - 1000.

3	10p on 1s3d (2)	£5.00
	Sheet of 12	£65.00

Nos: 4800. FDC: 2050

6/6/71. Emergency Supplementary Issue. Des: Douglas Ferreira. Ptr: R. H. Bethwaite. Letterpress single imperforate copies.

Dsgn: R.&E.R. motif

4	5p Black on pale green	£7.50
4a	5p Black on emerald green (29/2/72)	£7.50

Nos: 4) 1000; 4a) 1000. The heavy posting of covers by collectors, to use up surplus P.O. £sd stamps before they were demonetised, was responsible for the reprints of both No.4/4a and No.5/5a/5b, which are distinctive. FDC: 4) 73

25/8/71. Definitives. Des: T. Eric Ivens. Ptr: Historic Relics, London. Lithography in sheets of 6 (2 rows of 3). P11.

Dsgn: Facsimile of the original railway letter stamp

5	15p Red	£10.00
5a	15p - broken A	£12.00
5b	15p Brown red	£15.00
5ba	15p - broken A	£18.00
5bb	15p Light brown red	£15.00
5bba	15p - broken A	£18.00
(5)	Sheet of 6	£75.00
(5b)	Sheet of 6	£100.00
(5bb)	Sheet of 6	£100.00

Nos: 5) 4638; 5b) and 5bb) 1632. The flaw on the A of "Eskdale" appears on row 2, stamp 2. No.5 was printed on glossy paper; No.5b and 5bb were produced on plain paper and are shade differences in the same print run. A few stamps of No.5 exist with 'blind' perfs below row 2. See also footnote to No.4/4a. FDC: 5) 2815

3/6/74. Definitive. Des & Ptr: T. Stephenson & Sons Ltd.; Illus: from a photo by Douglas Ferreira. Lithography in sheets of 12 (3 rows of 4), num. 1 - 1000. P14.

Dsgn: R.&E.R. train

6	10p Multicoloured	£2.00
	Sheet of 12	£25.00

Nos: 12000. A variety of extra grey cinders in the loco's smoke, behind figure 0 of the value, appears on row 3, stamp 2. Examples are known on cover with a double black print. FDC: 2400

24/5/75. Railway Centenary. Des: Douglas Ferreira. Ptr: T. Stephenson & Sons Ltd. Lithography in sheets of 12 (4 rows of 3), num. 0001 - 0950. P14.

Dsgn: 3' gauge loco *Devon* with Furness squirrel emblem, inscribed "1875-1975"

7	10p Multicoloured	£1.25
	Sheet of 12	£15.00

Nos: 11400. One sheet is known with a significant shift to the left of the salmon colour, and one with a double print of the green resulting in a shadow image of the loco. FDC: 5000

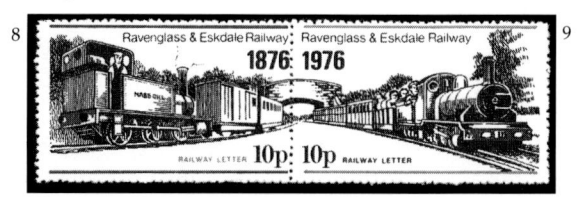

29/5/76. Passenger Centenary. Des & Ptr: Howe of Brampton, Cumbria, from a sketch by Douglas Ferreira. Lithography in sheets of 12 (6 rows of 2, se-tenant horiz. 8+9), num. 1 - 1000. Pin P14.

Dsgn: 8) Train hauled by 3' gauge 0-6-0T *Nab Gill*; 9) Train hauled by 15" gauge 0-8-2 *River Irt*

8	10p Black, red and green	
9	10p Black, green and red	
	Se-tenant pair	£3.50
	Sheet of 12	£21.50

Nos: 6000 of each. One sheet is known with red printing missing. Sheets are known with misaligned perfs. The paper is known in two thicknesses of cream, and also in white. FDC: 1574

28/5/77. The Queen's Silver Jubilee. Des: Douglas Ferreira. Ptr: T. Stephenson & Sons Ltd. Lithography in sheets of 12 (4 rows of 3), num. 0001 - 0600. P14.

Dsgn: R.&E.R. diesel multiple unit *Silver Jubilee*

10	10p Silver with red background	£2.75
	Sheet of 12	£35.00

Nos: 7200, later 1800 were surcharged for No.11, leaving an issue of 5400.   FDC: 1450

3/1/78. The Queen's Silver Jubilee Provisional. Surcharged in black by T. Stephenson & Sons Ltd, num. between 0001 and 0600.

11	15p on 10p (10)	£4.00
	Sheet of 12	£50.00

Nos: 1800.   FDC: 210

27/5/78. Definitive. Des: Douglas Ferreira. Ptr: T. Stephenson & Sons Ltd. Lithography in sheets of 12 (3 rows of 4), num. 0001 - 0600. P14.

Dsgn: R.&E.R. 2-6-2 *Northern Rock* and train, inscribed "Britain's First Radio Operated Railway"

12	15p Blue and yellow	£2.50
	Sheet of 12	£32.50

Nos: 7200. A flaw in the R of "Operated" appears on row 3, stamp 1, on sheets perf through the left-hand margin.   FDC: 1500

26/6/79. Second Season of Steam-hauled Excursion Trains through Ravenglass, B.R. Des: Douglas Ferreira; Illus: N. Stanbra (photography). Ptr: Blackburn Times Press. Lithography in sheets of 12 (4 rows of 3), num. 1 - 600. R4.5.

Dsgn: Trains side by side hauled by 2-6-2 *Northern Rock* and L.N.E.R. 4-6-2 No.4472 *Flying Scotsman*

13	15p Yellow, red and black	.80
	Sheet of 12	£10.00

Nos: 7200.   FDC: 1500

19/11/80. Definitive. Des & Ptr: T. Stephenson & Sons Ltd., from a sketch by Douglas Ferreira. Lithography in sheets of 10 (5 rows of 2), num. 1 - 750. P11.

Dsgn: R.&E.R. 'Flying Wheel' motif

14	20p Red, yellow, pale blue, green and black on cream background	.60
	Sheet of 10	£6.00

Nos: 10000; later 2500 were surcharged for No.15, leaving an issue of 7500. Sheets were printed as left and right hand panes, as indicated by the registration markings in the side margins. See also footnote to No.15.   FDC: 1475

24/11/80. Emergency Provisional. Surcharged in black by T. Stephenson & Sons Ltd, num. 751 - 1000.

15	15p on 20p (14)	.60
	Sheet of 10	£6.00

Nos: 2500. Sheets of No.14 were printed well in advance of the fee being increased. During the summer stocks of 15p stamps began to dwindle and it was feared that they would be exhausted before the 20p rate came into effect. So 250 sheets of the then unissued 20p stamp were surcharged to give a temporary 15p stamp if required. Stocks of previous issues did last out and No.15 was not needed. After No.14 was issued the Company decided to release No.15, but initially offered it only in sheets of 10. No fdc were serviced. It is understood it remains valid for use but additional stamps must be added to make up the rate.

26/9/81. 21 Years of Preservation. Des: Douglas Ferreira. Ptr: T. Stephenson & Sons Ltd. Photo-lithography in sheets of 10 (5 rows of 2), num. 1 - 600. P14.

Dsgn: Squirrel and stylised front view of loco, inscribed "Preservation Society 1960 - 1981".

16	20p Yellow, green, red and black	.60
	Sheet of 10	£6.00

Nos: 6000.   FDC: 1000

4/5/85. Definitive. Des: Douglas Ferreira. Ptr: T. Stephenson & Sons Ltd. Photo-lithography in sheets of 12 (4 rows of 3), num. 0001 - 0800. P14.

Dsgn: Outline of the front of a locomotive, inscribed "1985"

17	20p Brown	.40
	Sheet of 12	£4.80

Nos: 9600. FDC: 1050

LABELS

Early 1960s. Parcel Label. Single labels with selvedge at top, made up into booklets. Coloured R4.75 (in black) at top of label and imperf edges.

Dsgn: Ravenglass & Eskdale Railway motif (as No.4 and 4a)

L1	6d Black	£3.00

Examples are known with the design offset on the reverse.

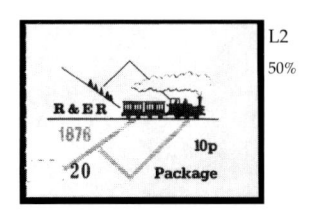

1976. Package Label. Single labels with selvedge at left, made up into booklets. R4.75 at left of label and imperf edges.

Dsgn: Stylised loco and carriages with Cumbrian hills in background

L2	10p Brown on cream	-

Packages conveyed with this label were often wrapped joints of meat from a butcher in Ravenglass to campers in Eskdale.

R.&E.R. SPECIAL CANCELLATIONS

1	1/2/71	80th Anniversary of the Railway Letter Service
2	15/2/71	Decimal Day
3	25/8/71	First Day of Issue [illus. side view of 2-8-2 loco]
4	6/11/71	Visit of Romney Hythe and Dymchurch Railway Locomotive *Northern Chief* [illus. loco]

P.O. SPECIAL CANCELLATIONS

A P.O. slogan postmark was used at Carlisle to celebrate the railway's centenary:

28/4/75   1875 1975 Centenary Year

FRANK J. WILSON
Railway Philatelist

57A Bourne Road, Spalding, Lincs. PE11 1JR

e-mail - stamps@mailbyrail.com
Internet site: www.mailbyrail.com

We always have a good range of Modern Railway Letter stamps and covers.
We also stock the Early Railway Letter Stamps, including covers, and Railway Newspaper and Parcel Stamps.
We usually have a good selection of TPOs, mostly 1950s onwards but with a selection of earlier available, and of GB Railway event covers.

We always have an extensive stock of Railway Thematics of the world including local and cinderella items.

Occasional lists issued, and photocopies of material in stock sent on request.

ROMNEY, HYTHE & DYMCHURCH LIGHT RAILWAY

Well known as the 'World's smallest public railway', the 15" gauge line was opened to the public between Hythe and New Romney in 1927, and from New Romney to Dungeness in 1929. It runs for nearly 14 miles across the Romney Marsh on the southeast coast of England. Built by Capt. J. E. P. Howey, passenger and goods traffic operated initially all year round, but the winter service was withdrawn in 1948, and goods traffic ceased in the 1950s. On Capt. Howey's death in 1963 the railway was continued by local business interests until increasing maintenance costs almost closed it in 1971. A new consortium rescued the line in 1972. Today the railway not only carries holiday-makers but operates school trains for pupils to and from New Romney.

The rolling stock includes 11 steam locomotives which are one-third sized reproductions of standard gauge prototypes, and a licensed buffet car. The railway aims to be a main line in miniature and many features are similar to contemporary practice at the time it was built. The introduction of a railway letter service coincided with the company's 50th anniversary in 1977.

The "Five pence 5p fee paid" rubber stamp, used to prepare the 15p+5p emergency provisionals issued on 1 February 1982 (No.6-8), was brought back into service as a cachet to make up the letter rate when it was increased to 25p on 1 January 1990. The railway signed the 1998 agreement.

Enquiries to: The R.H.D.R., New Romney Station, New Romney, Kent, TN28 8PL.

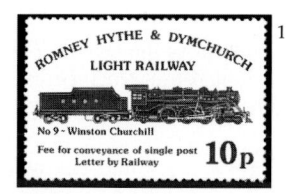

11/5/77. Definitive. Des & Ptr: The House of Questa Ltd, London. Lithography in sheets of 25 (5 rows of 5). P14.

Dsgn: Yorkshire Engineering Co. 4-6-2 No.9 *Winston Churchill*

1	10p Black, red and yellow	.75
1Sp	10p - ovptd in black	£10.00
(1)	Sheet of 25	
	Plate: 1A; 1B; 1C; or 1D	£15.00

Nos: 50000. Due to overprinting and surcharging only 18625 were issued in this original form. 1) 18425; 1Sp) 200. An imperf proof overprinted 'Specimen' and an official House of Questa proof-card exist.

16/7/77. 50th Anniversary. Overprinted "1927 1977" in gold by The House of Questa.

2	10p (1)	£4.00
2Sp	10p (1) - ovptd in black	£10.00
(2)	Sheet of 25	
	Plate: 1A; 1B; 1C; or 1D	£100.00

Nos: 2) 4800; 2Sp) 200. Imperf proofs, die proof cards, and an official House of Questa proof-card exist.

15/5/78. Provisional. Surcharged in black and gold by The House of Questa.

3	15p on 10p (1)	.40
3Sp	15p on 10p (1) - ovptd in black, or blue	£10.00
(3)	Sheet of 50	
	Plate: 1A+1B or 1C+1D	£20.00

Nos: 25000; later 1900 were surcharged leaving an issue of 3) 22900; 3Sp) 200. An imperf proof overprinted "Specimen" exists. FDC: 2250

31/5/78. Definitive. Des: A. Buckingham (Benham) Ltd. Ptr: The House of Questa. Lithography in sheets of 50 (2 panes of 25, each 5 rows of 5, separated by a gutter margin). P14.

Dsgn: Davey Paxman 4-6-2 No.8 *Hurricane*, inscribed "The Royal Train"

4	15p Black, blue and yellow	.45
4Sp	15p - ovptd in black, or blue	£10.00
(4)	Pane of 25 Plate: 1A, 1B, 1C or 1D	£12.00
(4)	Sheet of 50	
	Plate: 1A+1B or 1C+1D	£25.00

Nos: 50000; later 8625 were surcharged, leaving an issue of 4) 41175; 4Sp) 200. Some sheets were separated into panes of 25 before issue. FDC: 750

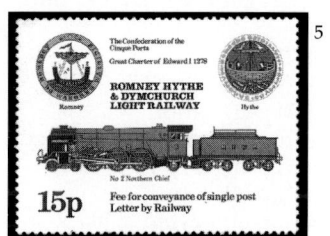

5/7/78. 700th Anniversary of the Cinque Ports. Des: The Railway and Cantuart. Ptr: The House of Questa. Lithography in sheets of 50 (5 rows of 5, in two panes separated by a gutter margin). P13.5.

Dsgn: Davey Paxman 4-6-2 No.2 *Northern Chief* and the badges of New Romney and Hythe

5	15p Black, green, gold and blue	.70
5Sp	15p - ovptd in black, or blue	£10.00
(5)	Pane of 25 Plate 1A or 1B	£16.00
(5)	Sheet of 50 Plate: 1A+1B	£35.00

Nos: 25000; later 5125 were surcharged, leaving an issue of 5) 19675, and 5Sp) 200. Some sheets were separated into panes of 25 before issue. Imperf proofs, die proof cards, and official House of Questa proof-cards exist. FDC: 1350

1/2/82. Emergency Provisionals. Handstamped "Five pence 5p fee paid" in black by the Railway.

6	5p+15p on 10p (3)	£6.00
6Sp	5p+15p on 10p (3) - ovptd in black	£12.50
7	5p+15p (4)	£6.00
7Sp	5p+15p (4) - ovptd in black	£12.50
8	5p+15p (5)	£6.00
8Sp	5p+15p (5) - ovptd in black	£12.50
	Pane of 25:	
(6)	Plate: 1A or 1B	£150.00
(6Sp)	Plate: 1A+1B or 1C+1D	-
(7)	Plate: 1A or 1B	£150.00
(7Sp)	Plate: 1A+1B or 1C+1D	-
(8)	Plate: 1A or 1B	£150.00
(8Sp)	Plate: 1A or 1B	-
	Sheets of 50:	
(6)	Plate: 1A+1B or 1C+1D	£300.00
(7)	Plate: 1A+1B or 1C+1D	£300.00

Nos: 6, 7 and 8) 1400 each; 6Sp, 7Sp and 8Sp) 100 of each - figures are approximate since no formal record was made. Some sheets of No.6 and 7 were separated into panes of 25 before issue.
FDC: 6, 7 & 8) 200; 8 only) 50

18/6/82 - 1983. Provisional Definitives. Surcharged in black and gold by Derek Smith Printers, Gillingham.

9	20p on 10p (1)	£7.50
9Sp	20p on 10p (1) - ovptd in black	£12.50
9a	20p on 10p (1) - error, black of surcharge omitted	£45.00
9b	20p on 10p (1)	£7.50
10	20p on 15p (4)	.60
10Sp	20p on 15p (4) - ovptd in black	£10.00
10a	20p on 15p (4) - error, black of surcharge omitted	£40.00
11	20p on 15p (5)	.60
11Sp	20p on 15p (5) - ovptd in black	£10.00
12	20p on 15p on 10p (3)	£40.00
12Sp	20p on 15p on 10p (3) - ovptd in black	£50.00
	Sheets of 25:	
(9)	Plate: 1B or 1D	£200.00
(9a)	Plate: 1B	-
(9b)	Plate: 1B or 1D (winter 1982-3)	£250.00
(10)	Plate: 1A; 1B; 1C; or 1D	£15.00
(10a)	Plate: 1B or 1?	-
(11)	Plate: 1A or 1B	£15.00
(12)	Plate: 1A; 1B; 1C; or 1D (winter 1982-3)	-

Nos: 9) 825; 9Sp) 100; 9a) 75; 9b) 375. 10) 6800; 10Sp) 200; 10a) 125. 11) 3425; 11Sp) 200. 12) 350; 12Sp) 50. Two printings of No.9 exist: No.9, 9Sp, and 9a - gold is coppery; No.9b and No.12 - gold is brassy or yellow. This second printing and the printing of No.12, were released during the winter of 1982-83.
FDC: 9, 10 & 11) 600

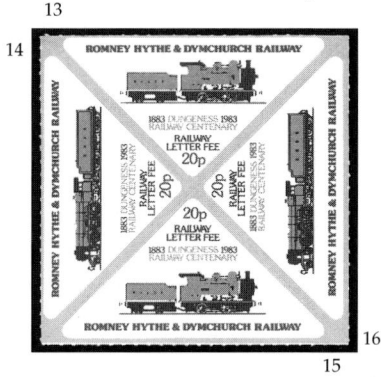

17/12/83. Dungeness Railway Centenary. Des: Joe Smith. Ptr: Derek Smith Printers. Photo-lithography in sheets of 12 (3 blocks of 4 triangular stamps horiz., se-tenant 13+14+15+16, with imperf vertical margins between), num. 1 - 1000. R9.

Dsgn: 13 and 15) Krauss 0-6-0 No.4 *The Bug*; 14 and 16) Davey Paxman 4-6-2 No.1 *Green Goddess*. All inscribed "1883 Dungeness Railway Centenary 1983"

13	20p Red, green, black and yellow (apex down)	
14	20p Red, green, black and yellow (apex down)	
15	20p Red, green, black and yellow (apex up)	
16	20p Red, green, black and yellow (apex up)	
13-16	Block of 4	£3.00
13Sp-16Sp	Block of 4 - ovptd in black	£9.00
(13-16)	Sheet of 12: Plate AAA	£9.00
(13Sp-16Sp)	Sheet of 12 - ovptd in black	£24.00

Nos: 13-16) 3000 of each; 13Sp-16Sp) Approx. 200 of each. The 'specimen' blocks of four stamps received two overprints. Imperf sheets are known. Three panes were printed together, below each other, on one sheet of paper: No.13-16 was coded "AAA"; No. 17-19 "AAB"; and a third planned issue, which was never completed, bore the code "AAC". Uncut sheets exist. Any sheets, panes or blocks without the value or commemorative inscription should not be regarded as errors but printer's waste from pane "AAC". The railway was not satisfied with the appearance of these stamps, destroying any sheets that remained unsold early in 1986.   FDC: 350

10/4/84. New Romney Steam Centenary. Details as for No.13-16.

Dsgn: As No.13-16, but inscribed "1884 New Romney Steam Centenary 1984"

17	20p Red, green, black and yellow (apex down)	
18	20p Red, green, black and yellow (apex down)	
19	20p Red, green, black and yellow (apex up)	
20	20p Red, green, black and yellow (apex up)	
17-20	Block of 4	£3.00
17Sp-20Sp	Block of 4 - ovptd in black	£9.00
(17-20)	Sheet of 12: Plate AAB	£9.00
(17Sp-20Sp)	Sheet of 12 - ovptd in black	£24.00

Nos: 17-20) 3000 of each; 17Sp-20Sp) Approx. 200 of each. Each 'specimen' block of four received two overprints. Imperf sheets are known. See also footnote to No.13-16.   FDC: 600

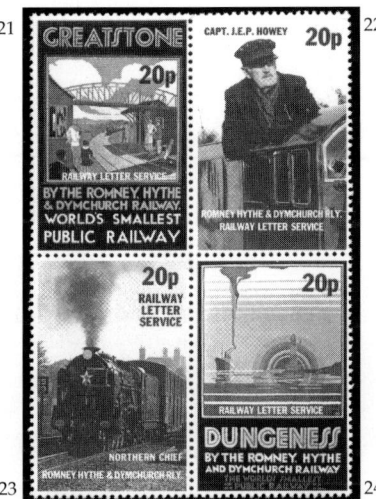

18/6/86. Pictorial Issue. Des: Derek Smith; Illus: 21 and 24) N. Cramer-Roberts (1930s posters), 22) George Barlow (photo), 23) P. H. Groom (photo). Ptr: Stephenson Print, Prescot. Lithography in miniature sheets of 4 (2 rows of 2), containing one example of each. P14.

Dsgn: 21) Greatstone poster; 22) Capt. J. E. P. Howey on footplate of No.1 *Green Goddess*; 23) No.2 *Northern Chief* storming away from New Romney; 24) Dungeness poster

21	20p Multicoloured	
22	20p Black	
23	20p Black	
24	20p Multicoloured	
(21-24)	Decor. Sheet of 4	£1.50
(21Sp-24Sp)	Decor. sheet of 4 - ovptd in black	£12.50

Nos: 7000 of each. The railway originally sold the miniature sheet for £1.00. Two different papers were used, a creamy white and a brilliant white. Approx 100 sheets of 4 were overprinted "Specimen", each sheet receiving one overprint.   FDC: 600

LABEL

28/7/86. Freud Commemorative. Des: Jan Littlemore. Ptr: Stephenson Print. Offset lithography in sheets of 4 (2 rows of 2). P11.

Dsgn: Portrait of Sigmund Freud, inscribed "Founder of psycho-analysis"

| L1 | 20p Blue and yellow | £7.50 |
| | Sheet of 4 | £40.00 |

FDC: 1500

The Freud Museum, London, privately produced a label, inscribed with the railway's name, to mail membership cards and publicity to those who had helped finance the setting up of the museum. The Museum paid the production costs and their name and 'rug design' logo appear in the upper margin. The envelopes were carried by the railway on 28/7/86, and then transferred to the postal system for delivery to addressees mainly in the U.S.A., and the U.K.. About 100 further covers were prepared for sale in the museum's shop and the last of these was sold on 2/10/86. Although produced with the co-operation of the R.H.D.R., they were neither publicised as railway letter stamps, nor regarded by the railway as being one of their own issues. Carried items, handed in to railway staff, bearing the label show that the label has been accepted on occasions as payment for the railway letter fee. Stamps remaining unsold were destroyed by the Museum on 31/12/87.

R.H.D.R. SPECIAL CANCELLATIONS

1	5/10/77	Dungeness [illus. Dungeness Lighthouse and lifeboat]
2	25/1/78	New Romney - Coal provides energy for R.H.D.R. [illus. outline of 0-4-0 loco]
3	2/6/78	25th Anniversary of the Coronation [illus. front view of loco - red]
4	5/7/78	New Romney - 700th Anniversary of the Cinque Ports [illus. Cinque Ports' crest]
5	5/7/78	Hythe - 700th Anniversary of the Cinque Ports [illus. Cinque Ports' crest]

P.O. ONE-DAY POSTMARKS

29/5/72	New Romney - 45th Anniversary [illus. stylised side view of loco. Used before letter service started]
11/5/77	Hythe - Queen Elizabeth II Silver Jubilee Special [illus. side view of 4-6-2 loco]
16/7/77	1927 Golden Jubilee 1977 *The Bug* [illus. side view of loco]
31/5/78	Hythe - Queen Elizabeth II 25th Anniversary of the Coronation [illus. side view of 4-6-2 *Winston Churchill*]
21/11/79	Cheriton, Folkestone - The Romney Hythe & Dymchurch Railway Salutes Cheriton & Morehall Traders Christmas Lights [illus. decorated Christmas tree]
25/8/84	New Romney - Appledore to New Romney Steam Centenary 1884-1984
28/7/86	London NW3 - Freud Museum Opening [Included as used on the covers produced by the sponsor of L1]

SNOWDON MOUNTAIN RAILWAY

This 4¾ mile long, 2'7½" gauge, passenger carrying line was first opened in 1896, and is Britain's only public rack railway. The Swiss ABT system, involving two toothed racks laid side by side in the centre of the track which are engaged by two cogged wheels (or rack pinions) fitted beneath the locomotive, was used to construct the line to the 3560' summit of Snowdon. There are seven steam locomotives, five of which are in service, all having been built at the Swiss Locomotive Works, Winterthur: Nos.2-5 in 1895 or 1896, and Nos.6-8 in 1922 or 1923. Two diesel locomotives, Nos.9 and 10 built in Leeds, were introduced in 1986-7, and a further two, Nos. 11 and 12, in 1991-2. A 3-car diesel-electric railcar set was built in 1995 by HPE Tredegar.

Apart from the diesel railcar a train consists of a single 59-seat passenger carriage which is pushed up the severe gradient by one locomotive. Trains do not run in bad weather, nor if there are insufficient passengers to warrant the journey. In the interests of safety the maximum speed permitted is 7.5mph.

Although not true railway letter stamps their issue has been approved by the Post Office, but the Company was required to omit a value from the design. The public is encouraged to buy the labels from a Hillday 1712P vending machine at the summit, which dispenses R.M. stamps along with the S.M.R. labels, and letters and cards bearing both are franked with the 'Snowdon Summit' cachet. All mail is brought down to Llanberis by train and posted there.

Enquiries to: The General Manager, The Snowdon Mountain Railway, Llanberis, Caernarfon, Gwynedd, LL55 4TY.

Styles of the label numbers. Details 200%

8/6/87. Definitive. Des: The Railway. Ptr: Hillday Ltd., Attleborough. Lithography in coil form (1000 stamps) for vertical delivery, num. as footnote below. P14.7 x 13.3.

Dsgn: Train crossing the lower viaduct, Llanberis

L1	(10p) Dark green and red	£1.00
L1a	(10p) - num. in black	£4.00
L1b	(10p) - num. in black (summer 1990)	.20
L1c	(10p) - num. in black (summer 1994)	.20
(L1+L1a)	Se-tenant strip of 5	£10.00
(L1b)	Strip of 5	£1.00
(L1c)	Strip of 5	£1.00

Nos: L1) 50000, in 50 coils; L1b) 50000, in 50 coils; L1c) 50000, in 50 coils. Throughout the original printing every fifth label on the coil (L1a) is numbered sequentially - "005", "010" etc., - being a standard feature in the production of 'stamps' by this printer. A second printing (L1b) was issued during the summer of 1990, with the same shades of colour, but having sequential numbering - "000001", "000002" etc. on every stamp. The third issue (L1c) has a larger dot-matrix style number on each stamp - "000001" etc. - first reported being used in summer 1994. The railway had difficulty distinguishing the printings and did not necessarily exhaust stocks of one batch before starting the next. Hence the use of L1b was reported being dispensed again from the summit machine after the first reports of L1c.

6/4/96. Centenary of the Snowden Mountain Railway. Des: The Railway. Ptr: Hillday Ltd. Lithography in coil form (1000 stamps) for vertical delivery. P9 x imperf sides.

Dsgn: Stylised silhouette of carriage and locomotive on a steep slope

1	(10p) Dark green and red	.20
	Strip of 5	£1.00

Nos: 50000. None of the stamps were numbered but all had perforations of two diameters separating the labels. The fdc was produced by the Talyllyn Railway but officially sanctioned by the S.M.R. Trains do not reach the summit so early in the year, therefore covers were conveyed to Clogwyn Station from where they were carried by foot to the summit to ensure the covers could receive the Snowdon Summit cachet. On return by train to Llanberis the envelopes had the cachet and the commemorative cancel applied in the Company's offices, before being taken by car to Abergynolwyn for servicing as railway letter items on the T.R. (see also T.R. No. 79 on pg 91.)   FDC: 500

S.M.R. SPECIAL CANCELLATIONS

All mail posted at the summit receives the circular summit cancellation.

1   6/4/96   Snowdon Mountain Rly
             1896 Centenary 1996
             Special Mail Service [undated]

TALYLLYN RAILWAY
RHEILFFORDD TALYLLYN

The Railway was built under powers obtained by Act of Parliament in 1865, to serve the Bryn Eglwys Slate Quarry which had opened in 1847. The 2'3" gauge line operated between the foot of the Cantrybedd incline, near Abergynolwyn, and the slate wharf at Tywyn, on the Aberystwyth and Welsh Coast Railway, later the Cambrian, and then the Great Western Railway. In 1867 a passenger service operated between Pendre and Abergynolwyn principally for quarry workers, but mail and parcels were also carried to and from the Quarry Office at Bryn Eglwys. Stations and halts were subsequently built for use by the inhabitants of farms and hamlets.

In 1911 the quarry (where the easier levels had been worked out) and the railway were sold to Sir Henry Haydn Jones, later M.P. for Merionethshire. He declared his intention to keep the railway running during his lifetime despite its poor finances. The Transport Bill of 1947, which nationalised all railways in Great Britain, omitted any reference to the T.R. and it retained its status as an independent statutory railway. In 1950 Sir Henry died, but a preservation society was formed on 10 October to restore and operate the line. From Wharf Station the line now serves Pendre (1/3), Rhydyronen (2 1/2), Brynglas (3 1/2), Dolgoch (5), Abergynolwyn (6 1/2), and Nant Gwernol, 7 1/4 miles from Tywyn.

Being a statutory railway the T.R. was the first to operate a post-war railway letter service under the 1891 Agreement. Initially only one denomination of stamp was issued, so when the fee increased, often some time after the official increase date because B.R. were slow to inform the company, a "1d extra fee" handstamp was used. A few covers sent to Northern Ireland or the Isle of Man received a "4d extra fee" endorsement.

Stamps can be bought at Wharf Station and from the brakevan on the train, and during the high summer at some of the intermediate stations. A single-circle undated handstamp was used at these stations until 1978-9 when they were replaced by distinctive dated cancellers. The railway has achieved continuity of operation by signing both the 1974 and 1998 Agreements when they were introduced.

Enquiries to: The Hon. Postmaster, The Talyllyn Railway, Wharf Station, Tywyn, Gwynedd, LL36 9EY.

23/5/57. Definitives. Des & Ptr: James Upton Ltd., Birmingham. Letterpress in miniature sheets of 6 (3 rows of 2), containing one of each design. R6.5.

Dsgn: 1 and 7) (row 1, stamp 1) Barclay 0-4-0WT No.6 *Douglas* at Dolgoch Station; 2 and 8) (row 1, stamp 2) Fletcher Jennings 0-4-0WT No.2 *Dolgoch* on Dolgoch Viaduct; 3 and 9) (row 2, stamp 1) No.2 *Dolgoch* at Abergynolwyn Station; 4 and 10) (row 2, stamp 2) Kerr Stuart 0-4-2ST No.4 *Edward Thomas* approaching Brynglas; 5 and 11) (row 3, stamp 1) Fletcher Jennings 0-4-2ST No.1 *Talyllyn* in pre-1951 livery; 6 and 12) Hughes 0-4-2ST No.3 *Sir Haydn* at Abergynolwyn Station

1	11d Black and red	£40.00
2	11d Black and green	£40.00
3	11d Black and green	£40.00
4	11d Black and red	£40.00
5	11d Black and red	£40.00
6	11d Black and green	£40.00
7	11d Black and green	£40.00
8	11d Black and red	£40.00
9	11d Black and red	£40.00
10	11d Black and green	£40.00
11	11d Black and green	£40.00
12	11d Black and red	£40.00

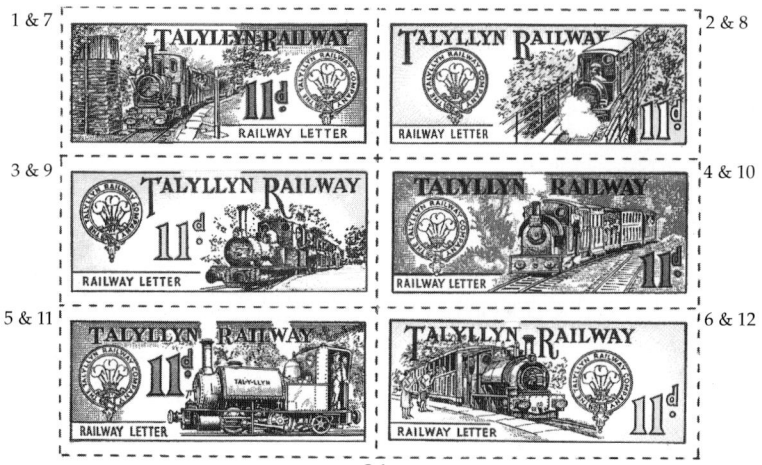

(1-6)	Sheet of 6	£300.00
(7-12)	Sheet of 6	£300.00

Nos: 1500 of each design; later approx 1052 of each were surcharged for No.13-24, leaving an issue of approx 448 of each. Issue was withdrawn from sale on 14/6/58. Imperf colour trials printed in brown, red and green are known to exist.

15/6/58. Provisionals. Surcharged in black by T. W. Robertson, London.

13	1s on 11d (1)	£25.00
14	1s on 11d (2)	£25.00
15	1s on 11d (3)	£25.00
16	1s on 11d (4)	£25.00
17	1s on 11d (5)	£25.00
18	1s on 11d (6)	£25.00
19	1s on 11d (7)	£25.00
20	1s on 11d (8)	£25.00
21	1s on 11d (9)	£25.00
22	1s on 11d (10)	£25.00
23	1s on 11d (11)	£25.00
24	1s on 11d (12)	£25.00
(13-18)	Sheet of 6	£200.00
(19-24)	Sheet of 6	£200.00

Nos: Approx 1052 of each. Red leading sheets appear scarcer than the green ones, probably because more of the former were split for the preparation of covers. The few remaining sheets were withdrawn from sale on 4/7/65. Pulls of the surcharge alone exist.

5/7/65. Railway Centenary. Des: Max Mason; Illus: Terence Cuneo (drawing). Ptr: Thomas de la Rue and Co. Ltd., London. Lithography in sheets of 10 (5 rows of 2). P14.

Dsgn: No.1 *Talyllyn* on Dolgoch Viaduct, inscribed "1865 1965"

25	1s Light brown and dark green	£2.50
	Sheet of 10	£25.00

Nos: 50000; later 6000 were surcharged, either as surcharge trials or provisionals, and approx 15000 were destroyed on withdrawal, leaving an issue of approx 29000. Although inscribed as if it was a commemorative, this issue served as a definitive until withdrawn and invalidated on 4/6/67. Stamp-sized colour roughs showing possible design layouts and colours, and proofs on card and paper exist. FDC: 8500

1966. Provisionals. Surcharged by Charles Norman Ltd, Birmingham.

26	1s1d on 1s (25) in red - "1s1d" style	£27.50
27	1s1d on 1s (25) in green - "1/1" style	£27.50
(26)	Sheet of 10 (1/6/66)	£250.00
(27)	Sheet of 10 (8/8/66)	£250.00

Nos: 2300 of each. Surcharge trials in both the two value styles (as No.26 and 27) exist in bright red, green and black. FDC: 800 of each

1967 - 1969. Definitives. Des: John Woodcock. Ptr: Walsall Lithographic Co. Ltd. Lithography in sheets of 10 (5 rows of 2, se-tenant horiz. as below). P11.

Dsgn: 28 and 30) No.1 *Talyllyn*; 29 and 31) No.2 *Dolgoch*

28	1s1d Black, sea green and red	
28a	1s1d - broken y	
28b	1s1d Black, dark green and red	
28ba	1s1d - broken y	
29	1s1d Black, sea green and red	
29b	1s1d Black, dark green and red	
28+29	Se-tenant pair	£10.00
28a+29	Se-tenant pair	£12.00
28b+29b	Se-tenant pair	£9.00
28ba+29b	Se-tenant pair	£11.00
(28+29)	Sheet of 10 (5/6/67)	£50.00
(28b+29b)	Sheet of 10 (?/9/68)	£45.00
30	1s2d Black, green and red	
30a	1s2d - broken y	
31	1s2d Black, green and red	
30+31	Se-tenant pair	£10.00
30a+31	Se-tenant pair	£10.00
(30+31)	Sheet of 10 (6/1/69)	£50.00

Nos: 28 and 29) 12725 of each, printed on very white paper; 28b and 29b) 5000 of each, printed in dark green on creamy paper; 30 and 31) 7500 of each, printed on a paper similar to that used for No.28b+29b. The 'broken y' variety [No.28a, 28ba, and 30a] appears on row 3, stamp 1, where the first y of "Talyllyn" has the upper left part of the character missing.

Examples of No.28+29 are known with the black part of the design offset on the reverse; and No.30+31 are known with the green offset. Proofs of the 1s1d, incorrectly formatted 2 rows of 5 and rouletted, and imperf proofs in the final format, exist. Up to six sheets of No.30+31 were handstamped "Specimen" in blue for publicity purposes.

FDC: 28 and 29) 4500 of each; 30 and 31) 1200 of each

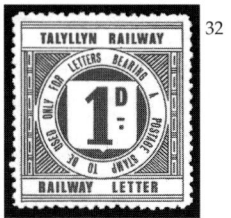

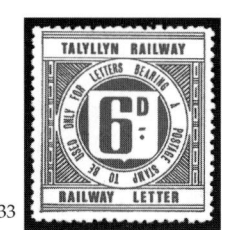

2/6/69. Low Value Definitives. Ptr: Walsall Security Printers. Lithography in sheets of 10 (5 rows of 2). P11.

Dsgn: Adapted from an unadopted railway letter stamp of the 1890s

32	1d Claret	£17.50
32	1d Claret (used on cover)	£1.50
32a	1d - extended A	£35.00
32a	1d - extended A (used on cover)	£3.00
32b	1d - Lilac red	.45
33	6d Bright blue	£17.50
33	6d Bright blue (used on cover)	£1.50
33b	6d - Dull blue	.80
(32)	Sheet of 10	£200.00
(32b)	Sheet of 10 (4/7/69)	£5.00
(33)	Sheet of 10	£200.00
(33b)	Sheet of 10 (4/7/69)	£8.00

Nos: 32) 5240; 32b) 15000; 33) 5000; 33b) 5240. Being very common on fdc, mint copies of No.32, 32a and 33 are scarce mint. The extended A variety on the 2nd A of "Railway Letter" on row 2, stamp 1, was corrected for the second printing. Imperf bromide proof panes in black exist for both values. FDC: 32 and 33) 2100 bearing two copies of each stamp.

2/6/69. Definitives. Des & Ptr: Bentley Photo-Litho Co. Ltd.; Illus: John Adams (photo). Lithography in sheets of 10 (5 rows of 2). P15.

Dsgn: No.4 *Edward Thomas* and No.1 *Talyllyn* at Tywyn Wharf Station

34	1s6d Multicoloured	£2.50
34a	1s6d - underprinted "T.R." in white	£3.00
	Sheets of 10:	
(34)	Plate 1B or 1C	£27.50
(34a)	Plate 1A (21/7/69)	£32.00

Nos: 34) 6500; 34a) 2900. Two proofs of No.34 exist denominated 1s2d. No.34a was produced at the request of the printer to demonstrate a printing technique and is almost invisible unless looked at obliquely to the light. Two sheets (of No.34) exist in a larger format (10 rows of 6), produced by the printers for a competition.   FDC: 34) 1400; 34a) 600

1/7/69. Investiture of H.R.H. The Prince of Wales. Des: Gordon Drummond. Ptr: Bentley Photo-Litho Co. Ltd. Lithography in sheets of 10 (5 rows of 2). P15.

Dsgn: No.1 *Talyllyn* and Prince of Wales' feathers

35	1s2d Multicoloured	£2.75
	Sheet of 10: Plate 1A	£30.00

Nos: 16490. Imperf proofs, and sets of progressive colour proofs of a single stamp and the complete sheet, exist.   FDC: 9700

1970. Definitives. Des & Ptr: Bentley Photo-Litho Co. Ltd.; Illus: John Adams (photos). Lithography in sheets of 10 (5 rows of 2). P14 x 13.

Dsgn: 36) No.3 *Sir Haydn* at Abergynolwyn Station; 37) No.3 *Sir Haydn* and train near Abergynolwyn

36	1s7d Multicoloured and red	£1.20
37	1s3d Multicoloured and blue	£1.20
	Sheets of 10:	
(36)	Plate 1B or 1D (7/4/70)	£12.00
(37)	Plate 1A or 1C (18/5/70)	£12.00

Nos: 24880 of each; later stocks were surcharged leaving an issue of 36) 9880; 37) 14880. Sets of progressive colour proofs and imperf proofs of a single stamp and the complete sheet exist. Black and white bromide trials were produced to determine the best size, shape, and lettering for the definitives.
FDC: 36) 2450; 37) 5400

1971. Decimal Provisionals. Surcharged by Charles Norman Ltd.

38	10p on 1s7d (36) in red	£1.20
39	15p on 1s3d (37) in blue	£1.20
	Sheets of 10:	
(38)	Plate 1B or 1D (12/2/71)	£12.00
(39)	Plate 1A or 1C (8/3/71)	£12.00

Nos: 38) 13310; 39) 10000. No.38 was withdrawn from sale on 24/6/81. Trial overprints in black exist for both values.   FDC: 38) 3900; 39) 2100

15/5/72. Decimal Definitives. As design No.36 but with the right-hand stamp in each row inscribed in

Welsh and valued in ceiniog (pence). Ptr: Bentley Photo-Litho Co. Ltd. Lithography in sheets of 10 (5 rows of 2, se-tenant horiz. 40+41). P14 x 13.3.

40	15p Multicoloured and brown (E)	
41	15c Multicoloured and brown (W)	
	Se-tenant pair	£6.00
	Sheet of 10: Plate 1B or 1D	£30.00

Nos: 12500 of each; later 480 of each were destroyed when withdrawn from sale on 24/6/81, leaving an issue of 12020 of each. FDC: 40 or 41) 2200 in all

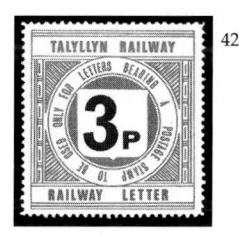

7/4/73. Low Value Definitive. Ptr: Walsall Security Printers. Lithography in sheets of 10 (5 rows of 2). P14.3.

Dsgn: As No.32 and 33

42	3p Blue and black	.35
	Sheet of 10	£3.50

Nos: 12000. A number of constant flaws are known. Stamps exist with the black value overlapping the solid blue around the shield. See also No.45, 49 and 52. FDC: 820

3/6/74. Decimal Definitives. Details as for No.40+41, but with design as No.37.

43	10p Multicoloured and green (E)	
44	10c Multicoloured and green (W)	
	Se-tenant pair	£6.00
	Sheet of 10: Plate 1A or 1C	£30.00

Nos: 12500 of each; later 3690 of each were surcharged and overprinted for No.50+51, leaving an issue of 8770 of each. A number of sheets had been found imperf and the majority of these were destroyed. There are some misperfed sheets and others with significant colour shifts. Issue was withdrawn from sale on 24/6/81.
FDC: 43 or 44) 5970 in all

13/7/75. Low Value Definitive. Details as for No.42.

45	1p Green and black	.35
	Sheet of 10	£3.50

Nos: 5950. Officially released on 13/7/75, it is thought that some were issued earlier in error.
FDC: 400. This refers to 9/10/75, when official 36p rate covers were carried through to Barmouth.

13/8/75. 150th Anniversary of the Stockton & Darlington Railway. Des: John Adams; Illus: Terence Cuneo (drawing). Ptr: Bentley Photo-Litho Co. Ltd. Lithography in sheets of 10 (5 rows of 2). P14.3.

Dsgn: *Locomotion No.1*

46	10p Blue and black	£2.75
(46)	Sheet of 10	£27.50

Nos: 9578. Some sheets, with imperf bottom margin, have a flaw in the vertical part of the T of "TR" on row 1, stamp 2. Colour trials and proofs exist.
FDC: 4500

22/5/76. Opening of Nant Gwernol Extension. Des: A. J. Bullimore. Ptr: Walsall Security Printers. Lithography in sheets of 10 (5 rows of 2). P14.3.

Dsgn: 'Steam'

47	10p Black and green	£1.10
	Sheet of 10	£11.00

Nos: 20000. A black and white proof on card, and an origination proof exist. FDC: 5000

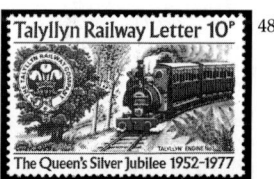

11/5/77. Silver Jubilee of H.M. Queen Elizabeth II. Des: Douglas Moyle. Ptr: Walsall Security Printers. Lithography in sheets of 10 (5 rows of 2). P14.

Dsgn: No.1 *Talyllyn* with train, and company seal

48	10p Black, green and red	£1.75
	Sheet of 10	£20.00

Nos: 19800. A proof card exists. FDC: 10800

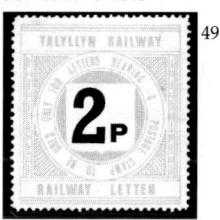

87

1/1/78. Low Value Definitive. Details as for No.42.

49	2p Green and red	.35
	Sheet of 10	£3.50

Nos: 6000. FDC: 620

31/5/78. Centenary of No.3 *Sir Haydn*. Overprinted "*Sir Haydn* 1878 - 1978" and surcharged 15p or 15c in red by Haydon Printing Co., Birmingham.

50	15p on 10p (E) (43)	
51	15c on 10c (W) (44)	
	Se-tenant pair	£9.50
	Sheet of 10: Plate 1A or 1C	£50.00

Nos: 3690 of each. Examples are known with green obliteration of the original value but no red overprint or surcharge, or with no obliteration of the original value but with the red overprint and surcharge. Some colour shifts and imperf stamps have been reported. Trials of No.50+51 exist with the overprint in green. A sheet of No.40+41 has the red overprint for No.50+51 applied as a trial.
FDC: 50 or 51) 3000 in all

26/9/79. Low Value Definitive. Ptr: Haydon Printing Co., Birmingham. R4.75.

Dsgn: As No.32 and 33

52	5p Magenta	.35
	Sheet of 10	£3.50

Nos: 5100. A flaw on the W of "Railway" appears on row 2, stamp 1. FDC: 200

12/3/80. 150th Anniversary of the Liverpool & Manchester Railway. Des: J. H. Kendall; Illus: S. G. Hughes after J. Shaw (aquatint). Ptr: G.B. Rotograph Ltd, Northampton. Lithography in sheets of 10 (5 rows of 2), num. 001 - 500. Coloured R9.5 (in black).

Dsgn: A L.&M. locomotive and carriage of 1830

53	15p Warm brown and black on buff	£3.25
53Sp	15p - ovptd in black	£25.00
(53)	Sheet of 10: Plate GBR1 & 2	£35.00
(53Sp)	Sheet of 10 - ovptd in black	£250.00

Nos: 53) 5000; 53Sp) 150 . Various constant flaws exist; the upper part of the "150" numerals in the stamp's legend is missing on row 3, stamp 1. The 'Specimen' overprint, applied on untrimmed sheets, was distributed for publicity purposes. Imperf stamps, Plate TR15, in other colours or on other papers are printer's colour trials: black and dark grey, or black and brown printing, on yellow, orange, or buff paper. FDC: 975

4/8/80. Great Little Trains of Wales Joint Issue. For full details see pg 26.

54	15p Black and red (E)
55	15c Black and red (W)

24/6/81. Locomotive Series. Des: Anthony Daffern. Ptr: T. Stephenson & Sons Ltd. Lithography in sheets of 10 (5 rows of 2, se-tenant horiz. 56+57), num. 1 - 1970. P14.

Dsgn: No.1 *Talyllyn*

56	20c Multicoloured (W)	
56Sp	20c - ovptd in black	
57	20p Multicoloured (E)	
57Sp	20p - ovptd in black	
56+57	Se-tenant pair	£1.25
56Sp+57Sp	Se-tenant pair - ovptd in black	£25.00
(56+57)	Sheet of 10	£6.25
(56Sp+57Sp)	Sheet of 10 - ovptd in black	£150.00

Nos: 56 and 57) 9850 of each; 56Sp and 57Sp) 150 of each. The 'specimen' sheets are num. 1971 - 2000. An imperf proof sheet exists. FDC: 5000

22/7/81. Locomotive Series. Details as for No.56+57, except sheets of 10 (5 rows of 2), num. 1 - 700.

Dsgn: No.4 *Edward Thomas*

58	20p Multicoloured	£3.00
58Sp	20p - ovptd in black	£25.00
(58)	Sheet of 10	£35.00
(58Sp)	Sheet of 10 - ovptd in black	£150.00

Nos: 58) 7000; 58Sp) 300. The 'specimen' sheets are unnumbered. FDC: 3200

12/8/81. Locomotive Series. Details as for No.56+57, except num. 1 - 2000.

Dsgn: No.2 *Dolgoch*

59	20c Multicoloured (W)		
59Sp	20c - ovptd in black		
60	20p Multicoloured (E)		
60Sp	20p - ovptd in black		
59+60	Se-tenant pair		£1.00
59Sp+60Sp	Se-tenant pair - ovptd in black		£25.00
(59+60)	Sheet of 10		£5.00
(59Sp+60Sp)	Sheet of 10 - ovptd in black		£150.00

Nos: 59 and 60) 10000 of each, 59Sp and 60Sp) 150 of each. The 'specimen' sheets are unnumbered.
FDC: 3500

23/9/81. Locomotive Series. Details as for No.56+57, except num. 1 - 2000.

Dsgn: No.3 *Sir Haydn*

61	20c Multicoloured (W)		
61Sp	20c - ovptd in black		
62	20p Multicoloured (E)		
62Sp	20p - ovptd in black		
61+62	Se-tenant pair		£1.00
61Sp+62Sp	Se-tenant pair - ovptd in black		£25.00
(61+62)	Sheet of 10		£5.00
(61Sp+62Sp)	Sheet of 10 - ovptd in black		£150.00

Nos: 61 and 62) 10000 of each; later 850 of each were overprinted for No.63+64, leaving an issue of 8750; 61Sp and 62Sp) 150 of each. The 'specimen' sheets are unnumbered.
FDC: 3000

31/8/85. 150th Anniversary of the Great Western Railway. Overprinted "GWR150 1835-1985" in red by Northampton Paper Company. 1st printing num. 830 - 949; 2nd printing num. 1060 - 1109.

63	20c (W) (61)	
63a	20c (W) (61)	
64	20p (E) (62)	
64a	20p (E) (62)	
63+64	Se-tenant pair	£40.00
63a+64a	Se-tenant pair	£40.00
(63+64)	Sheet of 10	£250.00
(63a+64a)	Sheet of 10	£250.00

Nos: 63 and 64) 600 of each; 63a and 64a) 250 of each. The railway seriously underestimated the number of stamps for immediate demand. Most of the first printing was used on fdc or affixed to envelopes for sale to the public. The printer, having completed the first run of 120 sheets, had preserved the forme intact and was able to print additional sheets with little difficulty. The red ink was a standard colour used straight from the same tin for both batches but, although the Railway was confident the two printings would be indistinguishable, a difference in shade seems apparent; the first batch being slightly darker than the second. A very few sheets have red lettering which is not horizontal, due to the gummed paper slipping when the letterpress overprint was applied. Several constant variations in the typesetting have been noted. Pulls of the overprint alone, in black, exist. FDC: 63 and 64) 800

3/7/88. Locomotive Series. Des: Anthony Daffern. Ptr: T. Clarke Printing Ltd., Northampton. Offset lithography in sheets of 10 (5 rows of 2, se-tenant horiz. 65+66). P11.

Dsgn: No.6 *Douglas*

65	20c Multicoloured (W)		
65Sp	20c - ovptd in red		
66	20p Multicoloured (E)		
66Sp	20p - ovptd in red		
65+66	Se-tenant pair		.80
65Sp+66Sp	Se-tenant pair - ovptd in red		£25.00
(65+66)	Sheet of 10		£4.00
(65Sp+66Sp)	Sheet of 10 - ovptd in red		£150.00

Nos: 65 and 66) 10000 of each; later 1000 sheets, 5000 of each, were overprinted for No.76+77, leaving an issue of 5000 of each (but see also footnote to No.76+77); 65Sp and 66Sp) 75 of each. The 'specimen' sheets are un-numbered. Progressive colour proofs and imperf proofs exist. The stamps were printed as two panes on one sheet of paper and uncut proof sheets are known.
FDC: 800

1/1/90. Low Value Definitive. Des: Neill Oakley. Ptr: Fisherprint, Peterborough. Offset lithography in sheets of 20 (4 rows of 5). R9.5.

Dsgn: Geometric design adapted from No.32 and 33

67	5c/p Green	.15
(67)	Sheet of 20	£3.00
(67Sp)	Sheet of 20 - ovptd in black	£30.00

Nos: 67) 12000; 67Sp) 500.
FDC: 125

25 untrimmed, imperforate 'specimen' sheets were

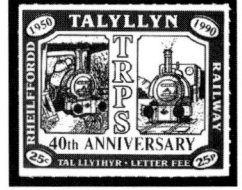

signed and numbered by the designer. Each sheet receiving two rubber stamped "Specimen" overprints applied horizontally.

5/7/90. 125th Anniversary of the Talyllyn Railway. Des: Neill Oakley. Ptr: Faulwood & Herbert Ltd., Brighton. Offset lithography in miniature sheets of 4 (2 rows of 2), containing one example of each. R4.75.

Dsgn: 68) No.4 *Edward Thomas* at Wharf Station in the early 1950s; 69) No.2 *Dolgoch* heading train down the Fathew Valley; 70) No.3 *Sir Haydn* crossing Dolgoch Viaduct; 71) No.1 *Talyllyn* arriving at Abergynolwyn in the early 1950s

68	25c/p Black and red	
69	25c/p Black and green	
70	25c/p Black and green	
71	25c/p Black and red	
(68-71)	Sheet of 4	£1.75
(68Sp-71Sp)	Sheet of 4 - ovptd in black	£37.50

Nos: 68-71) 3148 of each; 68-71Sp) 25 of each. 25 untrimmed but perforated 'specimen' sheets were overprinted, numbered and signed by the designer, General Manager and Postmaster, each sheet receiving one horizontal overprint. FDC: 68-71): 250

10/10/90. 40th Anniversary of the Talyllyn Railway Preservation Society. Des: Neill Oakley. Ptr: Faulwood & Herbert Ltd. Offset lithography in sheets of 10 (5 rows of 2). R9.5.

Dsgn: No.1 *Talyllyn* in the barn at Pendre in 1950, and in operational steam, inscribed "TRPS 40th Anniversary"

72	25c/p Black and ruby red	
72a	25c/p Black and ruby red	
72+72a	Se-tenant pair	£15.00
72b+72ba	Se-tenant pair	£1.75
(72+72a)	Sheet of 10	£125.00
(72b+72ba)	Sheet of 10	£10.00
(72bSp+72baSp)	Sheet of 10 - ovptd in black	£55.00

Nos: 72) 700; 72b) 1625; 72a) 400; 72ba) 1275; 72bSp+72baSp) 125 of each. 25 untrimmed, imperforate sheets were signed and numbered by the designer, each receiving one "Specimen" overprint applied vertically up the centre of the sheet.

A change in paper specification to reduce curl delayed the printing. When the stamps were supplied they were badly flawed and a reprint was agreed. It was hoped these could be delivered before the issue date so the first printing could be destroyed entirely but a further delay in the supply of replacement paper meant it was impossible to check and despatch them to the railway in time. A few first printing sheets were placed on sale in the railway shop at Wharf on the date of issue, and the rest were destroyed as being substandard. When the replacements arrived, a few days late, the remaining stock was removed from sale. Since the faults affected the original 'specimen' sheets, those that were issued came from a second printing.

The first printing is a strong ruby red and the gum has a grainy effect running horizontally across the paper; the second printing colour is slightly brick red in shade and the gum is completely smooth. Stamps in the right-hand column of both printings have a paler black image, resulting in the loss of fine detail. This fault, although known by the Railway, was not corrected for the second printing to accelerate delivery.

Only stamps from the left-hand column (No.72 and 72b) were used on commemorative covers, to avoid creating varieties, which accounts for the inequality of the figures in each printing. FDC: 72) 300

28/7/92. Definitive. Des: Neill Oakley. Ptr: Faulwood & Herbert Ltd. Offset lithography in sheets of 10 (5 rows of 2). R14.

Dsgn: No.1 *Talyllyn*

73	25p Steel blue	.40
	Sheet of 10	£3.50

Nos: 12000. FDC: 400

10/10/92. Definitive. Des: Neill Oakley. Ptr: Faulwood & Herbert Ltd. Offset lithography in sheets of 10 (2 rows of 5). R14.

Dsgn: Barclay/T.R. 0-4-2T No.7 *Tom Rolt*, shield and geometric background

74	25(c/p) Dark green	.40
	Sheet of 10	£3.50

Nos: 12000. FDC: 525

2/6/93. 40th Anniversary of the Coronation of Queen Elizabeth II. Des: Neill Oakley. Ptr: The House of Questa. Offset lithography in sheets of 10 (5 rows of 2). P14.2.

Dsgn: No.7 *Tom Rolt* and up train crossing Dolgoch viaduct

75	25(c/p) Multicoloured	.40
(75)	Sheet of 10	£3.50
75a	25(c/p) Multicoloured, plus set of proofs - imperf [see footnote]	£75.00

Nos: 75) 20000; 75a) 25   FDC: 525
25 card folders, containing an imperf example of the issued stamp and six individual progressive proofs mounted on a black stockcard, were released.

24/8/93. 40 Years Service on the Talyllyn Railway by No.6 *Douglas*. Surcharged "25" in red, and overprinted in black and "40 Years" in red by Faulwood & Herbert, se-tenant horiz. 76+77.

76	25(c) Multicoloured (W) (65)	
77	25(p) Multicoloured (E) (66)	
	Se-tenant pair	.80
	Sheet of 10	£4.00

Nos: 3330 of each. 1000 sheets of No.65+66 were sent to the printers but problems overprinting in two colours meant a significant number of sheets were destroyed as being unsatisfactory. Some examples, kept for a record, were marked in manuscript on the reverse as "printer's waste".   FDC: 300

8/5/95. 50th Anniversary of V. E. Day. Des: Neill Oakley. Ptr: Faulwood & Herbert Ltd. Offset lithography in sheets of 10 (5 rows of 2). R14.

Dsgn: No.6 *Douglas*, in 1940s condition with single buffer, beside a Lancaster bomber and ground crew, inscribed "Victory in Europe 50 1945 1995"

78	25p Multicoloured	.40
	Decor. sheet of 10	£3.50

Nos: 10000. FDC: 400

6/4/96. Definitive. Des: Neill Oakley; Illus: Terence Cuneo (oil painting). Ptr: Walsall Security Printers. Offset lithography in sheets of 9 (9 rows of 9). P14.

Dsgn: No.1 *Talyllyn* taking water at Dolgoch watertower

79	25p Multicoloured	.40
	Sheet of 9	£3.50

Nos: 18000. FDC 500
The fdc were carried over the Snowdon Mountain Railway and the T.R. See also S.M.R. L2 on pg 83.

31/12/96. 150th Anniversary of Slate Quarrying at Bryn Eglwys. Des: Neill Oakley. Ptr: Walsall Security Printers. Offset lithography in miniature sheets of 4 (2 rows of 2, se-tenant horiz. and vert., row 1: 80+81; row 2: 81+80). P14.

Dsgn: 80) No.2 *Dolgoch* at Wharf with slate wagons and man splitting slate; 81) No.1 *Talyllyn* and slate train passing through the winding house of the Abergynolwyn village incline

80	25(c/p) Multicoloured	
81	25(c/p) Multicoloured	
80+81	Se-tenant pair	.80
(80+81)	Decor. sheet of 4	£2.00
(80a+81a)	Decor. sheet of 4 - imperf	£20.00

Nos: 80 and 81) 12000; 80a and 81a) 120 of each. The 60 imperforate sheets were numbered and signed by the designer, and originally sold in pairs with sheets of No.83a-86a.   FDC: 500

1/1/97. Low Value Definitive. Des: Neill Oakley. Ptr: SJC Colour Printers. Offset lithography in sheets of 20 (4 rows of 5). R.26.

Dsgn: As 67

82	5c/p Ruby red	.15
	Sheet of 20	£2.50

Nos: 20000. FDC: 300

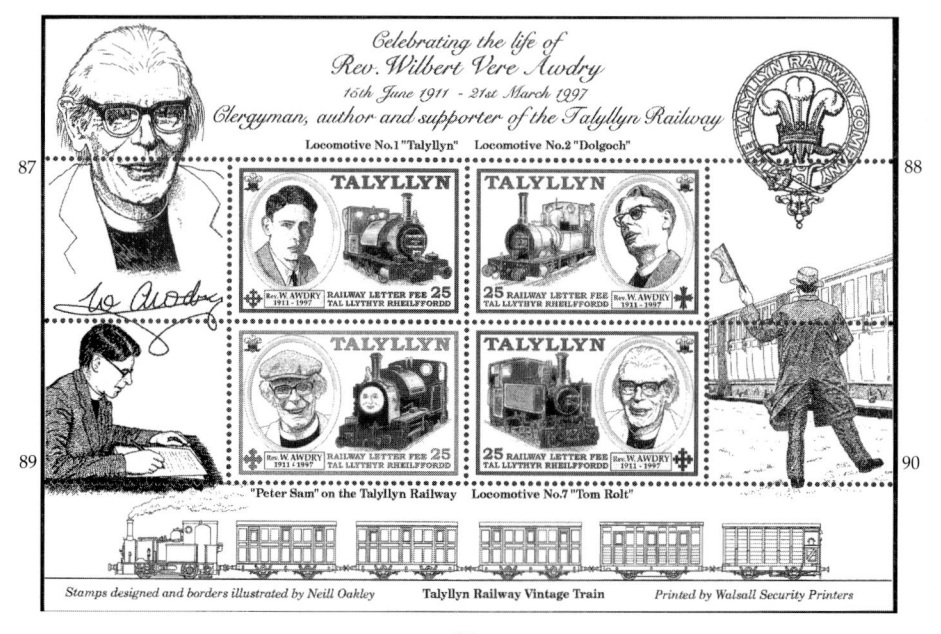

23/5/97. 40th Anniversary of the Talyllyn Railway Letter Service. Des: Neill Oakley; Illus: Neill Oakley, except 84) loco drawing adapted from the original T.R stamp design No.5 by James Upton Printers; 85) drawn from John Adams' photo used for No.37, 43 and 44). Ptr: Walsall Security Printers. Offset lithography in miniature sheets of 4 (2 rows of 2, containing one example of each). P14.

Dsgn: 83) No.2 *Dolgoch*, and four-wheel coaches, with 1891-style railway letter stamp and T.R. timetable heading; 84) No.1 *Talyllyn* in 1950s livery; 85) No.3 *Sir Haydn* heading an up train near Abergynolwyn; 86) No.3 *Sir Haydn* and Van No.5 at Wharf Station with guard receiving mail from a child

83	25(c/p)	Black, green and sepia
84	25(c/p)	Black and red
85	25(c/p)	Multicoloured
86	25(c/p)	Multicoloured
(83-86)	Decor. sheet of 4	£2.00
(83a-86a)	Decor. sheet of 4 - imperf	£20.00

Nos: 83-86): 2000 of each; 83a-86a): 60 of each. The 60 imperforate sheets were signed and numbered by the designer, and initially sold in pairs with sheets of No.80a+81a.
FDC 83-86): 500

22/6/97. Centenary of Queen Victoria's Diamond Jubilee. For full details see stationery envelope on pg 93.

21/3/98. Celebrating the Life of Rev. W. Awdry. Des: Neill Oakley. Ptr: Walsall Security Printers. Offset lithography in miniature sheets of 4 (2 rows of 2, containing one example of each). P14.

Des: 87) Portrait of Wilbert as a young man, No.1 *Talyllyn* and cross flory; 88) Portrait in the 1950s, No.2 *Dolgoch* and cross patonce; 89) Portrait in the 1980s, No.4 *Peter Sam* on the Talyllyn Railway and cross botonny; 90) Portrait in the 1980s, No.7 *Tom Rolt* and cross crosslet. All with T.R. feathers and inscribed "Rev. W. Awdry 1911 - 1997"

87	25(c/p)	Multicoloured
88	25(c/p)	Multicoloured
89	25(c/p)	Multicoloured
90	25(c/p)	Multicoloured
(87-90)	Decor. sheet of 4	£2.00
(87a-90a)	Decor. sheet of 4 - imperf	£15.00

Nos: 87-90): 2000 of each; 87a-90a): 60 of each.
FDC 83-86): 500

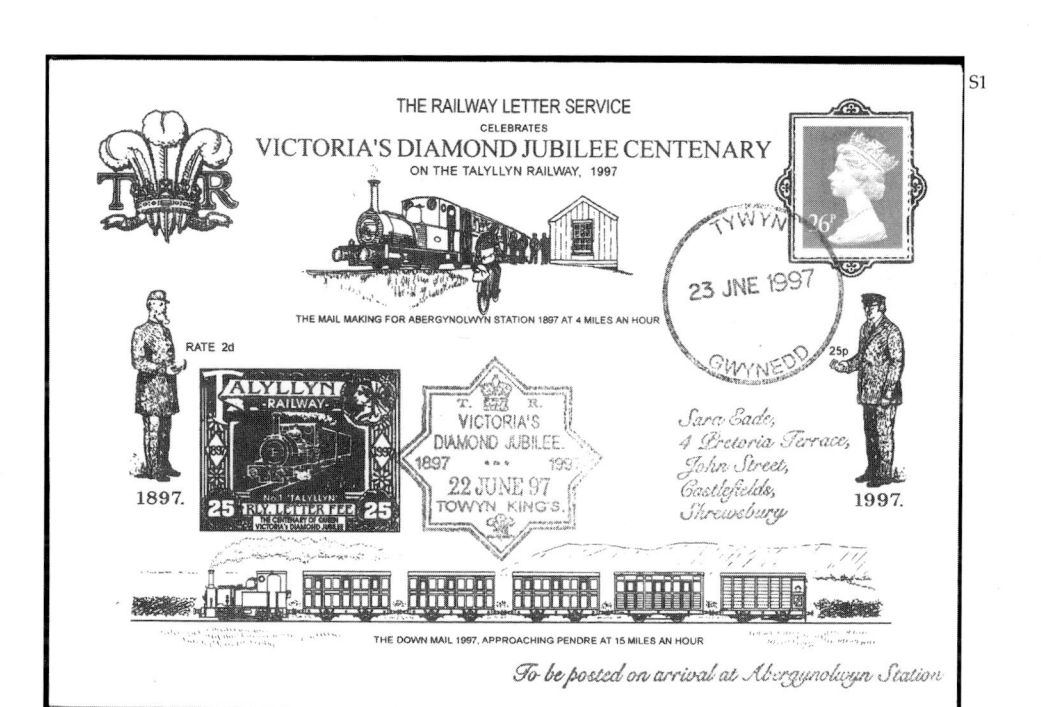

STATIONERY ENVELOPE

22/6/97. Centenary of Queen Victoria's Diamond Jubilee. Des: Neill Oakley. Ptr: PDC Print, Shrewsbury.

Dsgn: Envelope adapted from the design issued for the Post Office's Penny Post Jubilee in 1890. Stamp adapted from a New South Wales charity label issued in 1897, with No.1 *Talyllyn* and train and inscribed "The Centenary of Queen Victoria's Diamond Jubilee"

S1	25(p) Blue [see footnote]	£4.00
Nos: 1000		FDC: 500

Sold by the railway as carried and mint pairs. Each envelope contained a filler card, in the style of the Penny Post Jubilee portrait of Rowland Hill and decoration, which had portraits of Sara Eade "She runs the letter service", and Neill Oakley "He designs the RLS items", printed on either side.

T.R. SPECIAL CANCELLATIONS

1	1/7/69	Towyn - Loyal Greetings from the Talyllyn Railway [This is a translation of the P.O. handstamp sponsored by the Company on the same day; illus. Prince of Wales' feathers]
2	15/5/72	Tywyn - Dathlu penlwyd yn 21 ain ded owasanaeth trenau gan G.W.Rh.T.: Llythyr Rheilffordd Talyllyn [21st anniversary of operation of trains by the T.R.P.S.: Talyllyn Railway Letter; illus. Prince of Wales' feathers]
3	13/8/75	Tywyn - Talyllyn Salutes Stockton & Darlington
4	13/8/75	Tywyn - Cyfarchion Talyllyn i Stockton & Darlington
5	22/5/76	Tywyn - Extension Opened to Nant Gwernol [illus. stylised track with point]
6	11/5/77	Tywyn - Jiwbili arian Frenhines Elizabeth II [Used to commemorate the Silver Jubilee of H.M. The Queen]
7	31/5/78	Tywyn - Sir Henry Haydn Jones General Manager 1912-1950
8	5/7/78	Tywyn - The Iron Horse Salutes the Shire Horse [Used for P.O. Shire Horse issue]
9	25/11/82	Carried on Royal Train
10	22/1/85	Talyllyn Railway Salutes the Other Famous Trains [illus. T.R. and G.W.R. crests]
11	31/8/85	[As above, redated]
12	1/3/88	Mary Jones Welsh Bible
13	14/5/88	Inaugural Run *Peter Sam* on the Talyllyn Railway [illus. side view of *Peter Sam*]
14	3/7/88	Brynglas - *Mallard* 126mph 1938-1988 [illus. stylised side view of *Mallard* at speed]
15	3/7/88	Brynglas - [No.]6 1918-1988 [illus. front view of *Douglas*]
16	25/7/89	Cambrian Railways Company MDCCCLXIV [illus. crest of company]
17	23/6/90	Talyllyn Night T.P.O. - UP [double ring

18	23/6/90	Talyllyn Night T.P.O. - DOWN [as above]
19	5/7/90	1865 1990 T.R. 125 Years [oval metal plate illus. front view of loco No.1]
20	18/8/90	Race the Train [illus. shoeprints running inside a border of track - green]
21	10/10/90	1950 1990 T.R.P.S. 40 Years [oval metal plate design illus. Prince of Wales' feathers]
22	1/2/91	Abergynolwyn Station - RLS100 1881 [sic] 1991 [illus. railway letter]
23	6/5/91	Abergynolwyn - Loco No.7 Naming Ceremony *Tom Rolt* [illus. outline of loco]
24	2/11/91	Towyn Wharf - [No.]4 1921 - 1991 [stylised ticket design]
25	28/7/92	Abergynolwyn [illus. adapted reproduction of Penny Black stamp]
26	10/10/92	Tywyn Wharf - The T.R. celebrates with B.R. Cambrian 125 [illus. B.R. arrows symbol and T.R. crest]
27	2/6/93	Abergynolwyn - Vivat Regina! [illus. crown, sceptre and orb]
28	24/8/93	Dolgoch Falls [Celebrating 75 years of the R.A.F., 50 years of the R.A.F. Association, and 40 years service of No.6 on the T.R.; illus. R.A.F. badge, Spitfire and No.6 *Douglas* and train]
29	18/1/94	Pendre [illus. No.1 *Talyllyn* outside Pendre engine shed in the 1920s with railway staff]
30	1/3/94	Abergynolwyn - Investiture of the Prince of Wales Caernarfon 1 July 1969 Ich Dien [illus. Investiture crown]
31	16/7/94	Talyllyn T.P.O. NIGHT UP 2 [double ring T.P.O. style design]
32	16/7/94	Talyllyn T.P.O. NIGHT DOWN 2 [as above]
33	1/9/94	Tywyn - 100 Years British Picture Postcard [illus. a gull with postcard on a Victorian pillarbox]
34	1/4/95	Abergynolwyn - "The Quarryman" Scheduled Train Inaugural Run [illus. slate wagon]
35	23/4/95	Tywyn Wharf - Tywyn Postcard Festival [illus. elephant holding a postcard; the local Corbett Arms Hotel, where the event was held, has an elephant in its crest]
36	8/5/95	Pendre - Victory in Europe [illus. 'V' sign and morse code]
37	30/7/95	Abergynolwyn - 50 Years of the Rev. W Awdry "Railway Series Books" [illus. portrait of author and signature]
38	5/9/95	Towyn - Marconi Centenary of the 1st radio transmission [illus. stylised transmission tower and radio signal by the sea]
39	6/4/96	Abergynolwyn - The T.R celebrates the S.M.R.'s Centenary 100 [illus. S.M.R. crest]
40	31/12/96	Nant Gwernol [illus. slate worker's hammer and splitter]
41	23/5/97	Tywyn Wharf - T.R.L.S. 1957-1997 [illus. perforated stamp border and T.R. feathers]
42	23/5/97	Tywyn Wharf - Railway Letter Service 40th Anniversary Train [illus. two four-wheel carriages]
43	25/5/97	Talyllyn Travelling Post Office [illus. side view of Van No.7]
44	22/6/97	Towyn King's - T.R. Victoria's Diamond Jubilee 1897-1997 [illus. adapted cancel from the Penny Post Jubilee of 1890]
45	21/3/98	Tywyn Wharf - Rev. W. Awdry [illus. side view of 0-6-0T in steam]
46	20/8/98	Abergynolwyn - 50th Anniversary of the Corris Railway's Closure [illus. side view of Corris coach No.19]

P.O. ONE-DAY POSTMARKS

5/7/65	Towyn - Centenary [illus. Towyn's C33 postal cancellation used in 1865]
5/6/67	Towyn - A Hundred Years of Passenger Service
1/7/69	Tywyn - Cyfarchion diffuant oddi wrth [Loyal greetings from the Talyllyn Railway; illus. Prince of Wales' feathers]
22/5/76	Tywyn - Nant Gwernol Extension Opened [illus. stylised track with point]
17/6/85	Abergynolwyn Tywyn - GWR Celebrations [illus. side view of *Talyllyn*]

VALE OF RHEIDOL RAILWAY

This 1'11½" narrow gauge line, opened in 1902, runs from Aberystwyth alongside the Afon Rheidol and then climbs steeply to Devil's Bridge, 11½ miles inland, and 680' above sea level. En route to Devil's Bridge the line serves a number of small intermediate stations including Rheidol Falls.

The Cambrian Railway absorbed the line in 1913, and they in turn were incorporated in the G.W.R. from 1923. Since nationalisation in 1948 it was run by British Rail, latterly their only line operated by steam locomotives, with services confined to the summer season. At the end of 1988 B.R. sold the railway to the owners of the Brecon Mountain Railway

As the successor to most of the companies which signed the 1891 agreement to carry railway letters, British Rail issued stamps on the Vale of Rheidol Railway which had restricted validity. They were only valid on letters handed in at the V.o.R. terminal stations or to the guard on the train, and each of these three had an appropriate rectangular cancel. The stamps had no franking value on letters handed in elsewhere on B.R. The current owners have stated that they do not plan to re-introduce the letter service.

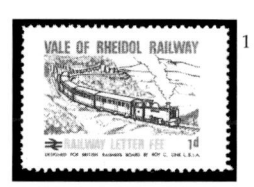

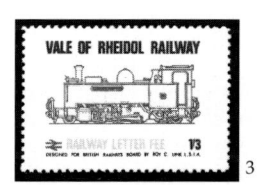

29/7/70. Definitives. Des: Roy C. Link. Ptr: Walsall Security Printers. Lithography in sheets of 12 (4 rows of 3), num. as below. P14.

Dsgn: 1) Train approaching Devil's Bridge; 2) Crest of Vale of Rheidol Company and British Rail motif; 3) G.W.R. 2-6-2T No.9 *Prince of Wales*; 4) G.W.R. 2-6-2T No.3 *Rheidol*

1	1d Yellow, green and blue	.25
2	6d Green, black and blue	.40
3	1s3d Yellow, purple and blue	.40
4	1s7d Grey, red and black	.40

Sheets of 12:

(1)	Num: 0001 - 1780	£3.00
(2)	Num: 0001 - 1545	£4.80
(3)	Num: 0001 - 1906	£4.80
(4)	Num: 0001 - 1825	£4.80

Nos: 1) 21360; 2) 18540; 3) 22872; 4) 21900. Imperf copies (proofs?) of No.3 exist.

15/2/71. Provisional Decimals. Surcharged in black by Davies Bros., Portmadoc.

5	5p on 1d (1)	£6.00
5a	5p on 1d - wider surcharge spacing	£10.00
5aa	5p on 1d - value to right of X	£15.00
6	10p on 1s3d (3)	£6.00
6a	10p on 1s3d - value to right of X	£25.00

Sheets of 12:

(5)	Num: 1956 - 2705	£72.00
(5a)	Num: 1783 - 1955 (?/10/71)	£120.00
(6)	Num: 1907 - 2426 (including 6a)	£72.00
(6a)	Num: 2032 - 2051(?)	-

Nos: 5) 8172; 5a) 2076; 6) 5904. Under two hundred exist of No.6a, and these are included in the total for No.6. These figures allow for spoilt sheets. In the original overprinting of the 5p the distance from the top of the 5 to the base of the "X" is 13-14mm; in the reprint, No.5a, this distance is 15-17mm. The variety No.5aa occurs in the central column of this latter printing. On sheets of both values the right foot of the obliteration X is broken off on row 4, stamp 3. Most of the 10p surcharges have the denomination above the "X"; in No.5aa and No.6a the 10p is positioned to the right so that the figure 1 of "10" is in a vertical line with the right-hand edge of the cross.

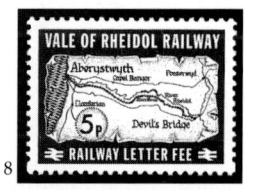

1971 - 1972. Decimal Definitives. Des: Lt. Col. H. B. L. Samways. Ptr: Walsall Security Printers. Lithography in sheets of 12 (4 rows of 3), num. as below. P11.

Dsgn: 7) Train approaching Devil's Bridge; 8) Map of the line

7	10p Black, blue and red	£1.10
8	5p Black and green	.75

Sheets of 12:

(7)	Num: 0001 - 1600 (7/7/71)	£13.50
(8)	Num: 0001 - 1375 (5/7/72)	£9.50

Nos: 7) 25200; later 5988 were surcharged for No.15, leaving an issue of 19200; 8) 16500.

28/2/73. Provisional. Surcharged in brown by Davies Bros., Portmadoc, num. 1546 - 1880.

9	16p on 6d (2)	£9.00
	Sheet of 12	£110.00

Nos: 3900.

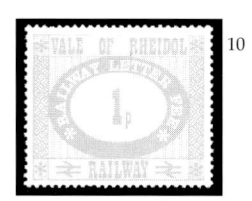

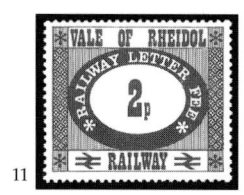

15/8/73. Low Value Definitives. Des: Roy C. Link. Ptr: Walsall Security Printers. Lithography in sheets of 12 (4 rows of 3), num. as below. P14.4 x 14.

Dsgn: Numeral and patterned background

10	1p Green	.40
11	2p Red	.40
	Sheets of 12:	
(10)	Num: 0001 - 1100	£4.50
(11)	Num: 0001 - 1092	£4.50

Nos: 10) 13200; 11) 13104.

16/7/75. Definitive. Des: Anthony Daffern. Ptr: T. Stephenson & Sons Ltd, Prescot. Lithography in sheets of 12 (4 rows of 3), num. 0001 - 1000. P13.5.

Dsgn: No.3 *Rheidol*

12	15p Blue and turquoise blue	£1.25
	Sheet of 12	£15.00

Nos: 12000.

4/8/80. Great Little Trains of Wales Joint Issue. For full details see pg 26.

13	15p Black and red (E)
14	15c Black and red (W)

13/5/81. Provisional. Surcharged in black by Shrewsbury Circular Printing and Publishing Co. Ltd, num. 1601 - 2100.

15	20p on 10p (7)	£1.75
	Sheet of 12	£21.00

Nos: 5988, sheet num. 1699 was spoilt.

16/6/82. Definitive. Des: Anthony Daffern. Ptr: T. Stephenson & Sons Ltd. Lithography in sheets of 12 (4 rows of 3), num. 1 - 1500. P14.

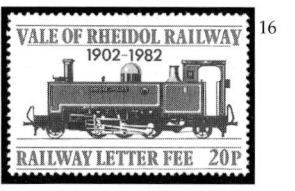

Dsgn: No.9 *Prince of Wales*, inscribed "1902-1982"

16	20p Bistre and black	.40
	Sheet of 12	£4.80

Nos: 18000.

17/6/85. G.W.R.150 Overprint. As B.R. stamps No.3-6, except overprinted "Vale of Rheidol Railway" and surcharged in black by Milbrooke Printers, Folkestone.

17	55p + 20p (BR 3)	
18	55p + 20p (BR 4)	
19	55p + 20p (BR 5)	
20	55p + 20p (BR 6)	
(17-20)	Miniature sheet of 4	£9.00
(17a-20a)	Miniature sheet of 4 - imperf	£25.00

Nos: 17-20) 10000 of each; 17a-20a) 200 imperf sheets. Some sheets were sold in presentation packs. See also B.R. No.3-6, pg 12.
FDC: G.W.R.150) 500 with sheets, 1200 with single stamps; V.o.R.) 200 with single stamps.

V.o.R. SPECIAL CANCELLATIONS

1	22/12/72	Aberystwyth - Vale of Rheidol Railway 70 Years of Service Rheidol Cambrian Great Western British Rail 1902-1972
2	4/9/73	Aberystwyth - No.7 and No.8 GWR 1923-1973 [illus. loco and GWR and BR logos]
3	25/7/77	Aberystwyth - 75 Years Vale of Rheidol Rly 1902-1977 [illus. No.2]
4	29/7/81	Aberystwyth - Devil's Bridge - No.9 "*Prince of Wales*" Royal Wedding Day H.R.H. Prince of Wales and Lady Diana Spencer [illus. No.9]
5	3/5/82	80 Years 1902-1982 Aberystwyth - Devil's Bridge [illus. No.9 - undated]
6	2/5/83	Aberystwyth - Devil's Bridge No.7 and 8 built Swindon 1923. Great Western Railway [illus. side view No.7]

P.O. ONE-DAY POSTMARKS

5/4/69	Aberystwyth - Devil's Bridge [illus. side view of No.8]
18/6/85	Shrewsbury - GWR150 Exhibition Train [illus. side view of 2-6-2T loco]

WELSHPOOL & LLANFAIR LIGHT RAILWAY
RHEILFFORDD TRALLWNG A LLANFAIR

This 2'6" gauge light railway was opened to passengers on 4 April 1903, when it was operated for the owners by neighbouring standard gauge Cambrian Railways. In 1922 it was taken over by the Great Western Railway who terminated the passenger service in 1931. The line existed on goods traffic until it was closed by British Railways in 1956. The present company re-commenced running passenger trains in 1963, and succeeded in buying the line from the British Transport Commission in 1974.

Originally passengers were carried between Llanfair Caereinion and Castle Caereinion (4 1/4 miles), followed by extensions to Sylfaen (5 1/2), and then Welshpool Raven Square (8), in 1981. The railway has an international collection of locomotives and carriages. The railway signed the 1974 and 1998 agreements.

Enquiries to: W.L.L.R. R.L.S., 3 Cathcart Green, Guilden Sutton, Chester CH3 7SR.

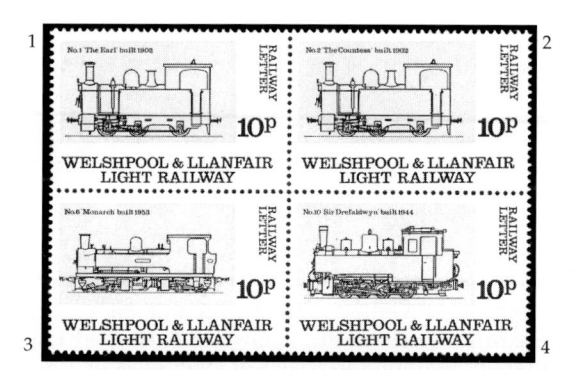

13/8/75. Definitives. Des: Robert Stocqueler. Ptr: Walsall Security Printers. Lithography in sheets of 12 (3 blocks of 4, containing one example of each, row 1: 1+2, row 2: 3+4, each block being separated by a horizontal gutter margin). P14.

Dsgn: 1) Beyer Peacock 0-6-0T No1 *The Earl*; 2) Beyer Peacock 0-6-0T No.2 *The Countess*; 3) 0-4-0+0-4-0T No.6 *Monarch*; 4) Franco-Belge 0-8-0T No.10 *Sir Drefaldwyn*

1	10p Black and yellow	
2	10p Black and yellow	
3	10p Black and yellow	
4	10p Black and yellow	
	Se-tenant block of 4	£20.00
	Sheet of 12 (3 of each design)	£75.00

Nos: 5000 of each; later 1500 of each were surcharged, leaving an issue of 3500 of each. Issue was withdrawn from sale on 30/6/80. FDC: 400

25/6/77. 50th Anniversary of No.12 *Joan*. Des: E. W. Basten and A. Wilkinson. Ptr: Walsall Security Printers. Lithography in sheets of 12 (3 rows of 4). P14.

Dsgn: Kerr Stuart 0-6-2T No.12 *Joan* and map

5	10p Brown, blue and black	.70
	Sheet of 12	£8.50

Nos: 10560; later 4800 were surcharged for No.16, leaving an issue of 5760. FDC: 1200

24/3/78. Provisionals. Surcharged in black by Walsall Security Printers.

6	15p on 10p (1)	
7	15p on 10p (2)	
8	15p on 10p (3)	
9	15p on 10p (4)	
	Se-tenant block of 4	£25.00
	Sheet of 12 (3 of each design)	£85.00

Nos: 1500 of each. FDC: 400

1/7/78. 75th Anniversary of Opening. Des: G. Nicholls. Ptr: T. Stephenson & Sons Ltd., Prescot. Lithography in sheets of 12 (4 rows of 3), num. 0001 - 0500. P14.

Dsgn: Hunslet 2-6-2T No.14 *SLR 85* and No.1 *The Earl*

10	15p Olive green, red and black	.70
	Sheet of 12	£8.50

Nos: 6000. FDC: 500

2/8/80. 150th Anniversary of the Liverpool & Manchester Railway. Des: Robert Stocqueler. Ptr: T. Stephenson & Sons Ltd. Lithography in sheets of 12 (4 rows of 3, rows 1 & 2: 11, rows 3 & 4: 12, se-tenant vert. 11+12 in rows 2 & 3), num. 1 - 350. P14.

Dsgn: No.1 *The Earl* and *Rocket*

11	15p Black, green and orange (E)	£1.25
12	15c Black, green and orange (W)	£1.25
	Se-tenant pair	£8.00
	Sheet of 12	£35.00

Nos: 2100 of each. There are only 3 vert. se-tenant pairs, formed by rows 2 and 3, on each sheet which accounts for the premium applied to them. On a few sheets (num. 338 - 350, and perhaps others at the end of the sequence) the top half of the figure 5s of "15p" and "15c" are filled in on the upper three stamps of the right-hand column. FDC: 400

4/8/80. Great Little Trains of Wales Joint Issue. For full details see pg 26.

13	15p Black and red (E)	
14	15p Black and red (W)	

17/4/81. Definitives. Details as for No.11+12, except num. 351 - 700.

15	20p (E) (as 11)	£1.25
16	20c (W) (as 12)	£1.25
	Se-tenant pair	£8.00
	Sheet of 12	£35.00

Nos: 2100 of each. There are only three vert. se-tenant pairs at the centre of each sheet. FDC: 500

16/5/82. Official Reopening to Welshpool. Des: Douglas Moyle. Ptr: T. Stephenson & Sons Ltd. Photolithography in sheets of 12 (4 rows of 3), with E or W text in the margins, num. as below. P14.

Dsgn: No.1 *The Earl*

17	20p Multicoloured	£1.00
	Sheets of 12:	
	Num: 1 - 349 (odd) E margin text	£15.00
	Num: 2 - 350 (even) W margin text	£15.00

Nos: 4200. Exceptions to the sheet numbering noted above exist. FDC: 600

30/5/87. 60th Anniversary of No.12 *Joan*. Overprinted "60th Year" and surcharged in black by Welshpool Printers, Welshpool.

18	20p on 10p (5)	.50
	Sheet of 12	£6.00

Nos: 4800. FDC: 252

10/5/88. Silver Jubilee of Reopening. Des: Mike Thomas and R. I. Cartwright. Printed by Faulwood & Herbert Ltd., Brighton. Offset lithography in sheets of 10 (5 rows of 2). R4.75.

Dsgn: No.1 *The Earl* and No.2 *The Countess*

19	20p Blue and black	.50
	Sheet of 10	£5.00

Nos: 6000. FDC: 190 rail & post; 99 rail only

10/4/90. 90th Anniversary of Zillertalbahn Coach. Des: Mike Thomas. Ptr: Faulwood & Herbert Ltd. Offset lithography in sheets of 10 (5 rows of 2, se-tenant horiz. 20+21). R4.75.

Dsgn: Austrian ex-Zillertalbahn open balcony coach built 1900, and inscribed "ZB coach 1900" in English and Welsh

20	25p Brown and green (E)	
21	25c Brown and green (W)	
	Se-tenant pair	£1.00
	Sheet of 10	£5.00

Nos: 3000 of each. FDC: 20+21) 70 rail & post; 20 or 21) 173 rail & post; 69 rail only.

9/4/93. 90th Anniversary of the First Passenger Service and 30th Anniversary of Passenger Services Restored. Des: Adam Swain and Peter Bailey. Ptr: Faulwood & Herbert Ltd. Offset lithography in sheets of 10 (5 rows of 2, se-tenant horiz. 22+23). R9.5.

Dsgn: 22) No.822 *The Earl*, in G.W.R. condition, inscribed "30 years passenger services restored"; 23) No.1 The Earl, in present condition, inscribed "90 Mlynedd Ers Cludo'r Teithwyr Cyntaf"

22	25p Blue and red (E)		
23	25c Blue and red (W)		
	Se-tenant pair		.90
	Sheet of 10		£4.50

Nos: 3000 of each. FDC: Not known.

Sheet of 10 £4.00
Nos: 1725 of each. FDC: 24+25) 150 rail & post

W.L.L.R. SPECIAL CANCELLATIONS

1	13/8/75	Welshpool & Llanfair Railway Letter First Day of Service
2	17/4/76	Llanfair Caereinion - First Steaming *Dougal* [illus. silhouette of loco]
3	11/5/77	Sylfaen - Silver Jubilee [of H.M. The Queen] 1952-1977 [illus. royal crown above circular border]
4	12/5/77	Llanfair Caereinion - Silver Jubilee [of H.M. The Queen] 1952-1977 [illus. royal crown above circular border]
5	25/6/77	Llanfair Caereinion - No.12 *Joan* Golden Jubilee 1927-1977
6	24/3/78	Sylfaen - First Day of Increased Rate
7	1/7/78	Castle Caereinion - 75th Anniversary of Opening 1903-1978
8	11/8/79	Castle Caereinion - Inauguration of Sierra Leone Train
9	2/8/80	Sylfaen - Liverpool & Manchester 150th Anniversary
10	4/8/80	Sylfaen - Narrow Gauge Railways of Wales Joint Marketing Panel 10th Anniversary [illus. Panel's logo]
11	17/4/81	Sylfaen - 1st Day of New 20p Rate
12	18/7/81	Llanfair Caereinion - Reopening to Welshpool [illus. town crest]
13	18/7/81	Welshpool Raven Square - Reopening to Welshpool [illus. town crest]
14	16/5/82	Official Reopening Welshpool Extension [oval cancel illus. town crest]
15	9/7/83	Welshpool RS - 80th Anniversary Celebration 1903-1983
16	30/5/87	Llanfair Caereinion - No.12 *Joan* 60th Year
17	10/5/88	Llanfair Caereinion - Silver Jubilee of Reopening [1963-1988]
18	10/5/90	Welshpool & Llanfair Light Railway New Railway Letter Stamp
19	25/7/92	Opening of the New Station Building at Welshpool Raven Square
20	9/4/93	Carried on the First Train Passenger and Reopening Anniversary Year
21	1/4/94	Carried on the First Train to Depart from the Reconstructed Station at Llanfair Caereinion
22	14/4/95	Carried on the First Train of the New Season
23	22/8/98	First Day of Issue [illus. W.L.L.R. Preservation Co. crest]

15/9/96. Definitive. Des: Ken Hooke. Ptr: Faulwood & Herbert Ltd. Offset lithography in sheets of 10 (5 rows of 2, se-tenant horiz. 24+25). R4.75.

Dsgn: Barclay 0-4-0T No.8 *Dougal*

24	25p Brown and black		
25	25c Brown and black		
	Se-tenant pair		.80
	Sheet of 10		£4.00

Nos: 2200 of each. FDC: 24+25) 200 rail & post

22/8/98. Definitive. Des: Ken Hooke; Illus: B. Webber (painting). Ptr: Faulwood & Herbert Ltd. Offset lithography in sheets of 10 (5 rows of 2, se-tenant horiz. 24+25). R4.75.

Dsgn: Tubize 2-6-2T No.15 *Orion*

26	25p Multicoloured		
27	25c Multicoloured		
	Se-tenant pair		.80

P.O. ONE-DAY POSTMARK

7/4/73   Welshpool - Welshpool & Llanfair 10th Anniversary [of reopening. Used before letter service started - illus. silhouette of Beyer Peacock 0-6-0T loco]

WEST SOMERSET RAILWAY

The original railway opened as a broad gauge line from Taunton to Watchet in 1862, and was later extended to Minehead by a separate company, the Minehead Railway, in 1874. Both parts of the line were operated by the Bristol & Exeter Railway until they were absorbed into the G.W.R. The whole branch was converted to standard gauge in 1882, and eventually British Rail closed the line in 1971.

Reopened in 1976, the service is currently operated from Minehead to Dunster (on request, 1 3/4 miles), Blue Anchor (3 1/2), Washford (5 3/4), Watchet (8), Williton (9 3/4), Stogumber (on request, 13), Crowcombe (on request, 15 3/4), and Bishops Lydeard (19 3/4). Some trains have bus connections into Taunton (24 3/4 miles), while in the holiday season some services have an immediate chartered coach connection. Occasionally special trains operate into the Taunton Cider Co. sidings at Norton Fitzwarren. Eventually the railway hopes to run services into Taunton B.R..

The Postmaster had to relinquish his post at the end of 1988, when his family moved from Somerset. The railway announced they were reluctantly suspending the railway letter service in April 1989, due to pressure on staff when trains arrived and departed during peak times. They have not signed the 1998 Agreement.

23/5/85. Definitive. Des: John Nash. Ptr: Gull Press, Watchet. Lithography in sheets of 10 (2 rows of 5). R7.

Dsgn: In the style of an old railway letter stamp

1	20p Green	.40
1Sp	20p - ovptd in black	£4.00
(1)	Sheet of 10	£3.50
(1Sp)	Sheet of 10 - ovptd in black	£35.00

Nos: 1) 10000; 1Sp) 300. There were a wide range of green shades. 30 specimen sheets were numbered and signed by the designer/Postmaster. FDC: 400

30/5/86. 10th Anniversary of the West Somerset Railway. Des: John Nash. Ptr: Status Stationery Printers, Minehead. Lithography in sheets of 10 (2 rows of 5). P12.

Dsgn: G.W.R. 0-6-0PT No.6412, inscribed "10 years 1976-1986"

2	20p Black, cocoa and yellow		.45
2Sp	20p - ovptd in red		£4.00
(2)	Sheet of 10		£4.50
(2Sp)	Sheet of 10 - ovptd in red		£35.00

Nos: 2) 10000; 2Sp) 300. 30 specimen sheets were numbered and signed by the designer / Postmaster. FDC: 250. Maxi cards were also prepared on the first day of issue and signed by the W.S.R. Postmaster.

31/3/87. 125th Anniversary of the Taunton - Watchet Section. Des: Bernard Parkinson. Ptr: Status Printers, Minehead. Offset lithography in sheets of 10 (5 rows of 2, se-tenant horiz. 3+4), num. 001 - 500. P11.

Dsgn: 3) B.&E.R. 4-4-0ST; 4) G.W.R. 2-6-2T

3	20(p) Orange and black		
4	20(p) Green and black		
3+4	Se-tenant pair		£1.25
3Sp+4Sp	Se-tenant pair - ovptd in purple		£7.00
(3+4)	Sheet of 10		£6.50
(3Sp+4Sp)	Sheet of 10 - ovptd in purple		£35.00

Nos: 3+4) 2500 of each; 3Sp+4Sp) 150 of each. 30 imperf 'specimen' sheets were produced. Colour proofs and trials exist. This issue was produced as a double pane printing with ship's mail labels for M.V. Balmoral; uncut sheets exist.
FDC: 250. 50 pairs of maxi cards of the stamp designs, num. 1 - 50, were also prepared.

W.S.R. SPECIAL CANCELLATIONS

1	23/5/85	Railway Letter Service Inaugural Run [illus. track and front view of loco No.6412 - red]
2	25/5/85	[illus. front view of loco No.6412 - green - undated]
3	25/5/85	Posted on Board Paddle Steamer "Waverley" [red - undated]
4	30/7/85	West Somerset Railway TPO UP
5	8/9/85	Minehead to Norton Fitzwarren Double Headed Steam [red]
6	14/12/85	Santa Special Christmas 1985 [illus. star - purple]
7	28/3/86	10 Years Minehead to Blue Anchor [illus. outline of 4-6-0 loco in steam]
8	30/5/86	First Day of Issue
9	28/8/86	10 Years Minehead to Williton [illus. outline of 4-6-0 loco in steam]
10	18/11/86	Christmas 1986 [illus. candle and holly - red]
11	31/3/87	Watchet - Taunton 125 Years 1852 - 1987
12	29/8/87	Washford Station - S & D Railway Trust [Used on a limited edition of postcards marking the first steaming of S.&D. 2-8-0 No.88 - see also "For the Record" pg 112.]

P.O. ONE-DAY POSTMARK

28/3/86   Minehead - West Somerset Railway 10th Anniversary [illus. 0-6-0ST and train]

The Railway Philatelic Group is the publisher of the following books of interest to the railway philatelist:

Travelling Post Offices of Great Britain & Ireland (Their history and postmarks with 41 photographs) -
      by H.S. Wilson   £21.00

Great Britain & Ireland T.P.O. Postmarks: A Guide & Catalogue -
      by Frank J. Wilson   £7.00

The Railway Sub Offices of Great Britain -
      by A.M. Goodbody   £3.00

Great Britain & Ireland Railway Letter Stamps 1957 - 1998
      by Neill Oakley   £10.00

Please add £4.00 postage and packing for the first book in the list and 50p each for the remainder. Available from:
H.S. Wilson, R.P.G. Publications Officer,
17 Heath Avenue, Littleover,
Derby DE23 6DJ

FOR THE RECORD

A number of labels that could be mistaken for railway letter stamps have been issued during the period covered by this catalogue. In some cases they have the appearance of being an official stamp; in others they are crudely printed. Those known to the compiler are listed briefly below.

ALDERNEY PACKET

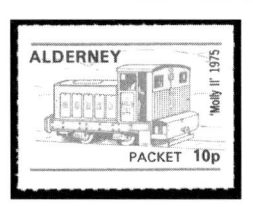

A parcel company which operates on this Channel Island has produced a number of labels with a transport or railway theme. In 1975 a set was issued with a 5p (blue) bus; 10p (green) Molly II diesel loco; 15p (orange) aircraft; 20p (red) ship. Diamond shaped labels with a 0-6-0T steam locomotive, inscribed "1847-1977", appeared on 1/1/78, with 5p (blue), 10p (green), 15p (brown), and 20p (red) values; perf and imperf labels, and colour trials exist.

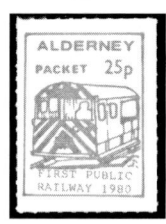

A green 25p label was issued inscribed "First Public Railway 1980"; one design on row 4 label 1, has a constant variety of a solid green driver. Black proofs are known. A cancellation with "Public Railway 1980" was used on fdc.

Since there was no longer a demand to send parcels off the island the scale of charges was revised so the delivery of a parcel on the island, regardless of weight, cost £1, and within 3 hours £2. A miniature sheet of four was issued on 2/3/93, showing 1944 Cowan Sheldon 8-ton steam crane; ex-L.T. Metro Cammell 1938 tube stock; Vulcan Drewry D100 *Elizabeth*; and ex-army Wickham railcar Type 27. On 7/7/95, a miniature sheet of four labels was issued which reproduced the transport designs originally issued in 1975 (see above). Each one was inscribed "1975-1995". The first three in the set had a £1 value, and the fourth £2.

BAGLEY WOOD RAILWAY

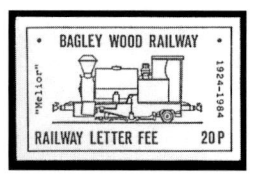

In the mid-1980s a railway enthusiast / philatelist produced a series of stamps featuring locomotives and rolling stock which ran on his model railway. Most designs were black on a coloured gummed paper and were sold as individual labels or in complete sheets. A series of covers, bearing the labels in the position a railway letter stamp would be affixed, was posted by the designer at philatelic counters around Great Britain.

BARDSEY / YNYS ENLLI

This island, 2 miles long and ¾ mile broad at the north end, lies 2½ miles southwest of the North Cardigan Bay peninsula. Labels have been issued for the postal service to the mainland. One set of se-tenant pairs (E & W horiz.), issued on 23/2/81 had a railway theme and used photographs depicting the Llechwedd Slate Caverns Railway / Rheilffordd Ceudyllau Llechwedd (12p/c value), Snowdon Railway / Rheilffordd Yr Wydda (13½p/c), Festiniog Railway / Rheilffordd Ffestiniog (15p/c), and Bala Lake Railway / Rheilffordd Llyn Tegid (20p/c). None of the designs have any franking value with the railways illustrated.

BODMIN & WENFORD RAILWAY

This railway marks the meeting of the two rival West Country railway companies, the G.W.R. and the L.S.W.R. In this area all lines were closed to passenger traffic in 1967, as part of the Beeching plan, and the Wenford branch, always a mineral only line, closed in 1983. In 1985 the Bodmin & Wenford Railway purchased the old G.W.R. line to Bodmin Road, with the track in situ, and obtained a Light Railway Order in 1989. It now runs 3½ miles east from Bodmin General down to the junction at Bodmin Parkway (formerly Bodmin Road), while another branch curves west round Bodmin for 3 miles and joins the Wenford branch at Boscarne Junction.

On 28/8/93, the railway introduced a '10p letter post'. It was never intended to be a railway letter service but because so many visitors could not find a convenient pillarbox the label showed a fee had been paid so that railway staff could post their mail for them.

It is known that visitors carried their own post, and the railway has sometimes arranged to convey items, between Bodmin General and Parkway. The railway would also cancel the label on postcards, using a handstamp showing a G.W.R. 2-6-2T, on demand. The labels were not available in 1997, but some 'low key' sales have been made from 1998.

Enquiries to: Bodmin & Wenford Railway plc, Bodmin General Station, Bodmin, Cornwall PL31 1AQ.

28/8/93. Letter Post Label. Des: Phillip Andrew. Ptr: Design & Print Group of Northamptonshire County Council. Offset lithography on self adhesive labels in sheets of 42 (7 rows of 6). Imperf.

Dsgn: Geometric design inscribed "Letter Post"

L1	10p Black	.35
	Sheet of 42	£6.50

B.&W.R. SPECIAL CANCELLATIONS

1 28/8/93 Bodmin Steam Railway [illus. railway's letterhead of G.W.R. 2-6-2T No.5552 and train - red - undated]

2 27/8/94 1st Anniversary of Bodmin & Wenford Letter Post - August 1994 [undated]

BOGUS ISSUES

A number of labels, purporting to be railway letter stamps were printed in the 1960s. It is thought they were produced by a stamp dealer on the Isle of Wight who may have been trying to encourage more preserved railways to launch letter services. Most of the examples known to the compiler are for railways who have operated letter services (including the Bluebell, Isle of Man, Welshpool & Llanfair, and British Rail), but there are some which have not (for example the Dart Valley Railway). All labels are printed black on a wide variety of coloured and gummed paper, and are perf or imperf.

Label, red handstamp, and special Christmas cachet applied in black

BRITISH RAIL

For convenience labels within this category have been listed from pg 12.

CALF OF MAN - ISLE OF MAN

The Calf of Man is a small rocky island close to the south west of the Isle of Man. Four labels illustrated with photographs of tramcars on the Manx Electric Railway and the Snaefell Mountain Railway were produced on 14/7/72, bearing legends including "Calf of Man" and the Scout Association trefoil logo. The labels were printed in panes of two, vert. se-tenant. On one sheet are illustrated M.E.R. Car 20 and trailer near the beauty spot of Mona (20m value), and Car 26 and trailer near Maughold Head (90m). On the other are Snaefell Car 2 (25m), and Car 6 near the summit (75m). Labels exist perf and imperf.

DUBLIN & KINGSTOWN RAILWAY

To commemorate the 150th Anniversary of this line, facsimiles of a 2d railway letter stamp were privately printed in red or green and overprinted "1834 1984" in black and red respectively. A quantity of stamps were not overprinted, and all exist perf or imperf. Labels illustrated by the D.&K.R. locomotive *Banshee* were printed (illustration indicated first) in blue and black, red and black, and black and red. None have any franking value.

DUBLIN - BELFAST EMERGENCY POSTAL SERVICE

On 27 April 1992, An Post suspended 550 postal workers from duty at the Central Sorting Office and as a result the Republic of Ireland's mail services effectively ground to a halt, apart from deliveries within provincial towns. An emergency commercial postal service, using a special courier, took mail between Dublin and Belfast by train from early May. On arrival in Belfast mail was placed in the normal post for distribution throughout Great Britain and the rest of the world. A special undenominated black on white self-adhesive label was fixed to each item of mail to indicate that the handling fee of £1 had been paid. About 1000 items of mail were carried during the period of operation, but no fdc were prepared. The dispute eventually ended on 25 May, but postal services did not return to normal until mid-June.

The labels were designed by Des Kiely, DKA Design, and 2000 were printed in sheets of 21 (7 rows of 3) by Mahons, Dublin. The design consists of a C.I.E. diesel locomotive and train emerging from a perforated label with Irish harp logo belonging to the firm of Whyte's. Some labels show poor registration of the design which bleeds off the edge.

GREAT EASTERN RAILWAY

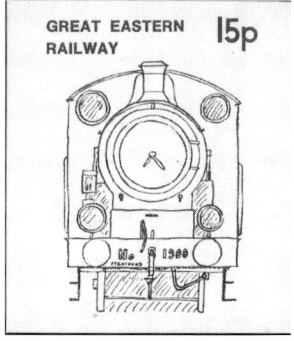

These appeared towards the end of 1972. They are crude letterpress designs on yellow paper, featuring the front elevation of a locomotive, with the inscription "Great Eastern Railway". 15p, 15p plus 1p surcharged in black, and 16p surcharged in red on 15p, denominations are known to exist. They were privately printed and have no franking value.

GREAT WESTERN RAILWAY AIRMAIL SERVICE

The 50th Anniversary of this service was commemorated by privately produced facsimiles of the 1933 design overprinted "1933-1983 50th Anniversary", in sheets of 3. Specimen sheets of the facsimile issue, and overprint trials on original G.W.R. airmail stamps, are known. They have no franking value and no service connection.

GWILI RAILWAY

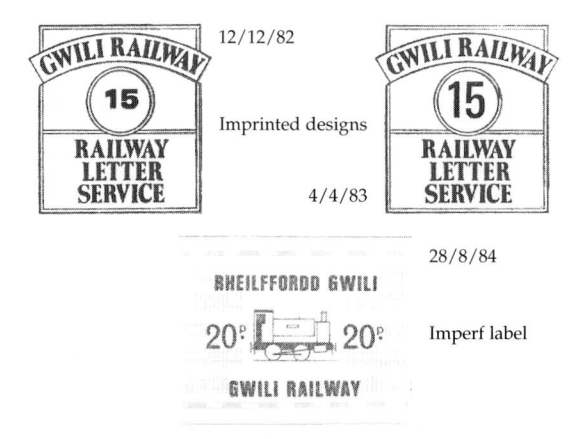

12/12/82

4/4/83

Imprinted designs

28/8/84

Imperf label

This railway runs for 2 miles from Bronwydd Arms to Llwyfan Cerrig at present. Postal envelopes with imprinted "railway letter service" stamps appeared in 1982 (black and orange) and 1983 (orange) incorrectly denominated 15(p). Covers with imperf 20p labels attached (lime green and yellow) appeared in 1984. They were apparently privately produced and not available from the railway. The railway has stated they will not consider a letter service until they have appropriate public access to both ends of the line.

ISLE OF WIGHT RAILWAY

The Isle of Wight boasted a network of over 45 miles, of which the I.W.R. preserves the 5 mile stretch from Wooton to Smallbrook Junction, via the line's headquarters at Havenstreet. This route was first operated by the Ryde & Newport Railway, which opened in 1875 and, like the others, struggled to make a profit and was closed to passengers on 21 February 1966. The I.W.R. has a rail link at Smallbrook Junction with the Ryde Pier to Shanklin line which is operated using ex-London Transport tube stock.

To mark the return to service of *Calbourne* commemorative covers were carried by steam train from Wooton to Smallbrook Junction on 29 March 1995, where they were transferred to the Network SouthEast electric service to Ryde Pier. The labels printed for the occasion cannot be regarded as railway letter stamps. The organisers of the issue hoped they could persuade the Railway to become a signatory to the R.L.S. Agreement but this was not achieved.

Enquiries to: Isle of Wight Railway Co. Ltd., The Railway Station, Havenstreet, Isle of Wight PO33 4DS.

29/3/95. Return to Steam of *Calbourne*. Des: Ray Harvey; Illus: Robert Barnes (drawing). Ptr: Robert Vale. Offset lithography in sheets of 6 (3 rows of 2). R9.5.

Dsgn: L.S.W.R. Class 02 0-4-4T No.209 (later S.R. No.24) *Calbourne*

L1	25p Green on cream (29/3/95)	£10.00
L1a	25p Green on white (16/8/98)	.40

Nos: L1) 600 approx; L1a) 1000.   FDC: L1) 450.
No fdc were officially prepared for the reprint.

In the 1980s a sheet of purely souvenir labels was produced by Vectis Philatelic Services and printed by the Isle of Wight County Press in full colour. These featured ten views of the island in two vertical columns of five with a third, central column divided into two half-width labels which bore appropriate crests. The ten scenes depicted included Godshill Village, The Needles Rocks and Lighthouse, Bembridge Windmill and, on row 3 stamp 1, Havenstreet Steam Railway. All the full-sized labels bear a 15p value and "Isle of Wight" logo in gold.

LOCAL POST

This company works with the Royal Mail in providing a 'very exclusive postal service'. Envelopes bearing Localpost labels can be mailed in R.M. post boxes anywhere in the U.K., just like ordinary letters, and do not require additional stamps. If sent to Localpost's head office address, covering the ultimate delivery address with a special label, special Localpost postmarks are applied and the envelope repacked in a clear protective cover to be delivered anywhere in the world.

On 6/5/94, Localpost issued two sheets of three labels to commemorate the opening of the Channel Tunnel. One sheet has: 75p "London to Paris", illustrated with Big Ben's clocktower; £1.50 "The Channel Tunnel The Opening Year 1994", with Eurostar train; and 75p "Paris à Londres", with Eiffel Tower. The second sheet has: 75p "United Kingdom", with map of U.K. and Union Flag; £1.50 "Channel Tunnel Opening 1994 First land route to Europe since prehistoric times", with symbolic tunnel portal; and 75p "France & Europe", with map of France, Tri-color and E.U. stars.

LONDON BRIGHTON & SOUTH COAST RAILWAY

Facsimiles of a 1d newspaper stamp were privately produced, in red, overprinted in black "50th Anniversary Brighton Belle 1933-1983". A blue facsimile stamp was incorrectly inscribed "Brighton Bell" in brown and rejected. A quantity of the red and blue stamps were not overprinted. They have no franking value.

LONDON UNDERGROUND

None of the London underground or tube companies have been signatories of the Post Office Agreements, and no regular railway letter service has been operated between London Underground stations. The Centenary Project Team consulted the British Telecommunications Act 1981, which allows private postal services to operate where the charge for each item is £1.00 or more. The minimum rate levied on mail carried by this service was £1.90 (2 x 95p labels)

The labels were only used on 4 November and 18 December 1990, the centenaries of the royal and public openings respectively.

Enquiries to: Printz P Holman, 74 Sterndale Moor, Buxton, Derbyshire SK17 9QB.

4/11/90. Centenary of the London Tube Railway. Des: Darren Pattenden. Ptr: Joh. Enschede en Zonen. Offset lithography in miniature sheets of 4 (2 rows of 2), containing one example of each. P12.8x14.

Dsgn: L1) 1890 tube locomotive; L2) 1923 tube stock; L3) 1938 tube stock; L4) 1972 tube stock; all ran on the Northern Line

L1	95p Multicoloured	
L2	95p Multicoloured	
L3	95p Multicoloured	
L4	95p Multicoloured	
	Sheet of 4	£5.50

Nos: 10000 of each.
FDC: A total of 5000 cards (in nine variations) were carried on the two anniversary dates.

LUNDY

The island, 11 miles northwest of Hartland Point in the Bristol Channel, has issued a large number of labels for its postal service to the mainland. An apparently bogus issue, since there are no railways on the island, has "Railway Fee Paid" overprinted in black on a 7½ puffin dull claret stamp.

MANCHESTER EXPRESS

These are 1971 British Postal Strike labels used in the Manchester area. Values known to the compiler are 2/- and 10p which were applied in blue, and 5/- and 25p applied in black. Although the strike began on 20/1/71 the service appears to have used the Lsd values from 25/1, and the decimal values from 15/2/71.

MID-HANTS RAILWAY

For convenience the labels issued on 30/4/77, and 7/6/77, and the postal envelope carried on 25/3/78, have been listed on pg 46.

MID-SUFFOLK LIGHT RAILWAY

This Museum based at Wetheringsett, near Stowmarket, has a short length of track to display two locomotives and rolling stock. The station buildings are restored from Mendlesham, Wilby and Brockford Stations. Having only one station it cannot operate a railway letter service between two points according to the regulations and does not qualify to sign the R.L.S. Agreement.

The M.S.L.R. has issued a series of labels which have been based on original letter, newspaper and parcel designs used by pre-grouping railways in East Anglia. Since they have been of interest to collectors they are briefly listed here. The museum identifies the designs by "S" or "L" codes which appear in the panels above each pane. The labels are listed here in chronological order with M.S.L.R. codes appended. They were designed by Barry R. Reynolds, with labels L1, and L3 to L6 printed by the Horseshoe Press, Stowmarket, and the remainder by Mr. Reynolds. L1 to L6 were imperf, but since L7 most label designs have been available perf and imperf, with perforated examples being the norm. To spread the workload most labels have been issued in advance of the event they commemorate - the difference in dates is indicated below.

The railway also used a circular "Railway Letter Service" cancellation with "25p" in the centre for the first day of issue of L1, and 16/7/95. Following comments and representations, made over several months, the railway changed how they described their operations from "M.S.L.R. Railway Letter Service" to "M.S.L.R. Philatelic Services".

Enquiries to Barry R, Reynolds, 24 Thirlmere Drive, Stowmarket, Suffolk IP14 1SE

11/9/94. 90th Anniversary of the Opening of the M.S.L.R. to Goods Traffic. Imperf.

Dsgn: Adapted from a C.V.R. letter stamp of February 1891

L1	25p Emerald green (S.01)	£1.25
	Pane of 10 (2 rows of 5)	£15.00
	Sheet of 30 (3 panes)	£50.00

Nos: 1500.   200 postcards carried 25/9/94.

107

11/1/95. Movement of Hudswell Clarke 0-6-0T to Brockford Station. Imperf.

Dsgn: Adapted from a G.E.R. newspaper stamp of April 1866

L2	25p Grey-blue (S.02)	£1.00
	Pane of 10 (2 rows of 5)	£12.50
	Sheet of 20 (2 panes)	£27.50

Nos: 1000. FDC: 170

5/5/95. 50 Years Since Victory in Europe. Imperf.

Dsgn: Adapted from a C.V.R. newspaper stamp and illustrating a Hudswell-Clarke 0-6-0T

L3	25p Magenta (S.03)	.60
	Pane of 10 (2 rows of 5)	£7.00
	Sheet of 20 (2 panes)	£15.00

Nos: 1000. 200 postcards carried 8/5/95.

24/6/95. Visit to the North Norfolk Railway. Imperf.

Dsgn: Adapted from a Y.N.R. newspaper stamp of about 1874

L4	25p Warm brown (S.006)	.40
	Pane of 10 (2 rows of 5)	£4.00
	Sheet of 20 (2 panes)	£8.00

Nos: 1000. FDC: 122

14/7/95. Tribute to the Great Eastern Railway. Imperf.

Dsgn: Adapted from a G.E.R. express parcel service stamp of May 1879

L5	25p Warm brown (S.004)	.40
	Pane of 10 (2 rows of 5)	£4.00
	Sheet of 20 (2 panes)	£8.00

Nos: 1000. 150 covers carried 16/7/95.

23/9/95. Edwardian Day. Imperf.

Dsgn: Adapted from a parcel stamp used by the C.V.R. from 1884

L6	25p Cyan (S.005)	.40
	Pane of 10 (2 rows of 5)	£4.00
	Sheet of 20 (2 panes)	£8.00

Nos: 1000. 180 covers carried 24/9/95.

26/4/96. Agricultural Weekend.

Dsgn: Adapted from a G.E.R. corn sample label of February 1878, and illus. Garrett traction engine

L7	25p Black and cerise (S.007)	.40
	Pane of 8 (2 rows of 4)	£3.20
	Sheet of 16 (2 panes)	£6.40

Nos: 966. 140 covers carried 5/5/96.

2/8/96. Centenary of the Light Railways Act.

Dsgn: Adapted from a L.&F. newspaper stamp and illus. No.1 *Haughley*

L8	25p Light blue and red (L.008)	.40
	Pane of 10 (2 rows of 5)	£4.00
	Sheet of 20 (2 panes)	£8.00

Nos: 1200. 100 covers carried 18/8/96.

13/9/96. 1930s Day.

Dsgn: Adapted from a G.E.R. parcel label issued from 1/5/1905, and illus. L.N.E.R. Class J15 used on M.S.L.R. from the 1930s

L9	25p Red and light blue (S.009)	.40
	Pane of 10 (5 rows of 2)	£4.00
	Sheet of 20 (2 panes)	£8.00

Nos: 1200 150 covers carried 29/9/96.

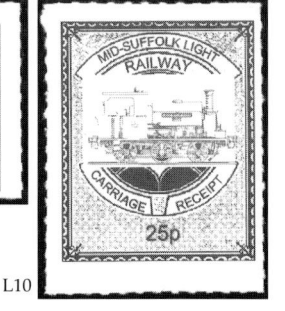

24/3/97. Railway Artists' Weekend.

Dsgn: Adapted from a G.E.R. parcels stamp of January 1880 and illus. 0-6-0T *Lady Stevenson*

L10	25p Red and blue	
	with yellow background (S.010)	.40
	Pane of 10 (2 rows of 5)	£4.00
	Sheet of 20 (2 panes)	£8.00

Nos: 1200.　　　　140 covers carried 4/5/97.

27/5/97. L.N.E.R. Day.

Dsgn: Adapted from a G.E.R. newspaper stamp issued from 2/4/1866, and illus. a Hudswell-Clarke 0-6-0T

L11	25p Red and blue (S.011)	.40
	Pane of 10 (2 rows of 5)	£4.00
	Sheet of 20 (2 panes)	£8.00

Nos: 1200.　　　　100 covers carried 6/7/97.

18/8/97. 1950s Day.

Dsgn: Adapted from a Y.N.R. newspaper stamp of about 1874, and illus. L.N.E.R. 0-6-0T No.8316

L12	25p Black and blue (S.012)	.40
	Pane of 10 (2 rows of 5)	£4.00
	Sheet of 20 (2 panes)	£8.00

Nos: 2000. 100 of 'Coronation' and 100 of 'Last Run' covers carried 21/9/97.

30/4/98. Bygones, Beer and Crafts Festival. 5 designs se-tenant horiz.

Dsgn: Adapted from a G.E.R. corn sample label used from 1/2/1878, but illus. one of five traction engines in the centre of each design: L13) Ransomes, Sims & Head No.5137; L14) Marshall; L15) Burrell No.3202 *Bampton Castle*; L16) Garrett No.32936 *Felstead Belle*; L17) Fowler Compound

L13	25p Black, warm brown and biscuit (S.013)
L14	25p Black, warm brown and biscuit (S.013)
L15	25p Black, warm brown and biscuit (S.013)
L16	25p Black, warm brown and biscuit (S.013)
L17	25p Black, warm brown and biscuit (S.013)
L13-L17	Se-tenant strip of 5　　£1.75
(L13-L17)	Pane of 15 (3 rows of 5)　　£5.25
(L13-L17)	Sheet of 30 (2 panes)　　£10.50

Nos: 1800.
100 covers, each bearing one label, carried 24/5/97.

24/8/98. 50th Anniversary of British Railways and 60th Anniversary of *Mallard*'s Steam Speed Record.

Dsgn: Adapted from a G.E.R. parcel label used from 1/5/1905, and illus. L.N.E.R. Class A4 No.4468 *Mallard*

L18	25p Black and blue (S.014)	.40
	Pane of 10 (2 rows of 5)	£4.00
	Sheet of 20 (2 panes)	£8.00

Nos: 1600.　　　　100 covers carried 30/8/98.

Detail from centre of L19　　75%

24/8/98. 90th Anniversary of M.S.L.R. Opening for Passenger Traffic.

Dsgn: Adapted from a L.&F. newspaper stamp with border as L8, but illus. 0-6-0T loco No.1 *Haughley*

L19	25p Yellow and red (S.015)	.40
	Pane of 10 (2 rows of 5)	£4.00
	Sheet of 20 (2 panes)	£8.00

Nos: 1600.　　　　100 covers carried 30/8/98.

M.S.L.R. SPECIAL CANCELLATIONS

1　25/9/94　Mid Suffolk Light Railway
　　　　　　25p Railway Letter Service [undated]

2	8/5/95	Mid Suffolk Light Railway celebrates 50 Years Since Victory in Europe 8 May 1945 - 8 May 1995 [illus. 'V', bells and wavy lines - green]
3	24/6/95	N. Norfolk Railway [green - undated]
4	4/5/96	Brockford Station - Agricultural Week-end [illus. cow outline - green]
5	18/8/96	Centenary of the Light Railway Act 1896 - 1996
6	29/9/96	Transported by Restored Morris FGN953 1930s Mail Van [silver]
7	4/5/97	Railway Artists Week-end 1997 [red]
8	6/7/97	LNER Day [LNER lozenge logo - green]
9	21/9/97	[illus. Coronation orb - gold - undated]
10	21/9/97	MSLR [red - undated]
11	12/10/97	Northampton & Lamport Railway [illus. wheel logo - green - undated]
12	24/5/98	Mauldon's Suffolk Real Ales [illus. beer mug - green]
13	28/8/98	MSLR [red with date applied below]
14	28/8/98	MSLR Railway Post

P.O. CANCELLATIONS

The M.S.L.R. has sometimes arranged for interesting or unusual P.O. cancels to be applied by favour to their commemorative covers, but most are carried by T.P.O. and receive the appropriate cancellations. Since none were sponsored by the railway they are not listed here.

MIDDLETON RAILWAY

Originally a waggonway from Leeds to the River Aire it became the first railway authorised by Act of Parliament. It was converted to standard gauge in 1881 and operated until 1958. A 1 mile length of track between Moor Road and Middleton Park, plus two additional short branches, are preserved from the Broom Colliery to Meadow Lane line.

Labels with a 6d denomination, illustrated by the Murray-Blenkinsop locomotive of 1812, first appeared on 20/6/70, to celebrate the tenth anniversary of reopening. Printed in letterpress, on various yellow papers, they are known with and without the legend identifying the locomotive.

NORTH YORKSHIRE MOORS RAILWAY

For convenience the parcel labels issued on 1/9/90, following the withdrawal of the original design of general parcel and railway letter stamps, have been listed on pg 66.

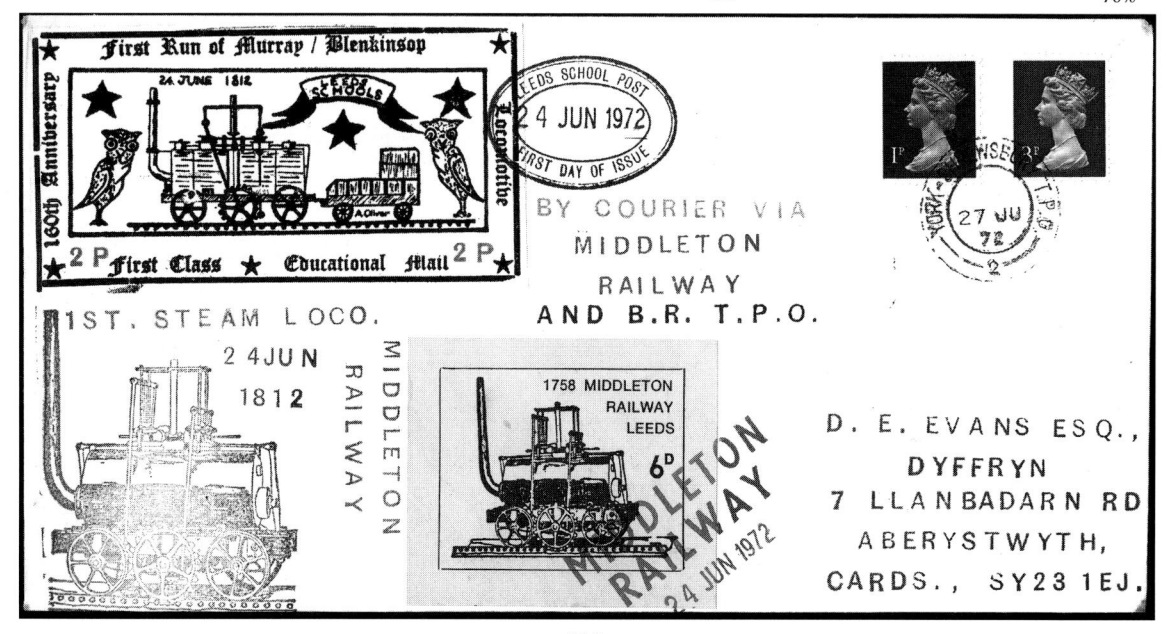

70%

NORTHERN IRELAND RAILWAYS

The Ulster Transport Authority was set up by the Northern Ireland legislative in 1948 to take over railway and road transport undertakings located wholly within the province. Severe cutbacks in rail route miles occurred from 1957. By the end of 1965 only the Dublin to Belfast line, and those serving Bangor, Portrush, and Londonderry via Coleraine, remained. Northern Ireland Railways became that authority's successor on 1 April 1968.

Despite the "Fee for post letter by rail" legend the labels produced in 1989 were promoted by the N.I.R. as a souvenir, rather than a stamp recording the payment of a charge for carrying mail. They were available at all stations on the N.I.R. network on the day of issue. A number of covers were carried from Belfast Central and Botanic Stations on various dates, including 30/11/89, with N.I.R., P.O. and station cancellations correctly applied. Such covers are scarce since few were carried during the period of use. Some were also carried aboard journeys of N.I.R. and R.P.S.I. special trains by the R.P.S.I. agent.

After receiving complaints that the company might not be operating a railway letter service the N.I.R. withdrew the labels from sale soon after issue.

30/11/89. 150th Anniversary of Railways in Northern Ireland.. Lithography in sheets of 4 (2 rows of 2), made up into booklets of 50 panes. R9.5.

Dsgn: N.I.R. steam locomotive and diesel multiple unit

L1	50p Black, dull orange and red	£2.50
	Sheet of 4	£10.00
	Booklet of 200	

RAILWAY PHILATELIC GROUP

To celebrate the annual conventions of 1970 and 1991 the R.P.G. printed labels in railway letter stamp styles. The green labels, printed in sheets of 10 (2 rows of 5) and issued on 10/10/70, were similar in design to the original 1891 railway letter stamps.

The multicoloured miniature sheet issued on 20/4/91 (see below), contained four designs featuring *The Great 'A'* of the Y.&N.M.R., built by Robert Stephenson's engineering company in 1845; *Sans Pareil* of the Y.N.&B.R. which was designed by Timothy Hackworth in 1849; *Aerolite* built in 1869 for the N.E.R.; and a Midland T.P.O., built in 1879, which ran on the M.&N.E.J.P.S. The sheet's margins contain illustrations of various railway thematic stamps and cancels, a bust of George Hudson, the railway engineer, and a view of York in 1865. 'Specimen' sheets also exist.

70%

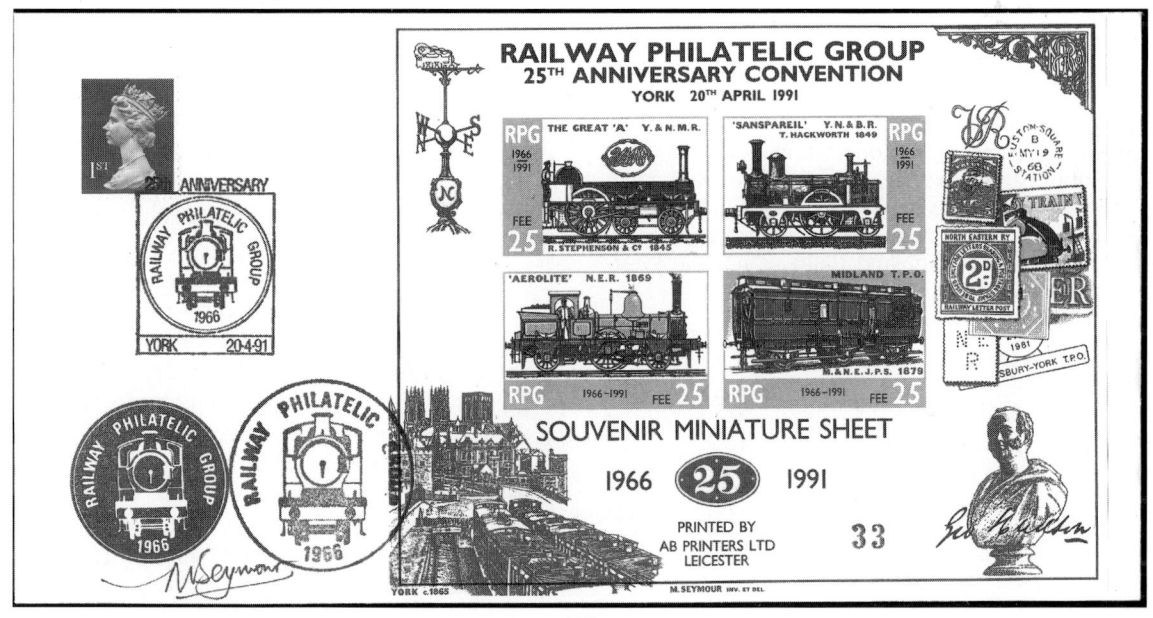

111

RAVENGLASS & ESKDALE RAILWAY

For convenience the parcel label issued in the early 1960s, and the package label issued in 1976, have been listed on pg 78.

ROMNEY HYTHE & DYMCHURCH RAILWAY

For convenience the commemorative label, featuring a portrait of Sigmund Freud, has been listed on pg 81 and 82.

SOMERSET & DORSET RAILWAY TRUST

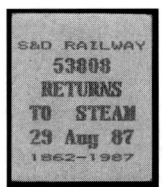

This society is based on the West Somerset Railway at Williton Station. A gummed label, produced on a dot-matrix printer, was used instead of a cachet to commemorate the first steaming of S.&D. 2-8-0 No.88 on 29/8/87. Only about six mint labels exist in addition to the 25 used on postcards (see also pg 101).

WELSH HIGHLAND RAILWAY

This railway runs two sections of track: one from Porthmadog to Pen-y-Mount (1/2 mile), and the other more recently from Caernarfon to Dinas (2 1/2 miles).

Covers were carried in conjunction with a special train from Crewe to Kyle of Lochalsh, in 9/71. The 10p label, with a blue value on a red design inscribed "Railway Post", had no franking value; it did not see use on the Welsh Highland Railway, nor the West Highland line.

WEST ANGLIA

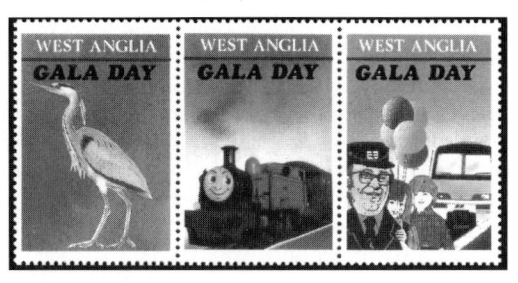

For their Gala Day, held in the West Anglia area on 29/9/90, Network SouthEast produced a sheet of nine undenominated commemorative labels (3 rows of 3) with three designs. One showed the West Anglia railway symbol of a heron (row 1 label 1; 2/2; 3/3); the second a portrait of Thomas the Tank engine (1/2; 2/3; 3/1); and the third a staff member, children with balloons and a Network SouthEast DMU in the background (1/3; 2/1; 3/2). Sheets had the legend "West Anglia Gala Day / Royal Mail Travelling Post Office - Special Issue" at the top of the sheets. Covers were serviced with the label remaining uncancelled and the postage stamp tied to the special envelope by a London Section T.P.O. handstamp.

PUBLICITY LABELS

A number of minor railways have, from time to time, issued undenominated publicity labels. These designs fall outside the scope of this catalogue.

I would welcome comments on whether the labels listed in the "For the Record" section should continue to be included in this catalogue. If included, should each section be restricted to a short paragraph or given the coverage displayed here? Alternatively if they are excluded they could be described in greater detail in a separate volume which would be updated less frequently than the railway letter stamp catalogue. If you wish to express an opinion please write to:
Neill Oakley, 7 Toll Bar Court, Basinghall Gardens, Sutton, Surrey SM2 6AT.   Thanks.